# The Legal Enforcement of Morality

BORZOI BOOKS IN LAW AND AMERICAN SOCIETY

# The Legal Enforcement of Morality

Thomas C. Grey
*Stanford University*

ALFRED A. KNOPF     NEW YORK

*This book was originally developed as part of an American Bar Association program on law and humanities with major funding from the National Endowment for the Humanities and additional support from the Exxon Education Foundation and Pew Memorial Trust. The ABA established this program to help foster improved understanding among undergraduates of the role of law in society through the creation of a series of volumes in law and humanities. The ABA selected a special advisory committee of scholars, lawyers, and jurists (Commission on Undergraduate Education in Law and the Humanities) to identify appropriate topics and select writers. This book is a revised version of the volume first published by the ABA. However, the writer, and not the American Bar Association, individual members and committees of the Commission, the National Endowment for the Humanities, Exxon Education Foundation, or Pew Memorial Trust, bears sole responsibility for the content, analysis, and conclusion contained herein.*

THIS IS A BORZOI BOOK
PUBLISHED BY ALFRED A. KNOPF, INC.

First Edition
9 8 7 6 5 4 3 2 1
Copyright © 1983 by Alfred A. Knopf, Inc.

LIBRARY OF CONGRESS CATALOGING IN PUBLICATION DATA
Main entry under title:

The Legal enforcement of morality.

(Borzoi books in law and American society)
Bibliography: p.
Includes index.
1. Law and ethics.  2. Sex and law—United States.
3. Dead bodies (Law)—United States.  4. Assistance in
emergencies—United States.  5. Assistance in
emergencies.  I. Grey, Thomas C.  II. Title.  III. Series
KF379.L43  1982          349.73          82-14869
                         347.3
ISBN 0-394-33192-3 (Paperbound)   394-33576-7 (Casebound)
Manufactured in the United States of America

# Preface

This book is a collection of legal materials about a traditional problem or set of problems in philosophy and practical politics. Philosophers tend to speak of the problem of "the enforcement of morals," lawyers and citizens of the problem of "victimless crimes." Neither of these expressions is very exact, nor do they mean the same thing, but most of us have a rough sense that there is a common core of issues to which they both refer.

To sharpen the focus on these vague issues, I have organized this book around John Stuart Mill's thesis that collective coercive power can be legitimately exercised only "to prevent harm to others." Both that thesis and the arguments responding to it have played a central role in contemporary controversy over morals enforcement and victimless crimes. Accordingly, I have supposed that most readers of these materials will have read *On Liberty* or significant excerpts from it—though the introductory part of Chapter 1 provides enough background to substitute, in a pinch, for consideration of Mill's own arguments in his own words. In general, the book should work best when read in conjunction with a collection of the standard philosophical texts on Mill's principle. In the absence of such readings, the second part of Chapter 1 is meant to raise the problems with Mill's thesis that most directly bear on the legal materials that make up the body of the book.

Each of Chapters 2, 3, and 4 is a set of legal texts dealing with a kind of regulation that potentially conflicts with Mill's principle. Chapter 2, on the legal prohibition of sexual deviance, addresses what has been the central question in the modern debate over law and morals. The celebrated Hart-Devlin exchange of the 1960s concerned the legitimacy of prohibiting homosexual acts between consenting adults, and much of the succeeding philosophical literature has had the same focus. The more recent introduction of this issue into American constitutional law has led lawyers and judges to argue the Millian issues of majority preferences and minority rights in the special institutional context of judicial review. Hence the chapter is largely made up of judicial opinions and legal commentaries drawn from constitutional law.

While the topic of sexual morality was chosen for treatment here largely because of its traditional centrality, the topics of Chapters 3 and 4 were selected in order to give a new twist to the familiar debates over legal moralism. Recent medical innovations, such as organ transplantation, have made the treatment of dead bodies a practical issue for the law, just as it was in the days when the use of cadavers for dissection by medical students affronted popular sentiment. Chapter 3 is meant to demonstrate the response of the legal system to rapidly developing new technology in an area where the relatively sparse existing law reflected the popular attitudes of prior generations. Another virtue of these materials is that many people who have no sympathy at all for sexual morals enforcement do have strong feelings of repugnance against desecration of human remains—feelings that stir an impulse toward legal moralism. Finally, many of the legal developments in this area are legislative in form, which permits the introduction of problems of reading and drafting statutes and corrects an otherwise unduly judge-centered view of the legal system.

The materials on rescue in Chapter 4 illustrate some connections between morals enforcement and broader themes of political philosophy: the antinomies of liberty and equality, individualism and collectivism, liberalism and Marxism. Lawyers have seen the problem of the good Samaritan as raising questions of the legitimacy and propriety of the law's enforcing moral duties. Both libertarians and leftist radicals are likely to see this issue as closely bound up with questions, like the issue of sexual morality, that are commonly thought to lie at the heart of the controversy over Mill's principle; on the other hand, traditional liberals are less likely to see the connection, at least at first. Here, as with Chapter 3, some pedagogically fruitful strain across standard ideological lines may be generated.

The legal materials used on the rescue issue introduce a comparative law perspective, because there are interesting differences among Anglo-American, Western European, and socialist legal systems in their treatment of this question. And the Anglo-American materials illustrate our characteristic common-law method in a sequence of tort cases, thus contrasting with the constitutional emphasis of Chapter 2 and the statutory emphasis of Chapter 3.

In selecting and editing the legal materials, I have assumed that my readers will mostly be without formal training in law. Thus technical legal problems have not been stressed. But to remove all technicalities from the materials would be to lose much of the benefit of confronting philosophical issues through legal texts. Philosophers commonly invent hypothetical cases to illustrate their points and to make their arguments. These hypotheticals have points in common with, but also points of difference from, the real disputes that the legal system must settle. A difference is that law can never put to one side the practical and administrative considerations that are often abstracted out in classroom hypotheticals. These sorts of considerations shape, often decisively, the way the legal system treats the merits of the substantive issues it confronts. Further, legal institutions *are institutions*, with a history, a customary way of doing things, and a concrete and sometimes parochial set of interests that all influence the way lawyers see things. All these points of difference would be lost if the law were treated only as a "rich storehouse" or "untoward cases"—the words of the philosopher J. L. Austin. I have thus deliberately retained in these materials some of the detail, contingency, parochialism, and technicality that characterize the law.

This book was originally prepared with the help—financial, editorial, and practical—of the Commission on Undergraduate Education in Law and the Humanities of the American Bar Association. I want to thank its Director, Gerald Fetner; its Chairman, Edward Levi; and its Law and Philosophy advisers, Joel Feinberg and Richard Wasserstrom. Thanks also go to John Kelley, Bruce MacEwen, and Rex Palmer for research assistance, and to Ann Babb for helping prepare the manuscript. Thanks most of all to Barbara Babcock for editorial help, and much more.

THOMAS C. GREY

# Contents

Preface .................................................V

Chapter 1: Introduction ..............................1

  A. The Context of the Dispute .........................3
    1. From Law Reform to Philosophy ..................4
    2. Transformation in Philosophy .....................5
    3. From Philosophy to Constitutional Law ............6
    4. The New Issues ...............................9

  B. Interpretation and Criticism ......................10
    1. Policy and Principle...........................10
    2. Decency and Offense ..........................13
    3. Property .....................................16
    4. Paternalism, Exploitation, and Economic
       Freedom.......................................20
    5. Causation, Action, and Omission .................25
    6. Collective Institutions .........................29

Chapter 2: Sexual Freedom and the Constitution ............37

  A. The Right to Privacy..............................40
    1. Griswold v. Connecticut .......................41
    2. Privacy After Griswold .........................55

  B. Obscenity and Privacy ...........................61
    Paris Adult Theater v. Slaton ....................62

  C. Homosexuality and Privacy .......................67

1. Doe v. Commonwealth's Attorney . . . . . . . . . . . . . 68
2. David Richards, "Sexual Autonomy and the
   Constitutional Right to Privacy" . . . . . . . . . . . . . . 74

D. Homosexual Marriage . . . . . . . . . . . . . . . . . . . . . . . . 78
   1. Baker v. Nelson . . . . . . . . . . . . . . . . . . . . . . . . . . . 79
   2. Note, "The Legality of Homosexual Marriage" . . . 82

E. Employment and Sexual Freedom . . . . . . . . . . . . . . . . 85
   1. Pettit v. State Board of Education . . . . . . . . . . . . . 86

F. Child Custody and Sexual Freedom . . . . . . . . . . . . . . 92
   1. Jarrett v. Jarrett . . . . . . . . . . . . . . . . . . . . . . . . . . . 93

G. Constitutional Privacy and Sexual Freedom: An
   Alternative View . . . . . . . . . . . . . . . . . . . . . . . . . . . . 97
   1. Thomas C. Grey, "Eros, Civilization and the
      Burger Court" . . . . . . . . . . . . . . . . . . . . . . . . . . . . 98

Chapter 3: The Treatment of the Dead . . . . . . . . . . . . . . . . . 103

A. The Law of Cadavers: Introduction and
   Historical Background . . . . . . . . . . . . . . . . . . . . . . . . 105
   1. "The Quick, The Dead, and the Cadaver
      Population" . . . . . . . . . . . . . . . . . . . . . . . . . . . . . . 105
   2. Rex v. Lynn . . . . . . . . . . . . . . . . . . . . . . . . . . . . . . 107
   3. M. J. Durey, "Bodysnatchers and
      Benthamites" . . . . . . . . . . . . . . . . . . . . . . . . . . . . 108
   4. State v. Bradbury . . . . . . . . . . . . . . . . . . . . . . . . . . 112
   5. Yome v. Gorman . . . . . . . . . . . . . . . . . . . . . . . . . . 115

B. The Transplant Problem: The Gift Act . . . . . . . . . . . . 118
   1. Alfred M. Sadler and Blair L. Sadler,
      "Transplantation and the Law" . . . . . . . . . . . . . . 119
   2. The Uniform Anatomical Gift Act . . . . . . . . . . . . 123
   3. Jesse Dukeminier, "Critique of the U.A.G.A." . . 127

C. Beyond Donation: Routine and Compulsory
   Salvaging . . . . . . . . . . . . . . . . . . . . . . . . . . . . . . . . . . 133
   1. Jesse Dukeminier, "Routine Salvaging of
      Cadaver Organs Unless There Is Objection" . . . . . 135
   2. Jesse Dukeminier, "Removal of Cadaver
      Organs Regardless of Objection" . . . . . . . . . . . . . 138

D. Commerce in Human Organs . . . . . . . . . . . . . . . . . . . 141

1. Jesse Dukeminier, "Sale of Cadaver Parts" .....141
2. Jesse Dukeminier, "Sales by Living Persons with Delivery During Life" ..................144

E. The Implications of Brain Death.................149
1. The California Brain Death Statute.............150
2. The "Neomort" Proposal ....................150
3. Hans Jonas, "Philosophical Reflections on Experimenting with Human Subjects ...........151

Chapter 4: The Duty to Rescue ........................155

A. The Traditional Anglo-American Doctrine .........157
1. Buch v. Amory Manufacturing Co. ............158
2. Thomas B. Macaulay, "Notes on the Indian Penal Code".................................159
3. Richard Epstein, "A Theory of Strict Liability"..163

B. The European Civil-Law Tradition ...............167
1. John Dawson, "Negotiorum Gestio: The Altruistic Intermeddler" .....................168
2. Note, "Stalking the Good Samaritan: Communists, Capitalists and the Duty to Rescue".................................171

C. The Common-Law Rescue Doctrine in Application..175
1. Hurley v. Eddingfield ......................176
2. O'Neill v. Montefiore Hospital ...............178
3. Wilmington General Hospital v. Manlove .......181
4. Tarasoff v. University of California ............185
5. Farwell v. Keaton..........................189
6. Ploof v. Putnam ..........................193
7. Warschauer v. Lloyd Sabaudo S.A. ............194

D. Conclusion: Vermont Joins Europe? .............198

Bibliographic Essay............................201
Index........................................203

*To my parents*

# INTRODUCTION

# A
## *The Context of the Dispute*

In his essay *On Liberty*, published in 1859, John Stuart Mill urged acceptance of a "simple principle" meant to "govern absolutely the dealings of society with the individual in the way of compulsion and control." Mill's principle is

> That the only purpose for which power can be rightfully exercised over any member of a civilized community, against his will, is to prevent harm to others.

Mill's principle requires that a free society must recognize two broad kinds of protected liberty. The first is "liberty of conscience in the most comprehensive sense," including free expression of opinion in speech and writing. On this point, Mill's views have achieved orthodoxy. The idea that freedom of speech and religion operate as limitations upon the legitimate reach of government power is today widely accepted in the liberal democracies.

The second freedom Mill asserts is a general liberty of action, or as he put it, "liberty of tastes and pursuits . . . of doing as we like, subject to such consequences as may follow: without impediment from our fellow-creatures, so long as what we do does not harm them, even though they should think our conduct foolish, perverse or wrong." This broader principle of liberty—liberty of "harmless action"—has remained controversial. Philosophers have argued that it is either wholly indeterminate or incoherent. Radical individualists have accepted the principle but urged that its implications require limitations upon government far beyond those Mill and his moderate adherents have recognized. Conservative critics have insisted that the practical conclusions Mill did draw from the principle are unacceptably restrictive of legitimate authority. At the same time, Mill's principle has served as a rallying cry for a diverse group of defenders of an equally varied assortment of unpopular forms of behavior.

The last twenty-five years have produced a vigorously renewed debate over Mill's principle. This debate provides the background for the materials in this book.

3

## I. FROM LAW REFORM TO PHILOSOPHY

The modern revival of the debate over Mill's principle was stimulated by two related efforts at criminal-law reform, both of which were part of a general contemporary critique of the punishment of "victimless crimes." In the United States, the drafters of the Model Penal Code proposed in 1955 to "exclude from the criminal law all sexual practices not involving force, adult corruption of minors, or public offense." In the drafters' view, "no harm to the secular interests of the community" resulted from "atypical sex practice in private between consenting adult partners." Such practices thus fell exclusively in the "area of private morals," and it was "inappropriate for the government to attempt to control behavior that has no substantial significance except as to the morality of the actor."

Two years later, in England, the Wolfenden Committee, which had been established to review the law governing prostitution and homosexuality, recommended repeal of the statute punishing homosexual acts between consenting adults. The committee argued that the functions of the criminal law were limited to the preservation of public order, the protection of the citizen against offense or injury, and the safeguarding of children and other especially vulnerable groups against exploitation. In particular, the committee stressed "the importance which society and the law ought to give to individual freedom of choice and action in matters of private morality" and concluded that "there must remain a realm of private morality and immorality which is, in brief and crude terms, not the law's business."

In 1958, the distinguished British judge Sir Patrick Devlin (later Lord Devlin) criticized the theoretical premises of the Wolfenden Report, arguing that no separate sphere of merely private morality could be marked off as in principle outside the concern of the criminal law. For him, the health of a society rested on its firm adherence to a binding moral code, so that the entire system of prevailing moral beliefs must be in principle subject to legal enforcement, though prudence might suggest limits on morals legislation.

Neither the Model Penal Code drafters, nor the Wolfenden Committee, nor Lord Devlin mentioned Mill's *On Liberty*. Nevertheless, the position of the reformers was recognizably in the spirit of Mill, and Lord Devlin's counterattack was recognizably critical of that spirit. At this point, the British legal philosopher H.L.A. Hart entered the dispute. In his book *Law, Liberty and Morality* (1963) Hart placed the controversy around the Wolfenden Report in the wider context of the century-old debate over Mill's principle, noting the similarity between the views of Lord Devlin and those expressed by Mill's nineteenth-century critic Sir James Fitzjames Stephen in his *Liberty, Equality, Fraternity* (1873).

At the same time, along with his review of the controversy, Hart offered a modern revision of Mill's principle. Lord Devlin responded, expanding his original position while criticizing Hart's views, in *The Enforcement of Morals* (1965). The Hart-Devlin debate attracted the attention of a number of the best-known Anglo-American writers on legal philosophy, and succeeding years saw a flurry of theoretical work on the modern implications of Mill's principle.

## 2. TRANSFORMATION IN PHILOSOPHY

The Hart-Devlin debate came at an important juncture for Anglo-American social philosophy. Over the preceding two decades, English and American philosophers had primarily pursued the technique of ordinary-language analysis, an approach that focused philosophers' professional attention on close examination of the use and meaning of the terms of everyday speech. The central thesis of the ordinary-language school was that traditional problems of philosophy could often be shown to result from the extension of ordinary terms outside their context in normal usage. A corollary was a consensus that philosophers had no special competence to speak on the merits of controversial moral and political questions. By the early 1960s, this consensus was ready to break down, and the Hart-Devlin dispute marked the renewal of debate by professional philosophers over live ethical and political issues. The hectic politics of the late 1960s accelerated the trend thus begun. Anglo-American academic philosophers have since addressed a wide range of social and political issues—income distribution, capitalism and socialism, race and sex discrimination, conservation and the environment, and the morality of war, among others.

The issues of the Hart-Devlin controversy reflect in microcosm a central concern of contemporary social philosophy—the question of the continued viability of liberalism, a world view identified with the spirit of Mill's principle. Thus recent liberal theorists like John Rawls and Ronald Dworkin have defended versions of Mill's theory, while libertarians like Robert Nozick have advocated an unregulated marketplace by expanding Mill's principle to encompass "capitalist acts between consenting adults." Libertarians have also argued that the classic common-law refusal to establish duties of rescue embodies a general principle of liberty prohibiting redistributive egalitarian measures. On the other hand, opponents of liberalism, both conservative and radical, have seen in Mill's principle what they find to be the vices of liberal theory generally: an abstract and unhistorical character, an excessive individualism, a blindness to economic power as distinguished from formal political authority.

## 3. FROM PHILOSOPHY TO CONSTITUTIONAL LAW

The modern dispute over Mill's principle began in the law with the Model Penal Code drafters and the Wolfenden Committee. The debate entered academic philosophy through the mediation of a judge and a law professor, Lord Devlin and Professor Hart. The philosophers' controversy has now had its own reciprocal influence on the practice and theory of law in the United States.

The Hart-Devlin debate was triggered by proposals for legislative reform of the law governing sexual behavior. The continuation of this criminal-law reform movement has achieved striking success in the years since, particularly with respect to the law concerning homosexual conduct. But it would be difficult to say that the revival of Mill's principle itself has played a large role in these legislative developments. The growth of a women's and later a gay political movement, the (apparently temporary) decline in power of the conservative churches, the changing technology of contraception, and other sociopolitical factors of this kind have no doubt been the dominant forces behind recent changes in the legislation governing sexual behavior.

But along with these legislative changes, American constitutional law has moved toward incorporating something like Mill's principle. Constitutional case law, because it is developed through opinions in which judges purport to justify their decisions, has always provided a bridge between practical politics on the one hand and more abstract theory on the other. At the constitutional level, the contemporary rebirth of normative moral and political theory inaugurated by the

Hart-Devlin debate has become intertwined with the development of new legal doctrines about the power of government to regulate morals.

The new doctrines were born with the United States Supreme Court's decision in *Griswold v. Connecticut* in 1965. In Griswold, the Supreme Court declared unconstitutional a Connecticut statute that prohibited to married couples as to others the use of contraceptives. The Court held that implicit in a number of constitutional provisions was a "right of privacy," which was violated by this sort of governmental intrusion into marital life. The dissenting Justices did not defend the justice or wisdom of the law but argued that the courts had no business inventing individual rights not to be found by reasonable exegesis of the text of the Constitution. They noted the parallels between the "right of privacy" invoked by the majority and the "liberty of contract" that a conservative Supreme Court had used to strike down economic regulatory legislation earlier in the century.

The *Griswold* dissenters were reflecting what had become an important strand in American constitutional thought during the 1940s and 1950s. This was the view, formed out of the clash between liberal legislatures and conservative courts during the Progressive era and the New Deal, that the Supreme Court was expected to defer to legislative judgment except where laws infringed specific limitations expressed in the text of the Constitution or clearly inferable from its history. Accepted as such specific limitations were the protections of freedom of speech and religion in the First Amendment, the specifications of fair criminal procedure in the Bill of Rights, and the prohibition of official racial discrimination implicit in the Equal Protection Clause of the Fourteenth Amendment. What was rejected by this view was the doctrine of "substantive due process"—that is, the use by the Court of the Due Process Clauses of the Fifth and Fourteenth Amendments as a vehicle to protect judicially selected "basic liberties" against legislative infringement, as the earlier Court had done with liberty of contract.

In the face of this New Deal-Progressive orthodoxy, the majority of the Court in *Griswold* revived a version of substantive due process with the new constitutional right of privacy, and, in the years since, the Court has continued to expand the scope of that right. Thus the right to use contraceptives without state interference was extended from married to unmarried couples and from adults to minors. The Court has also extended the rights of privacy to strike down restrictions on the right to marry, limits on the custodial rights of fathers of illegitimate children, and zoning restrictions on the right of extended families to live together in a single dwelling. Many lower courts have found that the new right of privacy protected individual autonomy in such matters as dress and hairstyle. The most dramatic extension of the new constitutional privacy came in 1973, when the Court in the case of *Roe v. Wade* struck down the restrictive abortion laws existing in a majority of American states, holding that these laws unduly infringed the right of women to determine their own procreative destiny.

From the first, the Court's development of a right to privacy has suggested to philosophical-minded commentators the possible elevation to constitutional status of Mill's principle of liberty. Critics of the new privacy developments have adapted a remark that Mr. Justice Holmes made while opposing the earlier doctrine of liberty of contract: "The Constitution does not enact Mr. Herbert Spencer's *Social Statics*." Nor, argue contemporary critics, does it enact John Stuart Mill's *On Liberty*. On the other hand, commentators friendly to the development of the privacy doctrine have argued that Mill's theory of liberty provides a sound theoretical basis for the doctrine, rebutting the charge that the new developments represent no more than the arbitrary invalidation of laws a majority of the justices find distasteful. Any number of academic legal commentaries in the years since *Griswold* have suggested that the Court is moving (or should move) to enshrine in the Constitution Mill's principle or one of its contemporary versions.

In the last few years, the trend in academic philosophy toward taking sides on controverted moral and policy issues has begun to affect constitutional-law commentary generally. Philosophers have analyzed and debated the issues in Supreme Court decisions—for example, abortion and affirmative action—while constitutional commentators have increasingly drawn on moral and political theorists as sources of legal doctrine and argument. John Rawls' reworking of social contract theory in *A Theory of Justice* has been especially popular with legal commentators. Emerging as the most influential legal philosopher in the United States in the later 1970s, Ronald Dworkin has argued that many difficult and controversial legal issues—particularly issues of constitutional law—*are* simply issues of normative moral and political philosophy. This trend has lent support to the idea that Mill's principle might be part of our constitutional law.

The Supreme Court itself has been less ready than have academic commentators to read philosophical theories in general—or Mill's principle in particular—into constitutional doctrine. In 1976, in its first confrontation with the precise question that began the Hart-Devlin debate, the Court upheld the constitutionality of laws punishing private homosexual acts between consenting adults against a challenge based on the *Griswold* privacy doctrine. Earlier the Court had held, though over vigorous dissent, that the Constitution did not prevent states from prohibiting the exhibition of pornographic movies to adults, in a decision with strongly Devlinesque overtones. But neither the civil liberties lawyers nor the academic commentators have been willing to take these decisions as the Court's last word on the constitutional version of the Hart-Devlin debate. Lawyers and critics have continued to argue that once the Court began to protect the rights of "consenting adults" in *Griswold*, it could not consistently stop short of reading into the Constitution some version of Mill's principle.

## 4. THE NEW ISSUES

The Hart-Devlin debate had its origins in, and was conducted largely in terms of, questions of the enforcement of traditional sexual morality by law. But Mill's principle has obvious application beyond sexual freedom for consenting adults. The principle purports to erect a clear barrier against all legal moralism, all coercive enforcement of communal ideals of decency or the sacred. Individual freedom can be legitimately constrained, according to Mill, only to protect the rights of individuals to life, liberty, and property.

While legally enforced sexual repression has retreated substantially in recent years, other regulatory impulses have arisen that seem to conflict with Mill's principle. Many of these impulses spring from recent advances in medicine and biology. Consider the movement to prohibit research on recombinant DNA, research that is aimed toward the artificial creation of new life forms. Some of the opposition to this kind of research is based upon traditional harm-based concern for public health and safety. However, others oppose DNA research on the ground that life-creating technologies violate some sense of the sacred, the idea that human beings should not play God. Similar objections are raised against research and development on extrauterine conception and gestation of human beings.

As in the days of the grave robbers, the development of medicine has generated public opposition to new uses of human cadavers. It is becoming technically feasible to maintain most of the functions of a human body by artificial means after the person in question has "died" (in the sense that the brain has irreversibly ceased functioning). Maintenance of bodies in their functioning state as objects of experiment, medical teaching devices, sources of organs for transplantation, and the like would, I believe, at the present time provoke widespread public outrage and ultimately legal prohibition. I doubt that it would be thought sufficient that the persons in question had consented to this treatment of their bodies after death or that their families had done so.

In this case and others like it that arise in the biomedical area, the grounds for prohibiting the practices are hard to square with Mill's principle. It is difficult to locate harm to the concrete interests of individual human beings in research on physiologically functioning dead bodies. What seems to be operating is a generalized sense of revulsion at the practice, akin to the nonrational "indignation, intolerance and disgust" that Lord Devlin believed justified the legal prohibition of homosexual acts.

But there has been no general rush by proponents of Mill's principle to defend the right of researchers to make free use of human cadavers. Instead, at least outside the reseach community itself, there has been a general acceptance of the propriety of regulation protective of public sensibilities. The general failure to place this new set of issues in the context of Mill's principle may mean only that there is a lag in casting new issues in traditional forms of dispute. Or it may suggest a decline in the vitality of the Millian discourse itself.

=============================  **B**  =============================

## *Interpretation and Criticism*

With its recent history in mind, it is now time to look at Mill's principle with an interpretive and critical eye. What is the principle and what can be said for and against it?

### I. POLICY AND PRINCIPLE

The debate between Mill's supporters and his critics has not been over the propriety of particular laws. The two sides do not divide fundamentally over the issue, for instance, whether there ought to be laws against private adult homosexual acts. Most of Mill's supporters oppose such laws, but it is by no means necessary that his opponents should generally favor them. What characterizes the Millian side of the debate is adherence to some general and reasonably definite *principle* of liberty of action. The exact formulation of the principle remains a matter of debate within the Millian camp.

The Devlinite camp then can be defined negatively as all those who deny that there is any such defensible general principle. The position is stated by Sir James Stephen ("I have no simple principle to assert on this matter") and by Sir Patrick Devlin ("I think . . . that it is not possible to set theoretical limits to the power of the State to legislate against immorality"). For the Devlinites, the question whether or not to have a particular piece of morals legislation is an open-ended matter of *policy*, to be decided by weighing all factors that might seem relevant in the circumstances. Such a weighing-up might lead to the conclusion that a particular law—for instance, prohibition of adult consensual homosexuality—does more harm than good, in which case Devlinites will oppose the law. But they have no theory, no general principle, that condemns the law in advance of their detailed examination of its effects and circumstances.

Of course, this formulation makes the line between the two camps seem clearer than it really is. A principle is not a mechanical rule. At the same time, for Devlinites each case is not unique; *general* policies are invoked in large classes of cases. For example, Stephen and Devlin both assert standards, more or less definite, to guide the decision whether to punish immorality. Stephen proposes that we consider "whether the object for which the compulsion is employed is good? whether the compulsion employed is likely to be effective? and whether it will be effective at a reasonable expense?" He notes some general dangers of prohibiting immorality; vice seldom does enough harm to be worth the suffering inflicted by criminal punishment, and its detection is typically expensive and threatening to privacy. Stephen urges that these considerations ought always to be taken into account, and he believes they will often tip the balance against invoking the criminal law against immorality as such. Devlin states three cautionary notes himself. Before immoralities are punished, the lawmaker should be satisfied that the vice in question "lies beyond the limits of tolerance. It is not nearly enough to say that a majority dislike a practice; there must be a real feeling of reprobation." Second, "in any new matter of morals the law should be slow to act." Finally, "as far as possible privacy should be respected," though this is not a "definite limitation" but rather "a matter to be taken into account."

How do these Devlinite policies differ from Millian principles? Devlin's own words can serve as a working formulation of the difference between the two camps. Millians assert "definite limitations" upon morals legislation; Devlinites only note "matters to be taken into account" in deciding for or against it. Especially when one concedes, as modern Millians characteristically do, that principles are not absolute, but only establish strong presumptions against their infringement, the issue between the camps becomes less a sharp division and more a question of degree. Is it enough of a division to justify the metaphor of two camps? Let us resist trying to answer in the abstract. First, we should work our way through some of the actual debate. But we are now alerted to examine proposed Millian principles for something more than their substantive appeal. We will focus as well on how *determinate* they are. If initially clear-sounding Millian formulations collapse into "matters to be taken into account," then the Devlinites have won the debate. They have defeated the claim that a *definite general principle* restricts the power of the state to enforce morals.

The controversy over whether liberty of action is a definite principle or a mere policy factor has a legal analog. Mill's principle purports to be at the very least a limitation on legitimate lawmaking authority. It is put forward, then, essentially as a *constitutional* limitation. Indeed the very question raised by the materials on sexual morality in this book is whether some version of Mill's principle is now being incorporated into American constitutional law. In our scheme of government, constitutional limitations are enforced by courts as legal restrictions on legislative power. Such limitations must thus be sufficiently definite to operate as legal rules in the decision of ordinary lawsuits. Not every verbal formula proclaiming a human right or a political ideal has seemed sufficiently definite to be judicially enforceable. For example, the courts have declined to enforce the constitutional requirements that federal spending must be "for the general welfare" and that each state must be guaranteed "a republican form of government." On the other hand, constitutional limitations apparently no more precisely worded than these *have* been found judicially enforceable (or "justiciable" as legal jargon has it). For example, courts interpret and apply the requirements that searches not be "unreasonable," that punishments not be "cruel and unusual," and that governments provide "due process of law" and "equal protection of the laws." History lends some content to these abstractions, but no one would pretend that the courts have clung close to the records of the past in their interpretations. Indeed one may fairly doubt whether there is anything but arbitrariness in the line drawn between justiciable and nonjusticiable general principles; one may suspect that the notion of "undue vagueness" is itself unduly vague. In any event, the debate over whether a proposed standard is definite enough to be applied in concrete cases is familiar to constitutional lawyers.

As these considerations should suggest, the discourse of the Millian-Devlinite debate takes on a characteristic form. First, Millians propose some version of the principle of liberty as a kind of constitutional limitation on the ordinary lawmaking power. Devlinites respond that the principle proposed is too broad, that it disables the polity from passing laws that all would agree should be within legislative discretion. They offer examples. Millians agree that some of the suggested results are unacceptable but argue that the principle of liberty as proposed has been too broadly interpreted; it can be qualified or amended to meet the difficulty. Now the Devlinites may respond that the amendment or reinterpretation has softened the proposed principle to the point where it is no longer definite enough to be a real principle; it has been reduced to a vague admonition against excessive moralistic zeal in lawmaking, a sentiment Devlinites can endorse, but a sentiment that is only a "matter to be taken into account" and no longer an enforceable "definite limitation." Millians respond that the Devlinites are creating an artificially rigid conception of what it is to be a principle . . . and the dialogue goes on.

## 2. DECENCY AND OFFENSE

Does making someone uncomfortable count as harming him? As all participants in the debate have recognized, if the answer is an unequivocal yes, then no version of Mill's principle can survive. It will always be the case that some people are upset and made uncomfortable that deviant activity is going on subject to no legal prohibition. If no one is bothered by an activity, there will be no pressure to prohibit it, and no issue of liberty can arise.

Millians thus seem driven to the position that "harm" must mean more than psychic discomfort. What then does it mean? One suggestion has been to confine the concept of harm to deprivation of property and physical injury. (The concept of "deprivation of property" is itself problematic, as we will see in the next section.) But surely this is unacceptably narrow. It is, for example, a crime (assault) to put someone in immediate fear of injury by threat of force. Are actions that cause only the psychic distress of fear to be protected by Mill's principle? Or consider laws that prohibit making obscene or threatening phone calls—surely these laws are not barred by Mill's principle. But if they are legitimate, what is the line between the psychic distress that they are meant to prevent and the distress generated in moralists by their knowledge that deviant sex is occurring with legal impunity?

More generally, there is the problem of conduct that is prohibited because it offends public sensibilities. The point can perhaps best be made with respect to prohibitions of public indecency, as applied, say, to public sexual intercourse. Can behavior that is embarrassing or distasteful to the majority when viewed in public be prohibited on that ground alone? Few Millians have come forward to argue that there can be no prohibition of public conduct on grounds of offense. Mill himself accepted the legitimacy of this sort of prohibition, as does Hart in his modern restatement of Mill's principle. Millians have typically drawn the line between public and private conduct. Public indecency can be suppressed, private deviance cannot.

The problem is to justify prohibition of some conduct on the basis of offended sensibilities without admitting offense or mental distress as a general ground for coercion, a concession that would wholly defeat Mill's principle. Professor Hart has given the best-known justification for disallowing " offense at the thought" as a ground for restriction:

> The fundamental objection surely is that a right to be protected from the distress which is inseparable from the bare knowledge that others are acting in ways you think wrong, cannot be acknowledged by anyone who recognizes individual liberty as a value. . . . To punish people for causing this form of distress would be tantamount to punishing them simply because others object to what they do; and the only liberty that could coexist with this extension of the utilitarian principle is liberty to do those things to which no one seriously objects.

On its most natural interpretation, this argument breaks down. Allowing people's distress at the thought of an activity they dislike to count as a ground for prohibition does not mean that *every* activity *anyone* seriously dislikes will be suppressed. Those who enjoy the activity will have their say on the other side, as will those who sympathize with them, those who love abstract liberty, and those who just dislike bluenoses. These forces, taken together, will frequently prevail in the political arena—as they have in Great Britain and many American states in recent years in effecting the repeal of anti-homosexual laws.

Perhaps Professor Hart did not mean to say that all *liberty* would disappear if pure distaste were admitted as a kind of harm. Perhaps he meant that no firm *right to liberty*, no *principle* protecting general individual freedom could survive under these circumstances. He would surely be right to claim that, but if offered as an argument against the Devlinites, it begs the question. For it is precisely the Devlinite position that there *is* no general right to liberty as a matter of principle; that the question of whether widely disapproved private activities shall be made criminal must be determined politically, on an issue-by-issue basis.

Finally, Professor Hart may mean that even generally accepted liberties, such as freedom of speech or religion, could not exist if pure distaste were a legitimate ground for suppression. A Devlinite response might be that it is only with respect to peculiarly important forms of human conduct that we create the special protection associated with the idea of a constitutional right. Speech and religious practice are immune from suppression on the ground of general offense only because substantive psychological, political, and moral arguments identify them as general realms of activity that deserve such extra immunity. No such special immunity can be claimed for the supposed all-embracing liberty of individuals to do as they please.

It may be that other spheres of human conduct can be brought within the category of special protection—for example, perhaps private adult sexual activity can. But to accumulate discrete particular rights is to abandon the Millian position that "nonharmful" behavior is *in general* protected, independent of any consideration of the value of that behavior.

Some Millians, recognizing the difficulties created for their principle by the prohibition of offense, have argued that even the suppression of public conduct on the grounds of decency must be rejected; if it is not, a prohibition against, for example, interracial couples' appearing together in public could be justified on the basis of the horror aroused in the breasts of racists at the very sight. But is it not the *racist* aspect of the prohibition, rather than its foundation in offended sensibilities, that makes it especially objectionable? It is hard indeed to defend the notion that no public display, however disgusting to average sensibilities, can be prohibited on grounds of decency.

### 3. PROPERTY

Why should spouses and relatives of the newly dead have anything to say about what is done with the remains? Suppose one dies without making any provision for one's burial or expressing any wishes about it. Why should not the hospital where the death occurred simply keep the cadaver and use it for dissection in the medical school anatomy classes, whatever the feelings and wishes of the family of the deceased?

There are two ways to answer this question. The straightforward way is to observe that the sensibilities of the relatives are protected by law, which gives them a limited veto over uses to which the body is put. This respect for their feelings is not absolute; for example, if the deceased died in suspicious circumstances, public authorities can require an autopsy even against the wishes of the family.

Another and more convoluted way of characterizing the matter introduces the familiar yet ultimately mysterious concept of property. It seems natural to determine what can be done with a body after death by asking who *owns* the body. Traditional law governing human remains is sometimes summarized in the statement that the next of kin own the body of the deceased, though this is usually qualified by saying that the relatives do not have "full ownership" but only a "quasi-property" right. What this murky language adds up to is that the "ownership" of a dead body does not include any right to sell the body, to give it away, to feed it to the hogs, or to keep it embalmed in the front parlor and charge admission to see it. The relatives' "ownership" means only that (1) they have a legal duty to see that the body receives a prompt decent burial, and (2) if anyone interferes with the body in a way that causes the family emotional distress, they can recover compensatory money damages. This is very far from what we usually mean in ascribing property ownership to someone.

In interpreting Mill's principle, it is common to assert as the two paradigms of harm, injury to the person and invasion of property.

The law of cadavers suggests some of the difficulties that lurk below the surface of the notion of property invasion. The first account given above of this area of law made no reference to property, but it raised a serious difficulty with Mill's principle. The hospital was forbidden by law to do something (dissect the body) on the sole basis that someone else (the relatives) would be shocked *at the thought* that the act was taking place. If the relatives are to have this control, must we not make the Devlinite concession that coercion based on distress "at the thought" is sometimes valid? If coercion is valid here, what in principle distinguishes coercion based on shock at the thought of deviant sex, drug use, and the like?

On the other hand, the second formulation seems to avoid the assault on Mill's principle by recasting the right to protect sensibilities as a property right. And of course it is uncontroversial that an invasion of a property right counts as a harm. But the very ease with which the reformulation is carried out should invite suspicion. Cannot every sensibility be recast as a property right, hence destroying Mill's principle? Why not legislatively create a property right in each person that will be infringed by anyone who engages in homosexual acts or who uses marijuana?

Before exploring possible Millian responses to this line of argument, let us consider a story that raises a related problem. Squatter moves in on an unused corner of Rancher's land with his tent and settles down. Rancher discovers he is there and tells him to leave. Squatter says he is not hurting Rancher in any way; he is not injuring the land or frustrating any practical purpose Rancher may have. He will move if and when Rancher wants to use the land in any way inconsistent with his remaining there. Rancher admits that he suffers no tangible injury or even inconvenience from Squatter's presence— he simply wants no one camping there, and it is his land. When Squatter won't go, Rancher sends for the Sheriff to arrest him for criminal trespass. Does Mill's principle protect Squatter, who insists he is not harming Rancher (or anyone else) in any way?

Of *course* not—so would say everyone accustomed to the property notions of our culture. Squatter *is* harming Rancher. He is trespassing on his land, thereby infringing his property rights. This is harm in the most classic and straightforward sense. But we must ask why Rancher is unaffected by Mill's principle, while my postulated statutory "property right" that no one shall have sex outside marriage would be dismissed by everyone as a play on words, a sham?

In order to answer this question, and resolve the dilemma posed by the law of cadavers, Millians must be able to formulate an intelligible concept of property rights. They must be able to say that not every entitlement a legislature enacts thereby becomes a property right, that indeed we have a definite and restrictive concept of what makes a legislated entitlement really a right of *property*.

Twentieth-century legal theory lends little help to Millians in their efforts to formulate such a conception. Two centuries ago, Blackstone defined property as "that sole and despotic dominion which one man claims and exercises over the external things of the world, in total exclusion of the right of any other individual in the universe." That definition may have made sense when it was written, and no doubt it closely corresponds to some inchoate popular sense of what property is even today. But it is wholly inadequate to capture present legal-economic arrangements.

First, it does not cover joint ownership. Ownership can be divided up in an almost infinite number of ways—different people can have property in parts of something, rights to use it, rights to profits from it, rights to time slices of it, and so on. Thus property is constituted of rights, not of things. Second, and more significantly, property rights need not have any connection with "things" (material objects) at all. Indeed present-day property is *mostly* made up of intangibles, like checking accounts, certificates of deposit, bonds, corporate shares, accounts receivable, pension rights, insurance policies, licenses, franchises, trademarks, copyrights, and business goodwill. It is still common to think of this kind of property in physical metaphors. An insurance policyholder "owns a piece of the rock"—but actually he has a complex set of legal claims against an abstract corporation, whose wealth itself is largely in the form of bonds, stocks, and the like. A bank depositor imagines herself to be "putting some money in the bank," as though she were placing some valued objects in a safe place. In fact she is engaging in a complex transaction giving her abstract contractual claims against an equally abstract financial institution. Shareholders in a corporation may think of themselves as part owners of the company's factory buildings outside of town. But really the corporation could sell off the buildings and still be "the same corporation." And the corporation's most valuable assets might not be its buildings but its name, its patents, and its trade secrets. Some businesses are valuable property, though they own nothing and produce nothing, because they have lost money in prior years and can provide tax benefits to another corporation that acquires them. The short of all this is that property rights can no longer be thought of as necessarily or even typically "rights in things." What, then, does property mean today?

The people who deal with the structures of the economy as professionals—lawyers, economists, financiers—have a multiplicity of technical definitions of property that have little correspondence to the classical Blackstonian definition. Let me give some examples of current technical usages. The Constitution prohibits infringing rights of "life, liberty or property without due process of law." A few years ago, the Supreme Court decided that this constitutional provision required that before individuals can lose their welfare benefits they must have the opportunity for a hearing on the question of eligibility. It was held that the statutory right to receive welfare when the stated conditions of eligibility were met was "property" within the meaning of the Constitution. Since then the Supreme Court has apparently concluded that all entitlements created by statutes are property—including, for instance, a young person's statutory right of attendance at public high school.

To take another of the disparate current conceptions of property, some lawyers have defined property rights as rights that are good against the world, as distinguished from rights (such as those established by contract) that are good only against certain people. If your neighbor sells you an easement to pass over his land, your right is good even against someone to whom he later sells the land. But if he merely makes a contract with you to let you use his land for a period in return for certain payments, that right cannot be enforced against someone who buys the land from him during the contract term. The first right is a property right, the second is not. This definition of property as all rights against the world is much broader than the popular concept of property; it includes, for example, your right not to be murdered or assaulted as a property right.

In summary, legal theory can no longer offer any generally accepted concept of property. Yet all versions of Mill's principle presuppose such a concept. Along with physical injury to the person, invasion of property rights is one of the two central categories of harms. Why is Squatter's trespass against Rancher a harm? If we are saying nothing independent of existing legal arrangements when we say "because it violates his property rights," then we are driven to seek another answer. Mill's principle is meant to be a critical standard by which existing legal arrangements may be evaluated.

### 4. PATERNALISM, EXPLOITATION, AND ECONOMIC FREEDOM

Do minimum wage laws violate Mill's principle? Most contemporary defenders of the principle would say no, and indeed would abandon the principle if it were thought to require economic laissez faire. On the other hand, left-wing critics sometimes argue that the personal freedoms liberals support are just window dressing for the fundamental core of liberalism, which is the "freedom of contract" of the capitalist marketplace. And classic liberals, or libertarians, echo this left-wing position, urging that those who argue for sexual freedom on liberal grounds cannot consistently abandon freedom to make voluntary economic transactions. In the words of the libertarian philosopher Robert Nozick, economic regulations such as minimum wage laws "prohibit capitalist acts between consenting adults."

Mill himself, though he supported laissez faire as a matter of policy, believed that market transactions fell outside the protection of his principle of liberty. As he said, "Trade is a social act. Whoever undertakes to sell any description of goods to the public does what affects the interest of other persons, and of society in general; and thus his conduct, in principle, comes within the jurisdiction of society."

What justifies Mill's saying that trade is a "social act," so that regulation of trade falls outside of the principle of liberty? It might be argued that laws like the minimum wage restrict only the employer, and do not interfere with the liberty of the worker but confer the benefit of higher pay on him. But this cannot be correct in all cases. The effect of a minimum wage must sometimes be to prevent a job being offered to a worker who is willing to work at less than the law requires, where the potential employer would rather do without the potential employee than pay the minimum. Here the state steps between two willing transactors, and the question of justification must arise; what harm is prevented?

An indirect answer is suggested by the fact that some workers *will* benefit from the minimum wage. While some who otherwise would have had jobs will go unemployed, other employees who would otherwise have received less will be raised to the minimum, unless highly unusual market conditions prevail. Exactly who will benefit and who will lose, and by how much, will generally be a technical and controverted economic question. This suggests a ground for Mill's conclusion that market regulations are "public" and hence outside the scope of the liberty principle. Such regulations are invariably redistributive, and this is typically part of their purpose. Some people benefit while others lose from such laws, just as with public taxing and spending programs. The fact that the redistributive effect of the minimum wage may be, on widely shared economic assumptions, antiegalitarian (creating unemployment among the poorest class) may be a policy argument against it, but it does not render the conduct regulated "self-regarding" in Mill's sense. Similar arguments would affect many other market regulations, including maximum hour laws, and maximum and minimum price regulation. Such laws can quite realistically be seen as taxes on those who lose and subsidies to those who gain by their redistributive effect.

On the other hand, many economic regulations seem to have no such purpose, and if they redistribute income or wealth do so only incidentally. Regulations of product or workplace safety are within this category. Thus requiring that new cars be sold with airbags, or that the workplace be free of harmful asbestos or radiation, seems primarily aimed at protecting people against harming themselves. Mill, at least, saw such laws this way and included them within the prohibition of the principle of liberty. All that could be allowed in such cases was the requirement that persons choosing an unsafe product or job be fully warned of the dangers before making the choice.

Most of Mill's modern supporters have deserted him on this point. For example, Professor Hart has proposed a major amendment to Mill's principle, striking out of it any condemnation of paternalistic regulation. Mill's principle, as modified by Hart, would allow coercive intervention to prevent harm to others *or to the actors themselves.* Hart justified this modification—a very substantial one, given the extent to which the argument of *On Liberty* was directed against paternalism—on the ground that the century since Mill wrote has seen "a general decline in the belief that individuals know their own interest best." Hart says that Mill saw the normal human being as "a middle-aged man whose desires are relatively fixed." We have had a century to learn that people are driven by unconscious desires and that their judgment about their own actions is deeply distorted by cognitive blind spots. We may still distrust paternalism, but few of us are any longer willing to accept a principle prohibiting it.

Such arguments expand on points Mill has made himself. He

excluded from the scope of the principle of liberty children and those not in full possession of their faculties. He allowed that the state could prohibit persons from selling themselves into slavery, recoiling from the paradox that a principle of liberty might protect a right to extinguish all liberty. He conceded that persons could be forcibly restrained from taking a risky step where it appeared that they might not know the risks involved. In the twentieth century we are more ready to see ourselves as in many respects children or idiots where our own welfare is concerned; as potential slaves to various addictions; and as incorrigibly unable to assimilate and properly weigh information about certain risks to our lives and safety.

Consider the question of automobile seatbelts. It can be shown that if people always fastened their seatbelts when they rode in cars, death and serious injuries occurring in accidents would be greatly reduced. This fact has been widely publicized and almost all cars are now equipped with seatbelts. Nevertheless, actual use of seatbelts remains very low. There is only a moment of inconvenience involved in fastening a seatbelt, and a slight sense of constriction, which for most people soon passes, involved in wearing one. The objective possibility of collision is a fact for anyone who rides in an automobile. What can explain the general pattern of nonuse?

The proponent of the Millian view that people know their own interests best must urge that seatbelt nonuse results from a rational weighing up of expected benefits from use (the preventable injury, discounted by its improbability) and expected costs (the actual inconvenience of buckling up). Into this equation must also be factored the individuals' attitudes toward risk of this sort—do they enjoy a gamble with life and health for its own sake, or are they averse to taking this kind of chance?

It is difficult to assign numbers with any assurance of accuracy to all these factors, but most people would agree that only rarely would anyone's fixed and considered views on the relative value of health and life, inconvenience, and risk lead to a decision not to wear a seatbelt. To explain the phenomenon of nonuse we must take account of irrational factors. In the age of Freud, it is not difficult to postulate what these might be. First, Freud himself said that we cannot truly imagine our own death. The same might be said, by extension, of very serious injury. Perhaps we are systematically unable to take effective account of the likelihood of drastic misfortune to ourselves in the subjective weighing process that underlies our daily decisions; in Freudian terms, we repress the possibility of our own death or injury. Second, many of us associate taking explicit health and safety measures with parental control, and freedom from such measures with adulthood and autonomy; thus driving without a seatbelt or riding a motorcycle without a helmet reenacts the psychic drama of the struggle to emancipate ourselves from our parents.

Of course, to assert these psychological claims is not to prove their truth. Perhaps equally familiar as denial of death and childish acting out are compulsive hand washing, safety obsession, and hypochondriasis. The point of introducing considerations of neurotic and unconsciously motivated behavior is not to settle the question of paternalism, but to argue that it must be treated as an issue of policy, to be resolved case by case in light of detailed facts and flexible guidelines, rather than prohibited once and for all as an issue of principle. We have strong grounds to doubt Mill's presumption that people are generally best able to decide in their own interests; very often *others* can by virtue of their detachment have clearer sight about rational behavior for an individual than he does.

If this sort of argument is accepted, so that Mill's principle is no longer read to prohibit paternalism, laws like the requirement of passive restraints (such as airbags) in cars, the requirement that motorcyclists wear helmets, the prohibition of known dangerous addicting drugs, all fall outside the scope of the principle. This is the conclusion that Professor Hart, among others, has reached, and it is probably the dominant position among contemporary Millians.

Once this concession is made, the question arises whether Mill's principle in its surviving aspect can stand by itself. In its original formulation the principle prohibits two kinds of coercive interference—the moralistic and the paternalistic. In its weaker version, it prohibits only legal moralism, leaving paternalism in the realm of policy.

Lord Devlin has argued that the same grounds Professor Hart cites as justifying paternalistic protection of health and safety likewise justify what he calls "moral paternalism." Does Hart mean to distinguish between "physical" and "moral" paternalism? Devlin asks. No such distinction can be sustained in principle. The same psychological discoveries that have led us to see that adults are not always the best judges of their own interests in matters of health and safety support similar conclusions in the sphere of morals. "If paternalism be the principle, no father of a family would content himself with looking after his children's welfare and leaving their morals to themselves. . . . If, on the other hand, we are grown up enough to look after our own morals, why not after our own bodies?" And yet, as Devlin says, if "moral paternalism" is accepted, this leaves nothing to be protected by Mill's principle. It makes little difference in practice whether we say we are prohibiting immoral acts for the sake of morality itself or to protect persons against their own moral weaknesses.

Against this argument of Devlin's, the response must be to draw an empirically based distinction between the state's authority to presume what individuals' best interests are in matters of health and safety on the one hand, and on matters of morals (Devlin has in mind chiefly sexual morals) on the other. A person who suffers serious physical injury which a fastened seatbelt would have prevented will *regret* not using the belt. He will unequivocally wish the injury hadn't happened; he has no doubt that he was harmed. Contrast the sexual sinner (you may choose your sin). In some cases he will regard himself as a compulsive person and wish he could stop; but in many others he will not. No longer is there a consensus as to what counts as "moral self-harm" in sexual matters. Any effective consensus would have to include the typical "perpetrator-victims" of the supposed self-harmful act. In the sexual case, even if 90 percent of the population thinks that some sexual pratice amounts to moral self-harm but most of the 10 percent who engage in the practice do not see it that way, then the analogy to physical paternalism does not hold. In the case of health, but not in the case of sexual deviance, we can say that the persons subject to paternalist restraint are injuring themselves on their own view of their interests.

Some paternalistic laws are also antiexploitative. Laws against sweatshop working conditions are aimed at exploitation, whereas laws requiring every new car sold to be equipped with an airbag are not. What is meant by exploitation is that one side of a transaction is taking advantage of some weakness in the other party. Housing codes, the unenforceability of contracts made by children with adults, and prohibition of psychiatrists' seducing their patients are other examples of prohibiting exploitation.

Mill himself was prepared to consider making an exception to his antipaternalistic stance in cases where people made exploiting human weakness their livelihood:

Fornication, for example, must be tolerated, and so must gambling, but should a person be free to be a pimp, or to keep a gambling house? . . . On the side of toleration it may be said that the following of anything as an occupation, and living or profiting by the practice of it, cannot make that criminal which would otherwise be admissible. . . . In opposition to this it may be contended that, although the public, or the State, are not warranted in authoritatively deciding, for purposes of repression or punishment, that such or such conduct affecting only the interests of the individual is good or bad . . . they cannot be acting wrongly in endeavoring to exclude the influence of solicitations which are not disinterested, of instigators who cannot possibly be impartial, who have a direct personal interest on one side, and that side the one which the State believes to be wrong, and who confessedly promote it for personal objects only.

The point is that where A has a financial incentive to close a transaction with B that is likely to be against B's interests, but toward which B is impelled by some recognized powerful motive known to have special power to override one's better judgment, there is an especially strong case for paternalistic intervention. In cases of economic exploitation, B's weakness is poverty, and his judgment is distorted by a powerful need for money in the short run. In the case of transactions between adults and children, we recognize the undeveloped impulse control of the young. Where the temptation offered is sex or gambling, there are again familiar distorting drives and compulsions at work.

## 5. CAUSATION, ACTION, AND OMISSION

Does Mill's principle allow every coercive intervention that is reasonably calculated to prevent harm from *occurring*? Or does it allow only coercion aimed at preventing the *doing* or *causing* of harm? In ordinary life, we draw a distinction between someone's causing harm on the one hand and merely allowing it to happen on the other.

The distinction I have in mind, between causing and allowing harm, presupposes that someone does suffer harm. We may imagine that someone dies or is badly injured. The distinction does not involve the degree of loss to the victim, but the causal contribution to it on the part of the person whom we are considering subjecting to coercion.

Thus this is not the distinction between causing harm and merely withholding a benefit. The harm versus nonbenefit distinction presupposes some benchmark of normal or appropriate welfare and designates a person's falling below that benchmark as harm, while misfortune that leaves the person above the benchmark is considered merely the absence of a benefit. The two distinctions are often confused with each other, especially under the terminology of "positive" versus "negative" duties.

A third distinction, variously phrased as the action-inaction, act-omission, or misfeasance-nonfeasance distinction, may or may not be separate from the first—the distinction between causing harm and merely allowing it to happen. Some would say that the notion of "cause" is so intimately linked to the notion of "action" that it would not make sense to say that someone caused an injury to someone else by inaction. But most would agree that where there is an independent duty to act, the inactive failure to discharge that duty *causes* harm in any case where discharge would have prevented that harm. Thus where a jailer is obligated to feed a prisoner and fails to do so, and as a result the prisoner starves, most people would say that the jailer's inaction caused the prisoner's death. Few would, I think, seriously argue that any principle of liberty should protect the jailer from being held legally responsible.

What many *do* believe is that liberty is violated where people are coerced to prevent harm they have not caused. Suppose that A needs a kidney transplant to survive and asks B, a stranger, to donate one. B refuses; no other donor comes forward; and A dies. Can B properly be said to have caused A's death? Nowhere does the law now hold B causally responsible for A's death in this situation; the question is, would a principle of liberty be violated if B were made responsible?

It is not clear whether Mill himself would have thought coercion in these circumstances to violate the principle of liberty. What *is* clear is that Mill thought coercion could be properly used to compel action where inaction would, in his words, "cause evil." He thought such duties to act for the aid of others should be the exception rather than the rule, but this was for him a matter of policy, which turned on the "special expediencies of the case." His language leaves open the possibility that there might be cases in which we would say that one person's inaction did not *cause* injury to another but merely allowed that injury to occur, and that in such cases holding the inactive person responsible would violate his liberty. Perhaps he would have seen the hypothetical reluctant kidney donor as raising such a case.

On the other hand, it is possible that Mill would not have thought there was any important distinction between "causing harm by inaction" and "merely allowing it to occur." One conception of causation would regard B, in the hypothetical kidney case, as unequivocally the *cause* of A's death through his refusal to donate a kidney, since a course of action was open to B that would have averted A's death—that is, donation of the kidney. This is what lawyers call the "but-for" conception of causation. Under it, event X is the cause of event Y if "but for" the occurrence of X, Y would not have occurred. Logicians would call it the "necessary condition" test; X causes Y if X is a necessary condition of Y. Under such a conception, we might not want to force B to donate his kidney to A, but we would have to say that B killed A—excusably or justifiably killed him, perhaps, but killed him nonetheless—in refusing to donate it.

Such a conception of causation is profoundly counterintuitive. To confirm this, consider another example. Each of the readers of this passage could, by dint of personal effort and expense, no doubt save some *one* of the many children who will die of malnutrition or disease throughout the world in the next year. To do it, you might have to give up your present station in life, at least temporarily; raise all the money you can; travel to Bangladesh or Somalia. Or it might turn out that you could be assured of the result if you just gave one half of your income to a reliable charitable organization. It would take some considerable time and effort to find out how one could be reasonably sure to save a single child, but you could do it.

It is a fair prediction that few readers of this passage will follow this course. Shall it be said of each of you, and also of me, that we have each of us *caused the death* of the child (presently unknown to us) whom we each would have saved had we undertaken this enterprise? Note that the argument is further subject to reiteration. Even the person who *does* undertake the saving mission for one child could presumably, with greater effort and expense, save *two*. Indeed the only limit placed on the saving capacity of each of us is our need for survival—in this version of causation, we *cause* the deaths of children as long as we leave ourselves *any margin* of money, time, or energy above what is needed to avert our own death.

Does this story make out a successful *reductio ad absurdum* argument against the conception of "causing harm" under which B has caused harm to A as long as there is some action open to B that would save A from harm? The notion that each of us causes all the death and misery in the world that we could conceivably prevent almost entirely eliminates the usefulness of the concept of causation in the ascription of human responsibility. It may be that we will want to accept this consequence and admit that each of us has caused the death of (i.e., *killed*) those children; we will certainly depart from ordinary usage if we say so, but perhaps this is a reform of ordinary language we will want to undertake. Dropping causation as a limiting concept forces us to confront in more explicitly normative terms the scope of our responsibilities. We would no longer be able to say of each dead child, "Well, *I* didn't kill him." We will have to conclude that we value our comfort, our plans, our range of individual options more than we value the lives of children personally unknown to us, and we will have to then justify these priorities to ourselves.

I suspect that no such reform of ordinary language and ordinary moral thought can possibly be carried through with any consistency. The consequences of sincerely attempting it would not be more altruism or wider moral vision, but helpless anxiety and endless hypocrisy on the part of most of those making the experiment. If I am right, some limiting notion of what it is to *cause* harm by inaction must be recognized. When that is done, it will be plausible to say that Mill's principle prohibits coercion to prevent harm that is not caused or threatened by the person against whom the coercion is directed.

Some have argued that no such intelligible line can be drawn between those events that are actually *caused* and those that are merely occasioned by inaction. The argument is that the common notion of human causation is intimately linked to the common notion of action; only when persons act can it be intelligibly said that they have caused consequences. Persons holding this view may argue that Mill's principle ought to be extended to protect against any coercive requirement that persons take positive action to avert avoidable harm. On this view, associated with modern libertarianism, the state violates liberty if it imposes civil or criminal sanctions on a doctor who refuses emergency treatment to a badly injured patient, even when no other doctor is unavailable, and however trivial the reasons for the doctor's refusal to give treatment. As the passage quoted above (see p. 26) indicates, Mill himself held no such view; but he did not address himself to the difficult question of what the limitations were to be on the extent to which inaction could be said to cause harm. As the materials in Chapter 4 will illustrate, the Anglo-American common law has long incorporated a general principle that inaction (or as the legal jargon has it, nonfeasance) will not give rise to criminal or civil liability. That doctrine has long been subject to intense criticism because it legally permits instances of dreadful callousness and selfishness. But at the same time, it has been defended by libertarians as a necessary if troubling consequence of the principled protection of individual liberty and autonomy.

## 6. COLLECTIVE INSTITUTIONS

Under Mill's principle, what is the justification for punishing espionage, perjury, contempt of court, or tax evasion? Very often these crimes do no direct harm to any individual. Take the case of someone who perjures himself so that a criminal escapes punishment—who is hurt by this? The natural answer, easily accepted by most defenders of Mill's principle, is that this action tends to undermine the deterrent effect of the criminal law, which in turn is needed to protect individuals against concrete injury to person or property.

But this natural answer opens up what is in many ways the most sweeping of objections to Mill's principle. Perjury against the state—or the other crimes catalogued above—typically cause harm to individuals only indirectly, through the undermining effect such actions have on important collective institutions. Furthermore, the concrete injury to these institutions of any particular violation is typically undetectable—it is only when one considers that *many* people may perjure themselves, or not pay taxes, if these matters are left to private decision that one can locate the harm justifying coercion.

Opponents of Mill's principle urge that many of the main examples of "morals legislation" or "victimless crime" are justified as laws protecting collective institutions. For example, it is said that the laws prohibiting sex outside marriage are designed to protect the family. If one believes that stable monogamous marriage is a socially valuable institution, and that the institution is in part defined by the designation of sexual relations outside marriage—fornication, adultery, and homosexuality—as illegitimate, then the argument for these laws has exactly the same form as the argument for the laws against perjury or tax evasion. The claim is not that isolated nonmarital sex acts harm particular individuals or that these acts are punishable because they violate some abstract moral code; rather, the claim is that some legal restraint is needed in addition to social or customary sexual mores to protect the social structure of monogamous marriage against being undermined by general disregard of its limitations.

It is not necessary here to resolve the factual issues that this argument raises. One can argue about how important sexual fidelity is to marital stability and about how important marital stability is to child-rearing and the other social goals promoted by the family. One can debate how useful or necessary legal sanctions are in enforcing sexual mores. One can further separate out the various sorts of sexual aberration—perhaps adultery is more threatening to the stable family than fornication, and so on. The point is not how one *comes out* when one enters into these factual and value disputes; the point is that as soon as one ventures onto the terrain of balancing values and guessing at debatable social facts, the Millian position is in jeopardy. Where the legitimacy of particular laws against sexual activity turn on the assessment of such contingent, debatable, and fluctuating matters, it becomes increasingly difficult to treat the question as one of principle; the question looks more like one of policy, one in which sexual liberty, privacy, family stability, and so on are all "matters to be taken into account" in striking the legislative balance.

Devlinites need not conclude as an empirical matter that criminal punishment is a useful deterrent to adultery or that widespread adultery is threatening to the family as a stabilizing social structure. Some of them will come out one way and some the other on this question. They will all agree, however, that the question is one that will be answered differently from time to time and from place to place; none of them will believe it is a question that can be answered independent of the facts and outside of history and concrete politics by an abstract principle such as Mill's.

Contemporary Millians have seen the threat to their position in the argument that conduct should be prohibited because, if generalized, it will undermine valued collective institutions. Their response has been to attempt to place the argument under a double handicap. They have dubbed the argument from collective institutions "the disintegration thesis"—the thesis, that is, that society will disintegrate if the law does not protect its central institutions by legally enforcing the *mores* that constitute them. Millians have not generally denied that it would be right to prohibit a social practice that had so disastrous an effect, but they have urged that the burden of proof must rest on the proponents of coercion to demonstrate a serious threat of *social disintegration* before interference with liberty on this ground can be justified. Of course such a burden is in practice impossible to meet.

Why should the *proponents* of legal regulation have the burden of proof, and why must they prove a threat of *disintegration*? Let us take the second question first. It seems absurd to say that society can protect one of its valued institutions against injury only if there is a threat of the total disintegration of society itself. Take the example of perjury. Suppose we removed all criminal penalties against committing perjury in favor of a defendant in a criminal trial, on the ground that such perjury is a victimless crime. No one could believe that the system would be very seriously damaged, much less that society would disintegrate. Many witnesses would continue to testify truthfully, because they thought it wrong to lie generally, or because they felt especially bound by an oath to tell the truth, or because they wanted the defendant punished, or because they feared humiliation and disgrace if their false testimony were exposed. Many other witnesses would lie, probably more than do now. But many witnesses lie under oath today anyway; they are very rarely prosecuted and less often convicted.

We cannot be sure that any serious negative consequences would result from the "decriminalization" of perjury against the state; perhaps the only thing we *can* be sure of is that society would not disintegrate as a result. Yet no one would think of arguing that making perjury against the state a crime violates some basic principle of liberty because it neither harms individuals nor threatens social disintegration. It is enough that there is some betrayal of a valued collective institution.

Similar stories can be told with respect to other crimes against the state, such as bribery and tax evasion. In many countries there is a virtual decriminalization in practice of certain forms of these two activities. Those societies do not disintegrate as a result. Indeed some of them have flourished as great civilizations with essentially no legal suppression of some varieties of bribery or tax evasion for hundreds and even thousands of years. That this is so provides no argument for striking these "victimless crimes" off our statute books in the name of some principle of individual liberty. In short, we do not need a threat of disintegration to find ourselves justified in protecting collective institutions. Minor injury will suffice.

Now let us return to the first question: assuming that collective institutions may be legally protected against injury if they are merely useful to society's functioning, though not necessary to its survival, why should the proponents of such legal protection bear the burden of proof that any concrete injury will result? Suppose this burden were placed upon defenders of the laws against perjury or bribery. Could they show, with any sort of convincing scientific evidence, that decriminalizing these activities would lead to *any* serious social detriment at all? You may believe as I do that a society is better where the law tells witnesses they must not lie under oath and tells officials they must not use their office for private gain. Many people likewise believe that societies are better, cleaner, more vigorous, where strict sexual morality is practiced and enforced by law. In neither case could the proponents of these views prove their case conclusively; in either case, they could give examples from history and comparative politics that would cut in their favor, examples that could be countered by competing examples from their opponents. Do you prefer Sparta or Athens; republican or Augustan Rome; contemporary China or contemporary Italy?

Mill recognized that his principle of liberty could be realized only in an advanced and complex society, one characterized by stable collective institutions. He never doubted that society could legitimately protect its basic institutional fabric by law, in addition to punishing acts that harmed individuals directly. The difficulty with his position is in drawing any principled distinction between those customary institutional norms and practices that are, and those that are not, part of the fundamental fabric. We think of the courts and government fiscal apparatus as unquestionably fundamental, legitimately to be protected by law, even against "victimless crimes." Should the traditional family be seen in this light? The evidence of history and anthropology suggests that all known societies have placed some restrictions, flowing from their kinship and family structure, on sexual activity. The content of the restrictions has varied with the different family structures that have existed—just as the content of the law of theft has varied with the different property structures in effect in different cultures.

What about the social structures defined by burial customs? Again, all known societies have had established procedures and rituals for disposing of the bodies of the dead. In most cases, breaches of these procedures have been treated as serious offenses against the social order. Do our traditions with respect to the handling of human remains deserve similar legal protection, apart from any particular harm to an individual that might be caused by breaches of these traditions? To modify an example used earlier, suppose a group asked that bodies unclaimed at the morgue be turned over to them so that they might remove and shrink the heads, which would then be used as objects of amusement. On what basis would the law say no to this? Doubtless reasons of health or hygiene would be given, but surely all can recognize that such grounds would be specious. Human burial is treated differently from the disposal of the bodies of animals for reasons other than health. Are not those reasons rooted in a sense that collectively defined and transmitted restrictions on burial customs are part of what makes up the institutional framework of our society? No harm would be done by shrinking human heads for souvenirs in a society in which that was customary, but in ours that is *not* what is done with human remains. The "harm" or "injury" from the practice is the inconsistency with our collective self-definition. Here, no more than in the case of our approach to taxes or witnesses' oaths, can we do more than guess that a different collective self-definition might not be, in some Olympian sense, just as good.

This introduction has aimed at flagging a number of difficulties that are raised by the effort to establish Mill's principle as a reasonably definite protection of "freedom of harmless action." It is by no means a comprehensive discussion, or even a comprehensive introductory sketch, of all the important philosophical issues that can arise out of the debate over Mill's principle.

In the first place, I have not given equal time to arguments for Mill's principle. I have assumed an audience on the whole inclined to agree with Mill, and have played the gadfly to this inclination.

Second, I have almost entirely ignored the issues of ethical theory that are often discussed in connection with these matters. It is often debated whether Mill's principle can rest on a utilitarian foundation, as Mill himself thought. Many contemporary philosophers would disagree with Mill, arguing that the principle can be justified only by some separate, deontological doctrine—some individual right to be considered as an autonomous person, categorically entitled to treatment with dignity and respect equal to that accorded all other persons.

Such questions of ethical theory are important in their own right. While there is room for some skepticism about how often views on these matters affect resolution of the more concrete disputes that are the focus of this book, I would not carry such skepticism too far. On even the most mundane issue of policy, there exist divergent views that are recognizably linked to belief in Bentham's calculus of utility on the one hand or Kant's kingdom of ends on the other.

The characteristic mind-set of the Anglo-American lawyer is intuitionistic and biased toward the concrete and particular. Offer a lawyer trained in our tradition a theory or principle, and he will respond in terms of cases—first asking for a typical case to illustrate what the theory means in application, then challenging the theory with a "hard case," where application seems to produce a counter-intuitive result. If you respond by holding to the principle while agreeing that the result it compels seems wrong, you are not speaking the lawyer's language. He will expect you to recast or reconstrue the theory, however much it seems to you rooted in the nature of things. On the whole, the Anglo-American lawyer's case-law intuitionist approach dominates this book. The reader should be on guard against this bias, recalling that there are those who believe this is a false and dangerous way to proceed in ethical argumentation.

No one has spoken more vigorously against basing moral conclusions on intuitions about cases than did Immanuel Kant. He argued that moral principles cannot, without circularity, be tested by merely considering examples. "For each example of morality which is exhibited to me must itself have been previously judged according to principles of morality to see whether it is worthy to serve as an original example." Reliance on intuitions and examples in the first instance produces mere "popular practical philosophy" whose measure is not truth but only popularity, a "disgusting jumble of patched-up observations and half-reasoned principles." For Kant, this is because intuitions follow from mere "incentives of feeling and inclination" which can never sustain a consistent framework of moral principles. "Principles must be erected on concepts; on any other foundation there are only passing moods which give the person no moral worth and not even confidence in himself, without which the consciousness of his moral disposition and character, the highest good in man, cannot arise."

I tend to believe, with Hume as against Kant, that moral judgments *inevitably* arise in large part from feelings and inclinations and that the ideal that one should decide these matters on the basis of abstract concepts stripped of feeling is more likely to result in hypocrisy and self-delusion than in integrity of character and purity of heart. We can discover and clarify our moral sentiments in no better way than by stimulating them through the use of examples and the confrontation of concrete cases. In so clarifying our sentiments, we discover where they clash and may then begin work on the difficult task of forming them as nearly as may be into a working whole—the task of pulling ourselves together.

Relying on concrete intuition does not mean being uncritical. It is true that if we not only begin but end with our immediate intuitive responses to situations, we do no more in ethical or legal reasoning than to rationalize the prejudices we have been taught. But in my view we cannot effectively subject our views to criticism by struggling to detach judgment from feeling. Rather we should try to confront one feeling with another, by changing the way in which we represent to ourselves the concrete situations we encounter. Our intuitions flow not from the situation as a thing-in-itself but from the situation-as-represented. Perhaps you have seen the ambiguous drawing, used in perception psychology, that can be seen as either a rabbit or a duck. If you have always seen it only as a rabbit, you react to it only as a rabbit. One of the tasks of philosophy is to get ourselves to see ducks and rabbits where we have previously seen only rabbits or only ducks.

# SEXUAL FREEDOM
# AND THE CONSTITUTION

The question of the legitimacy of legal enforcement of sexual morality has been the centerpiece of the modern debate over Mill's principle, as the Introduction has indicated. To many people the term "morality" *means* no more than sexual morality, and the debate over the enforcement of morality is just an abstract way of talking about the question whether the law should punish unorthodox sex acts between consenting adults. In this book we are working from the assumption that Mill's principle has wider implications than that, but it does seem sensible to start with a detailed consideration of what to most people is the heart of the matter.

As the Introduction suggested, the modern debate over Mill's principle has come to intersect with an important controversy within American constitutional law—the legitimacy and content of the constitutional "right to privacy" developed by our courts since the mid-1960s. This constitutional debate has two dimensions. First, it echoes older debates over the extent to which American courts can properly "invent new rights" not to be found by normal methods of interpretation within the text of the Constitution. This debate is in many ways parallel with the distinction drawn in the Introduction between Millians, who think in terms of a principle of liberty, and their opponents, who regard general liberty of action as rather a policy, a matter to be taken into account, than a definite limitation on collective power. The analogue among constitutional lawyers is the division between those who think that these questions of privacy and liberty are matters for the courts finally to decide on grounds of principle and those who think that in the absence of clear consti-tutional textual guidance they should be treated as questions of prudence and policy, left to the legislative process for final res-olution.

Second, once one accepts the existence of a constitutional right to privacy, there remains the question of its content. In particular, some would argue privacy should draw content from the Millian idea that individuals must be left alone in their behavior unless they can be shown to be doing definite harm; while on the other hand, others would confine it to the protection of various discrete and historically valued areas of immunity from collective intrusion, particularly the area of traditional family life.

39

# A.

# The Right to Privacy

The right to privacy was introduced into American constitutional law in the famous case of *Griswold v. Connecticut*. Extensive excerpts follow from the six separate opinions delivered by Supreme Court Justices in the decision of the case. You will notice that the four opinions of the Justices in the majority differ in the grounds they give for reaching the same result. Justice Douglas, writing for a majority of the Court, places the decision on the basis of a "right to privacy" which makes its first constitutional appearance in this case. Justice White and Justice Harlan do not join this opinion; rather, they base their decisions in different ways on the Fourteenth Amendment's prohibition against depriving persons of liberty without due process of law. Justice Goldberg adopts a middle position, joining the Douglas opinion on the one hand, while agreeing with White and Harlan that the Connecticut law also invades a protected "liberty" and further arguing that the Ninth Amendment lends additional support to the decision.

To understand the debate among the majority Justices, which may seem a mere verbal dispute over what label to give to their decision, you should know some historical background.

In *Griswold*, the Court was operating under the shadow of the now-discredited earlier decision of *Lochner v. New York*, 198 U.S. 45 (1905), in which the Court struck down a law limiting the hours bakery employees could work to sixty a week. The Court held that the law violated the "liberty"—in particular the "liberty of contract"—implicit in the Due Process Clause. In his famous dissent in *Lochner*, Justice Holmes wrote:

> This case is decided upon an economic theory which a large part of the country does not entertain. If it were a question whether I agreed with that theory, I should desire to study it further and long before making up my mind. But I do not conceive that to be my duty, because I strongly believe that my agreement or disagreement has nothing to do with the right of a majority to embody their opinions in law. . . . The liberty of the citizen to do as he likes as long as he does not interfere with the liberty of others to do the same, which has been a shibboleth for some well-known writers, is interfered with by school laws, by the Post Office,

by every state or municipal institution which takes his money for purposes thought desirable, whether he likes it or not. The Fourteenth Amendment does not enact Mr. Herbert Spencer's *Social Statics*. . . . A constitution is not intended to embody a particular economic theory, whether of paternalism and the organic relation of the citizen to the State or of *laissez faire*. It is made for people of fundamentally differing views, and the accident of our finding certain opinions natural and familiar or novel or even shocking ought not to conclude our judgment upon the question whether statutes embodying them conflict with the Constitution of the United States. . . . I think that the word liberty in the Fourteenth Amendment is perverted when it is held to prevent the natural outcome of a dominant opinion, unless it can be said that a rational and fair man would admit that the statute proposed would infringe fundamental principles as they have been understood by the traditions of our people and our law.

Later, during the New Deal (when Hugo Black and William Douglas were appointed Justices), the Court repudiated the doctrine of freedom of contract and endorsed Holmes's *Lochner* dissent.

## 1. *Griswold v. Connecticut**

*In reading the Griswold opinion, consider the following: (a) Do the majority Justices escape the reproach leveled by Justice Black that they are committing, from a different political point of view, the mistake of Lochner as Holmes analyzed it? (b) From the opinions, are the right to privacy, the Ninth Amendment, and substantive due process significantly different justifications for the Court's decision? How do they differ? (c) Justice Harlan says the enforcement of morality as such constitutes a legitimate basis for state coercion. Why isn't the Connecticut birth-control statute sustained on this ground?*

MR. JUSTICE DOUGLAS delivered the opinion of the Court.

Appellant Griswold is Executive Director of the Planned Parenthood League of Connecticut. Appellant Buxton is a licensed physician and a professor at the Yale Medical School who served as Medical Director for the League at its Center in New Haven—a center open and operating from November 1 to November 10, 1961, when appellants were arrested.

They gave information, instruction, and medical advice to *mar-

* 381 U.S. 479 (1965).

*ried persons* as to the means of preventing conception. They examined the wife and prescribed the best contraceptive device or material for her use. Fees were usually charged, although some couples were serviced free.

The statutes whose constitutionality is involved in this appeal are §§ 53-32 and 54-196 of the General Statutes of Connecticut (1958 rev.). The former provides:

> Any person who uses any drug, medicinal article or instrument for the purpose of preventing conception shall be fined not less than fifty dollars or imprisoned not less than sixty days nor more than one year or be both fined and imprisoned.

Section 54-196 provides:

> Any person who assists, abets, counsels, causes, hires or commands another to commit any offense may be prosecuted and punished as if he were the principal offender.

The appellants were found guilty as accessories and fined $100 each, against the claim that the accessory statute as so applied violated the Fourteenth Amendment. . . . Coming to the merits, we are met with a wide range of questions that implicate the Due Process Clause of the Fourteenth Amendment. Overtones of some arguments suggest that *Lochner v. New York*, 198 U.S. 45, should be our guide. But we decline that invitation. . . . We do not sit as a super-legislature to determine the wisdom, need, and propriety of laws that touch economic problems, business affairs, or social conditions. This law, however, operates directly on an intimate relation of husband and wife and their physician's role in one aspect of that relation. . . . [S]pecific guarantees in the Bill of Rights have penumbras, formed by emanations from those guarantees that help give them life and substance. . . . Various guarantees create zones of privacy. The right of association contained in the penumbra of the First Amendment is one. . . . The Third Amendment in its prohibition against the quartering of soldiers "in any house" in time of peace without the consent of the owner is another facet of that privacy. The Fourth Amendment explicitly affirms the "right of the people to be secure in their persons, houses, papers, and effects, against unreasonable searches and seizures." The Fifth Amendment in its Self-Incrimination Clause enables the citizen to create a zone of privacy which government may not force him to surrender to his detriment. The Ninth Amendment provides: "The enumeration in the Constitution, of certain rights, shall not be construed to deny or disparage others retained by the people." . . .

The present case, then, concerns a relationship lying within the zone of privacy created by several fundamental constitutional guarantees. And it concerns a law which, in forbidding the *use* of contraceptives rather than regulating their manufacture or sale, seeks to achieve its goals by means having a maximum destructive impact upon that relationship. Such a law cannot stand in light of the familiar principle, so often applied by this Court, that a "governmental purpose to control or prevent activities constitutionally subject to state regulation may not be achieved by means which sweep unnecessarily broadly and thereby invade the area of protected freedoms." . . . Would we allow the police to search the sacred precincts of marital bedrooms for telltale signs of the use of contraceptives? The very idea is repulsive to the notions of privacy surrounding the marriage relationship.

We deal with a right of privacy older than the Bill of Rights— older than our political parties, older than our school system. Marriage is a coming together for better or for worse, hopefully enduring, and intimate to the degree of being sacred. It is an association that promotes a way of life, not causes; a harmony in living, not political faiths; a bilateral loyalty, not commercial or social projects. Yet it is an association for as noble a purpose as any involved in our prior decisions.

MR. JUSTICE GOLDBERG, whom THE CHIEF JUSTICE and MR. JUSTICE BRENNAN join, concurring.

I agree with the Court that Connecticut's birth-control law unconstitutionally intrudes upon the right of marital privacy, and I join in its opinion and judgment. . . . I . . . agree that the concept of liberty protects those personal rights that are fundamental, and is not confined to the specific terms of the Bill of Rights. My conclusion that the concept of liberty is not so restricted and that it embraces the right of marital privacy though that right is not mentioned explicitly in the Constitution is supported . . . by the language and history of the Ninth Amendment. . . .

The Ninth Amendment reads, "The enumeration in the Constitution, of certain rights, shall not be construed to deny or disparage others retained by the people." The Amendment is almost entirely the work of James Madison. It was introduced in Congress by him and passed the House and Senate with little or no debate and virtually no change in language. It was proffered to quiet expressed fears that a bill of specifically enumerated rights could not be sufficiently broad to cover all essential rights and that the specific mention of certain rights would be interpreted as a denial that others were protected.

In presenting the proposed Amendment, Madison said:

> It has been objected also against a bill of rights, that, by enumerating particular exceptions to the grant of power, it would disparage those rights which were not placed in that enumeration; and it might follow by implication, that those rights which were not singled out, were intended to be assigned into the hands of the General Government, and were consequently insecure. This is one of the most plausible arguments I have ever heard urged against the admission of a bill of rights into this system; but, I conceive, that it may be guarded against. I have attempted it, as gentlemen may see by turning to the last clause of the fourth resolution [the Ninth Amendment].

Mr. Justice Story wrote of this argument against a bill of rights and the meaning of the Ninth Amendment:

> In regard to . . . [a] suggestion, that the affirmance of certain rights might disparage others, or might lead to argumentative implications in favor of other powers, it might be sufficient to say that such a course of reasoning could never be sustained upon any solid basis. . . . But a conclusive answer is, that such an attempt may be interdicted (as it has been) by a positive declaration in such a bill of rights that the enumeration of certain rights shall not be construed to deny or disparage others retained by the people. J. Story, *Commentaries on the Constitution of the United States*, 626−627 (5th ed. 1801).

He further stated, referring to the Ninth Amendment:

> This clause was manifestly introduced to prevent any perverse or ingenious misapplication of the well-known maxim, that an affirmation in particular cases implies a negation in all others; and, *e converso*, that a negation in particular cases implies an affirmation in all others. . . .

These statements of Madison and Story make clear that the Framers did not intend that the first eight amendments be construed to exhaust the basic and fundamental rights which the Constitution guaranteed to the people. . . .

MR. JUSTICE HARLAN, concurring in the judgment.

I fully agree with the judgment of reversal, but find myself unable to join the Court's opinion. The reason is that it seems to me to evince an approach to this case very much like that taken by my Brothers BLACK and STEWART in dissent, namely: the Due Process Clause of the Fourteenth Amendment does not touch this Connecticut statute unless the enactment is found to violate some right assured by the letter or penumbra of the Bill of Rights. . . . In my view, the proper constitutional inquiry in this case is whether this Connecticut statute infringes the Due Process Clause of the Fourteenth Amendment because the enactment violates basic values "implicit in the concept of ordered liberty," . . . For reasons stated at length in my dissenting opinion in *Poe v. Ullman, supra,* I believe that it does. . . .

[The following passage is from Mr. Justice Harlan's opinion in the earlier Connecticut birth-control case of *Poe v. Ullman,* 367 U.S. 497 (1961).]

. . . I consider that this Connecticut legislation, as construed to apply to these appellants, violates the Fourteenth Amendment. I believe that a statute making it a criminal offense for married couples to use contraceptives is an intolerable and unjustifiable invasion of privacy in the conduct of the most intimate concerns of an individual's personal life. . . .

[T]he basis of judgment as to the constitutionality of state action must be a rational one, approaching the text which is the only commission for our power not in a literalistic way, as if we had a tax statute before us, but as the basic charter of our society, setting out in spare but meaningful terms the principles of government. . . . But as inescapable as is the rational process in constitutional adjudication in general, nowhere is it more so than in giving meaning to the prohibitions of the Fourteenth Amendment and, where the Federal Government is involved, the Fifth Amendment, against the deprivation of life, liberty or property without due process of law.

It is but a truism to say that this provision of both Amendments is not self-explanatory. As to the Fourteenth, which is involved here, the history of the Amendment also sheds little light on the meaning of the provision. . . . It is important to note, however, that two views of the Amendment have not been accepted by this Court as delineating its scope. One view, which was ably and insistently argued in response to what were felt to be abuses by this Court of its reviewing power, sought to limit the provision to a guarantee of procedural fairness. . . . The other view which has been rejected would have it that the Fourteenth Amendment, whether by way of the Privileges and Immunities Clause or the Due Process Clause, applied against the States only and precisely those restraints which had prior to the Amendment been applicable merely to federal action. However, "due process" in the consistent view of this Court has ever been a broader concept than the first view and more flexible than the second.

Were due process merely a procedural safeguard it would fail to reach those situations where the deprivation of life, liberty or property was accomplished by legislation which by operating in the future could, given even the fairest possible procedure in application to individuals, nevertheless destroy the enjoyment of all three. . . .

[I]t is not the particular enumeration of rights in the first eight Amendments which spells out the reach of Fourteenth Amendment due process, but rather, as was suggested in another context long before the adoption of that Amendment, those concepts which are considered to embrace those rights "which are . . . *fundamental*; which belong . . . to the citizens of all free governments," . . . for "the purposes [of securing] which men enter into society.". . . Indeed the fact that an identical provision limiting federal action is found among the first eight Amendments, applying to the Federal Government, suggests that due process is a discrete concept which subsists as an independent guaranty of liberty and procedural fairness, more general and inclusive than the specific prohibitions. . . .

Due process has not been reduced to any formula; its content cannot be determined by reference to any code. The best that can be said is that through the course of this Court's decisions it has represented the balance which our Nation, built upon postulates of respect for the liberty of the individual, has struck between that liberty and the demands of organized society. If the supplying of content to this Constitutional concept has of necessity been a rational process, it certainly has not been one where judges have felt free to roam where unguided speculation might take them. The balance of which I speak is the balance struck by this country, having regard to what history teaches are the traditions from which it developed as well as the traditions from which it broke. That tradition is a living thing. A decision of this Court which radically departs from it could not long survive, while a decision which builds on what has survived is likely to be sound. No formula could serve as a substitute, in this area, for judgment and restraint.

[T]he liberty guaranteed by the Due Process Clause . . . is not a series of isolated points pricked out in terms of the taking of property; the freedom of speech, press, and religion; the right to keep and bear arms; the freedom from unreasonable searches and seizures; and so on. It is a rational continuum which, broadly speaking, includes a freedom from all substantial arbitrary impositions and purposeless restraints . . . and which also recognizes, what a reasonable and sensitive judgment must, that certain interests require particularly careful scrutiny of the state needs asserted to justify their abridgment. . . .

Appellants contend that the Connecticut statute deprives them, as it unquestionably does, of a substantial measure of liberty in carrying on the most intimate of all personal relationships, and that it does so arbitrarily and without any rational, justifying purpose. The State, on the other hand, asserts that it is acting to protect the moral welfare of its citizenry, both directly, in that it considers the practice of contraception immoral in itself, and instrumentally, in that the availability of contraceptive materials tends to minimize "the disastrous consequence of dissolute action," that is fornication and adultery.

It is argued by appellants that the judgment, implicit in this statute—that the use of contraceptives by married couples is immoral—is an irrational one, that in effect it subjects them in a very important matter to the arbitrary whim of the legislature, and that it does so for no good purpose. Where, as here, we are dealing with what must be considered "a basic liberty," . . . "there are limits to the extent to which the presumption of constitutionality can be pressed," . . . and the mere assertion that the action of the State finds justification in the controversial realm of morals cannot justify alone any and every restriction it imposes. . . .

[T]he very inclusion of the category of morality among state concerns indicates that society is not limited in its objects only to the physical well-being of the community, but has traditionally concerned itself with the moral soundness of its people as well. Indeed to attempt a line between public behavior and that which is purely consensual or solitary would be to withdraw from community concern a range of subjects with which every society in civilized times has found it necessary to deal. The laws regarding marriage which provide both when the sexual powers may be used and the legal and societal context in which children are born and brought up, as well as laws forbidding adultery, fornication and homosexual practices which express the negative of the proposition, confining sexuality to lawful marriage, form a pattern so deeply pressed into the substance of our social life that any constitutional doctrine in this area must build upon that basis. . . .

It is in this area of sexual morality, which contains many proscriptions of consensual behavior having little or no direct impact on others, that the State of Connecticut has expressed its moral judgment that all use of contraceptives is improper. Appellants cite an impressive list of authorities who, from a great variety of points of view, commend the considered use of contraceptives by married couples. What they do not emphasize is that not too long ago the current of opinion was very probably quite the opposite, and that even today the use is not free of controversy. Certainly, Connecticut's judgment is no more demonstrably correct or incorrect than are the varieties of judgment, expressed in law, on marriage and divorce, on adult consensual homosexuality, abortion, and sterilization, or euthanasia and suicide. If we had a case before us which required us to decide simply, and in abstraction, whether the moral judgment implicit in the application of the present statute to married couples was a sound one, the very controversial nature of these questions would, I think, require us to hesitate long before concluding that the Constitution precluded Connecticut from choosing as it has among these various views. . . .

But, as might be expected, we are not presented simply with this moral judgment to be passed on as an abstract proposition. The secular state is not an examiner of consciences: it must operate in the realm of behavior, of overt actions, and where it does so operate, not only the underlying, moral purpose of its operations, but also the *choice of means* becomes relevant to any Constitutional judgment on what is done. . . .

Precisely what is involved here is this: the State is asserting the right to enforce its moral judgment by intruding upon the most intimate details of the marital relation with the full power of the criminal law. Potentially, this could allow the deployment of all the incidental machinery of the criminal law, arrests, searches and seizures; inevitably, it must mean at the very least the lodging of criminal charges, a public trial, and testimony as to the *corpus delicti.** Nor could any imaginable elaboration of presumptions, testimonial privileges, or other safeguards, alleviate the necessity for testimony as to the mode and manner of the married couples' sexual relations, or at least the opportunity for the accused to make denial of the charges. In sum, the statute allows the State to enquire into, prove and punish married people for the private use of their marital intimacy. . . .

It is clear, of course, that this Connecticut statute does not invade the privacy of the home in the usual sense, since the invasion involved here may, and doubtless usually would, be accomplished without any physical intrusion whatever into the home. What the statute undertakes to do, however, is to create a crime which is grossly offensive to this privacy, while the Constitution refers only to methods of ferreting out substantive wrongs, and the procedure it requires presupposes that substantive offenses may be committed and sought out in the privacy of the home. But such an analysis forecloses any claim to Constitutional protection against this form of deprivation of privacy, only if due process in this respect is limited to what is explicitly provided in the Constitution, divorced from the rational purposes, historical roots, and subsequent developments of the relevant provisions. . . .

It would surely be an extreme instance of sacrificing substance to form were it to be held that the Constitutional principle of privacy against arbitrary official intrusion comprehends only physical invasions by the police. . . .

Certainly the safeguarding of the home does not follow merely from the sanctity of property rights. The home derives its preeminence as the seat of family life. . . .

Of [the] whole "private realm of family life" it is difficult to imagine what is more private or more intimate than a husband and wife's marital relations. . . .

Of course, . . . "[t]he family . . . is not beyond regulation," . . .

---

* Literally "the body of the crime," here meaning evidence of the use of contraceptives in sexual intercourse.

and it would be an absurdity to suggest either that offenses may not be committed in the bosom of the family or that the home can be made a sanctuary for crime. The right of privacy most manifestly is not an absolute. Thus, I would not suggest that adultery, homosexuality, fornication and incest are immune from criminal enquiry, however privately practiced. . . .

Adultery, homosexuality and the like are sexual intimacies which the State forbids altogether, but the intimacy of husband and wife is necessarily an essential and accepted feature of the institution of marriage, an institution which the State not only must allow, but which always and in every age it has fostered and protected. It is one thing when the State exerts its power either to forbid extramarital sexuality altogether, or to say who may marry, but it is quite another when, having acknowledged a marriage and the intimacies inherent in it, it undertakes to regulate by means of the criminal law the details of that intimacy. . . .

MR. JUSTICE WHITE, concurring in the judgment.

In my view this Connecticut law as applied to married couples deprives them of "liberty" without due process of law, as that concept is used in the Fourteenth Amendment. I therefore concur in the judgment of the Court reversing these convictions under Connecticut's aiding and abetting statute. . . .

As I read the opinions of the Connecticut courts and the argument of Connecticut in this Court, the State claims but one justification for its anti-use statute. . . . There is no serious contention that Connecticut thinks the use of artificial or external methods of contraception immoral or unwise in itself, or that the anti-use statute is founded upon any policy of promoting population expansion. Rather, the statute is said to serve the State's policy against all forms of promiscuous or illicit sexual relationships, be they premarital or extramarital, concededly a permissable and legitimate legislative goal.

Without taking issue with the premise that the fear of conception operates as a deterrent to such relationships in addition to the criminal proscriptions Connecticut has against such conduct, I wholly fail to see how the ban on the use of contraceptives by married couples in any way reinforces the State's ban on illicit sexual relationships. . . . Connecticut does not bar the importation or possession of contraceptive devices; they are not considered contraband material under state law, . . . and their availability in that State is not seriously disputed. The only way Connecticut seeks to limit or control the availability of such devices is through its general aiding and abetting statute whose operation in this context has been quite obviously ineffective and whose most serious use has been against birth-control clinics rendering advice to married, rather than unmarried, persons. . . . Indeed, after over 80 years of the State's proscription of use, the legality of the sale of such devices to prevent disease has never been expressly passed upon, although it appears that sales have long occurred and have only infrequently been challenged. This "undeviating policy . . . throughout all the long years . . . bespeaks more than prosecutorial paralysis." . . . Moreover, it would appear that the sale of contraceptives to prevent disease is plainly legal under Connecticut law.

In these circumstances one is rather hard pressed to explain how the ban on use by married persons in any way prevents use of such devices by persons engaging in illicit sexual relations and thereby contributes to the State's policy against such relationships. Neither the state courts nor the State before the bar of this Court has tendered such an explanation. . . . I find nothing in this record justifying the sweeping scope of this statute, with its telling effect on the freedoms of married persons, and therefore conclude that it deprives such persons of liberty without due process of law.

MR. JUSTICE BLACK, with whom MR. JUSTICE STEWART joins, dissenting.

I do not to any extent whatever base my view that this Connecticut law is constitutional on a belief that the law is wise or that its policy is a good one. In order that there may be no room at all to doubt why I vote as I do, I feel constrained to add that the law is every bit as offensive to me as it is to my Brethren of the majority and my Brothers HARLAN, WHITE and GOLDBERG who, reciting reasons why it is offensive to them, hold it unconstitutional. There is no single one of the graphic and eloquent strictures and criticisms fired at the policy of this Connecticut law either by the Court's opinion or by those of my concurring Brethren to which I cannot subscribe—except their conclusion that the evil qualities they see in the law make it unconstitutional. . . . The Court talks about a constitutional "right of privacy" as though there is some constitutional provision or provisions forbidding any law ever to be passed which might abridge the "privacy" of individuals. But there is not. There are, of course, guarantees in certain specific constitutional provisions which are designed in part to protect privacy at certain times and places with respect to certain activities. Such, for example, is the Fourth Amendment's guarantee against "unreasonable searches and seizures." . . .

One of the most effective ways of diluting or expanding a constitutionally guaranteed right is to substitute for the crucial word or words of a constitutional guarantee another word or words, more or less flexible and more or less restricted in meaning. This fact is well illustrated by the use of the term "right of privacy" as a comprehensive substitute for the Fourth Amendment's guarantee against "unreasonable searches and seizures." "Privacy" is a broad, abstract and ambiguous concept which can easily be shrunken in meaning but which can also, on the other hand, easily be interpreted as a constitutional ban against many things other than searches and seizures. . . . For these reasons I get nowhere in this case by talk about a constitutional "right of privacy" as an emanation from one or more constitutional provisions. I like my privacy as well as the next one, but I am nevertheless compelled to admit that government has a right to invade it unless prohibited by some specific constitutional provision. For these reasons I cannot agree with the Court's judgment and the reasons it gives for holding this Connecticut law unconstitutional.

This brings me to the arguments made by my Brothers HARLAN, WHITE and GOLDBERG for invalidating the Connecticut law. . . . The due process argument which my Brothers HARLAN and WHITE adopt here is based, as their opinions indicate, on the premise that the Court is vested with power to invalidate all state laws that it considers to be arbitrary, capricious, unreasonable, or oppressive, or on this Court's belief that a particular state law under scrutiny has no "rational or justifying" purpose, or is offensive to a "sense of fairness and justice." If these formulas . . . are to prevail, they require judges to determine what is or is not constitutional on the basis of their own appraisal of what laws are unwise or unnecessary. The power to make such decisions is of course that of a legislative body. Surely it has to be admitted that no provision of the Constitution specifically gives such blanket power to courts to exercise such a supervisory veto over the wisdom and value of legislative policies and to hold unconstitutional those laws which they believe unwise or dangerous. I readily admit that no legislative body, state or national, should pass laws that can justly be given any of the invidious labels invoked as constitutional excuses to strike down state laws. But perhaps it is not too much to say that no legislative body ever does pass laws without believing that they will accomplish a sane, rational, wise and justifiable purpose. While I completely subscribe to the holding of *Marbury v. Madison*, . . . that our Court has constitutional power to strike down statutes, state or federal, that violate commands of the Federal Constitution, I do not believe that we are granted power by the Due Process Clause or any other constitutional provision or provisions to measure constitutionality by our belief that legislation is arbitrary, capricious or unreasonable, or accomplishes no justifiable purpose, or is offensive to our own notions of "civilized standards of conduct." . . . My Brother GOLDBERG has adopted the recent discovery that the Ninth Amendment as well as the Due Process Clause can be used by this Court as authority to strike down all state legislation which this Court thinks violates "fundamental principles of liberty and justice," or is contrary to the "traditions and [collective] conscience of our people." Moreover, one would certainly have to look far beyond the language of the Ninth Amendment to find that the Framers vested in this Court any such awesome veto powers over law-making, either by the States or by the Congress. . . . That Amendment was passed, not to broaden the powers of this Court or any other department of "the General Government," but, as every student of history knows, to assure the people that the Constitution in all its provisions was intended to limit the Federal Government to the powers granted expressly or by necessary implication. . . . I realize that many good and able men have eloquently spoken and written, sometimes in rhapsodical strains, about the duty of this Court to keep the Constitution in tune with the times. The idea is that the Constitution must be changed from time to time and that this Court is charged with a duty to make those changes. For myself, I must with all deference reject that philosophy. The Constitution makers knew the need for change and provided for it. Amendments suggested by the people's elected representatives can be submitted to the people or their selected agents for ratification. That method of change was good for our Fathers, and being somewhat old fashioned I must add it is good enough for me. And so, I cannot rely on the Due Process Clause or the Ninth Amendment or any mysterious and uncertain natural law concept as a reason for striking down this state law. The

Due Process Clause with an "arbitrary and capricious" or "shocking to the conscience" formula was liberally used by this Court to strike down economic legislation in the early decades of this century, threatening, many people thought, the tranquility and stability of the Nation. See, *e.g., Lochner v. New York*, 198 U.S. 45. That formula, based on subjective considerations of "natural justice," is no less dangerous when used to enforce this Court's views about personal rights than those about economic rights. I had thought that we had laid that formula, as a means for striking down state legislation, to rest once and for all. . . .

In *Ferguson v. Skrupa*, 372 U.S. 726, 730, this Court two years ago said in an opinion joined by all the Justices but one that

> the doctrine that prevailed in *Lochner, Coppage, Adkins, Burns,* and like cases—that due process authorizes courts to hold laws unconstitutional when they believe the legislature has acted unwisely—has long since been discarded. We have returned to the original constitutional proposition that courts do not substitute their social and economic beliefs for the judgment of legislative bodies, who are elected to pass laws.

. . . [M]y concurring Brethren . . . would reinstate the *Lochner, Coppage, Adkins, Burns* line of cases, cases from which this Court recoiled after the 1930s, and which had been I thought totally discredited until now. Apparently my Brethren have less quarrel with state economic regulations than former Justices of their persuasion had. But any limitation upon their using the natural law due process philosophy to strike down any state law, dealing with any activity whatever, will obviously be only self-imposed. . . .

. . . MR. JUSTICE STEWART, whom MR. JUSTICE BLACK joins, dissenting.

Since 1879 Connecticut has had on its books a law which forbids the use of contraceptives by anyone. I think this is an uncommonly silly law. As a practical matter, the law is obviously unenforceable, except in the oblique context of the present case. As a philosophical matter, I believe the use of contraceptives in the relationship of marriage should be left to personal and private choice, based upon each individual's moral, ethical, and religious beliefs. As a matter of social policy, I think professional counsel about methods of birth control should be available to all, so that each individual's choice can be meaningfully made. But we are not asked in this case to say whether we think this law is unwise, or even asinine. We are asked to hold that it violates the United States Constitution. And that I cannot do.

At the oral argument in this case we were told that the Connecticut law does not "conform to current community standards." But it is not the function of this Court to decide cases on the basis of community standards. We are here to decide cases "agreeable to the Constitution and laws of the United States." It is the essence of judicial duty to subordinate our own personal views, our own ideas of what legislation is wise and what is not. If, as I should surely hope, the law before us does not reflect the standards of the people of Connecticut, the people of Connecticut can freely exercise their true Ninth and Tenth Amendment rights to persuade their elected representatives to repeal it. That is the constitutional way to take this law off the books.

## 2. Privacy After Griswold

*Griswold* announced a constitutional right of privacy, but the decision to strike down the Connecticut anticontraception statutes did not determine the nature of that right and did not specify its contents. Justice Douglas observed that "specific guarantees in the Bill of Rights have penumbras, formed by emanations from those guarantees that give them life and substance," and concluded that "[v]arious guarantees create zones of privacy." The following cases illustrate the Supreme Court's expansion of the right of privacy in a number of areas in the years since 1965. To what extent do these cases involve the constitutionalization of Mill's principle?

### MARRIAGE

In *Loving v. Virginia*, 388 U.S. 1 (1967), a unanimous Court invalidated Virginia's antimiscegenation law, stating: "Marriage is one of the 'basic civil rights of man,' fundamental to our very existence and survival. . . . To deny this fundamental freedom on so unsupportable a basis as the racial classifications embodied in these statutes [would deny due process]." In *Zablocki v. Redhail*, 434 U.S. 374 (1978), the Court struck down a Wisconsin statute providing that anyone "having minor issue not in his custody and which he is under an obligation to support by any court order" could not marry without special court approval. Justice Marshall elaborated upon the inclusion of a right to marry as

> part of the fundamental "right of privacy" implicit in the Fourteenth Amendment's Due Process Clause. It is not surprising that the decision to marry has been placed on the same level of importance as decisions relating to procreation, childbirth, child-rearing, and family relationships. As the facts of this case illustrate, it would make little sense to recognize a right of privacy with respect to other matters of family life and not with respect to the decision to enter the relationship that is the foundation of the family in our society. . . . [I]f appellee's right to procreate means anything at all, it must imply some right to enter the only relationship in which the state of Wisconsin allows sexual relations legally to take place.

## PRIVACY OF THE HOME

Another strand of the *Griswold* decision emphasized the privacy of the home. In *Stanley v. Georgia*, 394 U.S. 557 (1969), the defendant was convicted under Georgia law for possession of obscene materials. In a prior decision, *Roth v. United States*, 354 U.S. 476 (1957), the Supreme Court had resolved that "obscenity is not within the area of constitutionally protected speech or press." Since Stanley's obscene materials were not protected by the First Amendment, Georgia claimed that it could freely exercise the police power to control what it regarded as an affront to public morality. Justice Marshall, writing for the Court, refused to accept the State's contentions:

> . . . Whatever may be the justifications for other statutes regulating obscenity, we do not think they reach into the privacy of one's own home. If the First Amendment means anything, it means that a State has no business telling a man, sitting alone in his own house, what books he may read or what films he may watch.
> . . . As we have said, the States retain broad power to regulate obscenity; that power simply does not extend to mere possession by the individual in the privacy of his own home.

## CONTRACEPTION

While there is a sense in which the decision in *Griswold* rested upon the protected zones of privacy found in the home and the family, subsequent cases have also affirmed a general right of free choice in matters of procreation. *Eisenstadt v. Baird*, 405 U.S. 438 (1972), reversed a conviction for public distribution of contraceptive foam to an unmarried person in violation of Massachusetts law. The Court did not accept the State's argument that the statute discouraged premarital sexual intercourse: "It would be plainly unreasonable to assume that Massachusetts has prescribed pregnancy and birth of an unwanted child as punishment for fornication." Nor could the statute be upheld as a simple prohibition on contraception deriving from the judgment that contraceptives are inherently immoral:

> If under *Griswold* the distribution of contraceptives to married persons cannot be prohibited, a ban on distribution to unmarried persons would be equally impermissible. It is true that in *Griswold* the right to privacy in question inhered in the marital relationship. Yet the marital couple is not an independent entity with a mind and heart of its own, but an association of two individuals each with a separate intellectual and emotional makeup. If the right of privacy means anything, it is the right of the *individual*, married or single, to be free from unwarranted governmental intrusion into matters so fundamentally affecting a person as the decision whether to bear or beget a child.

And in *Carey v. Population Services International*, 431 U.S. 678 (1977), the Court invalidated prohibitions on the sale of nonprescription contraceptives by persons other than licensed pharmacists and to persons under 16, stating "[t]he decision whether or not to beget or bear a child is at the very heart" of the right of privacy. State statutes that substantially limit "access to the means effectuating that decision" must be closely scrutinized. Limiting distribution of contraceptives to licensed pharmacists imposes "a significant burden on the right of the individuals to use contraceptives if they choose to do so . . ." because it "renders contraceptive devices considerably less accessible to the public, reduces the opportunity for privacy of selection and purchase, and lessens the possibility of price competition." Justice Brennan, writing for a plurality of four Justices, also rejected the ban on distribution to persons under 16. The prohibition could not be justified "as a regulation of the morality of minors, in furtherance of the State's policy against promiscuous sexual intercourse among the young." As in *Eisenstadt*, the State could not impose pregnancy as a punishment for fornication. The restrictive statutes were an unacceptable means of impressing upon "young people the seriousness with which the State views the decision to engage in sexual intercourse at an early age." Justice White, in a separate opinion, concurred in this result on the narrower ground that "the State has not demonstrated that the prohibition against distribution of contraceptives to minors measurably contributes to the deterrent purposes which the State advances as justification for the restriction."

## ABORTION

In *Roe v. Wade*, 410 U.S. 113 (1973), the Court struck down Texas criminal abortion statutes that prohibited abortions except to save the life of the mother. Justice Blackmun's opinion for the Court applied the privacy right to the decision to abort:

> This right of privacy, whether it be founded in the Fourteenth Amendment's concept of personal liberty and restrictions upon state action, as we feel it is, or, as the District Court determined, in the Ninth Amendment's reservation of rights to the people, is broad enough to encompass a woman's decision whether or not to terminate her pregnancy.

The Court made a threefold division of the term of pregnancy. During the first trimester, a woman and her physician could elect to obtain an abortion. After this time, the State could intervene to regulate the abortion procedure in order to protect maternal health. Once the fetus became viable, the State could regulate and even proscribe abortion, except when necessary to preserve the life of the mother.

Justice Rehnquist, in dissent, argued against the application of the notion of privacy to abortions:

> A transaction resulting in an operation such as this is not "private" in the ordinary usage of that word. Nor is the "privacy" that the Court finds here even a distant relative of the freedom from searches and seizures protected by the Fourth Amendment to the Constitution, which the Court has referred to as embodying a right to privacy.

He also objected to the manner in which the Court reached its final conclusion:

While the Court's opinion quotes from the dissent of Mr. Justice Holmes in *Lochner v. New York*, the result it reaches is more closely attuned to the majority opinion of Mr. Justice Peckham in that case. . . . [S]ubstantive due process standards . . . will inevitably require this Court to examine legislative policies and pass on the wisdom of these policies. . . . The decision here to break pregnancy into three distinct terms and to outline the permissible restrictions the State may impose in each one, for example, partakes more of judicial legislation than it does a determination of the intent of the drafters of the Fourteenth Amendment.

Justice White also attacked the majority's decision as a usurpation of legislative prerogative:

As an exercise of raw judicial power, the Court perhaps has authority to do what it does today; but in my view its judgment is an improvident and extravagant exercise of the power of judicial review. . . . In a sensitive area such as this, involving as it does issues over which reasonable men may easily and heatedly differ, I cannot accept the Court's exercise of its clear power of choice by interposing a constitutional barrier to state efforts to protect human life and by investing mothers and doctors with the constitutionally protected right to exterminate it. This issue, for the most part, should be left with the people and to the political processes the people have devised to govern their affairs. . . .

## FAMILY LIFE

During the era of the now-discredited *Lochner* decision, the Court had established in *Meyer v. Nebraska*, 262 U.S. 390 (1923), and *Pierce v. Society of Sisters*, 268 U.S. 510 (1925), that among the basic liberties protected by the doctrine of substantive due process was a right of parents to control their children's upbringing. In *Griswold* the Court reaffirmed the holding of these cases. Subsequent cases have established a more general right to family integrity. Thus in *Stanley v. Illinois*, 405 U.S. 645 (1972), the fathers of illegitimate children were held to have a right to custody of the children upon the mother's death, unless they could be shown to be unfit parents.

*Moore v. East Cleveland*, 431 U.S. 494 (1977), involved a local zoning ordinance that restricted occupancy within a dwelling unit to members of a single family. The applicable definition of a "family" prevented Mrs. Moore from living with her two grandsons, who were first cousins rather than brothers. The city argued that a "constitutional right to live together as a family," recognized in cases such as *Stanley v. Illinois*, was limited to "the nuclear family—essentially a couple and its dependent children." The Court held otherwise. Justice Powell's plurality opinion addressed the question of the extension of constitutional protections:

> Appropriate limits on substantive due process come not from drawing arbitrary lines but rather from "careful respect for the teachings of history [and] solid recognition of the basic values that underlie our society." Our decisions establish that the Constitution protects the sanctity of the family precisely because the institution of the family is deeply rooted in this Nation's history and tradition. . . . Ours is by no means a tradition limited to respect for the bonds uniting the members of the nuclear family. The tradition of uncles, aunts, cousins, and especially grandparents sharing a household along with parents and children has roots equally venerable and equally deserving of constitutional recognition. . . . The Constitution prevents East Cleveland from standardizing its children—and its adults—by forcing all to live in certain narrowly defined family patterns.

While history and tradition support the extended family, not every living arrangement is accorded the same degree of constitutional protection. In *Hollenbaugh v. Carnegie Free Library*, 439 U.S. 1052 (1978), the Court denied a petition to review a decision upholding the discharge of public library employees for "living together in a state of 'open adultery.' " Justice Marshall dissented, arguing:

> Petitioners' rights to pursue an open rather than a clandestine personal relationship and to rear their child together in this environment closely resemble the other aspects of personal privacy to which we have extended constitutional protection. . . . [I]ndividuals' choices concerning their private lives deserve more than token protection from this Court. . . .

## "LIFESTYLE"

In determining the contents of the right of privacy, the Supreme Court has been reluctant to protect idiosyncratic lifestyles. For example, the Constitution has never been applied to protect private drug use, though the Alaska Supreme Court, in *Ravin v. State*, 537 P. 2d 494 (1975), held that a right to privacy in the Alaska Constitution protected the use and cultivation of marijuana in the home. In *Kelley v. Johnson*, 425 U.S. 238 (1976), the Supreme Court rejected a challenge to a local regulation stipulating the length and style of policemen's hair. Justice Rehnquist analyzed the extent of the liberty interest protected by the Due Process Clause of the Fourteenth Amendment. The cases from *Meyer* through *Roe* circumscribed the right of privacy.

> Each of those cases involved a substantial claim of infringement on the individual's freedom of choice with respect to certain basic matters of procreation, marriage, and family life. But whether the citizenry at large has some sort of "liberty" interest within the Fourteenth Amendment in matters of personal appearance is a question on which this Court's cases offer little, if any, guidance. . . .

Justice Rehnquist found that the regulation should be evaluated under the relatively lenient "rational relation" standard favored in cases involving regulation of economic interests and concluded that it was justified as a "chosen mode of organization" for the local police force. Uniformity in appearance "may be based on a desire to make police officers readily recognizable to the members of the public, or a desire for the esprit de corps which such similarity is felt to inculcate within the police force itself." Justice Marshall took issue with this conclusion in a forceful dissent:

> An individual's personal appearance may reflect, sustain, and nourish his personality and may well be used as a means of expressing his attitude and lifestyle. In taking control over a citizen's personal appearance, the Government forces him to sacrifice substantial elements of his integrity and identity as well. To say that the liberty guarantee of the Fourteenth Amendment does not encompass matters of personal appearance would be fundamentally inconsistent with the values of privacy, self-identity, autonomy, and personal integrity that I have always assumed the Constitution was designed to protect.

# B.

## Obscenity and Privacy

The Supreme Court's first explicit confrontation with Mill's principle came in 1973 in *Paris Adult Theater v. Slaton*, a case involving the problem of obscenity regulation. As noted above, the Court had earlier held that obscene material was not protected by the free speech and free press provisions of the First Amendment. After *Griswold*, and especially after *Stanley v. Georgia*, the argument was naturally made that the right of privacy guaranteed to consenting adults free access to pornography; the argument treats using pornography not as an act of reading or viewing, but as simply a harmless sexual practice.

## *Paris Adult Theater v. Slaton**

*Here is the Supreme Court's response to the argument stated above. In reading it consider the following questions:*

*(a) The Court draws an analogy between pornography prohibition based on aesthetic grounds and environmental legislation protecting natural beauty. Are there important differences between moral and physical "pollution"? Can Mill's principle accommodate infringement of liberty on aesthetic grounds?*

*(b) The Court argues that the theory underlying compulsory and public education—the notion that books, ideas, and dramatic portrayals form character—also supports pornography prohibition. Is the fact that we have compulsory education only for minors a decisive objection to this argument? What about using tax money to support high culture and adult education—isn't this compulsion in the service of particular intellectual, aesthetic, and moral ideals?*

*(c) Many feminists argue that pornography should be suppressed because it promotes a degrading view of women. Is this argument different from those suggested by Chief Justice Burger? Is it consistent with Mill's principle?*

. . . MR. CHIEF JUSTICE BURGER delivered the opinion of the Court.

Petitioners are two Atlanta, Georgia, movie theaters and their owners and managers, operating in the style of "adult" theaters. On December 28, 1970, respondents, the local state district attorney and the solicitor for the local state trial court, filed civil complaints in that court alleging that petitioners were exhibiting to the public for paid admission two allegedly obscene films, contrary to Georgia Code Ann. § 26-2101. The two films in question, "Magic Mirror" and "It All Comes Out In The End," depict sexual conduct characterized by the Georgia Supreme Court as "hard core pornography" leaving

* 413 U.S. 49 (1973).

"little to the imagination." . . . We categorically disapprove the theory . . . that obscene, pornographic films acquire constitutional immunity from state regulation simply because they are exhibited for consenting adults only. . . . Although we have often pointedly recognized the high importance of the state interest in regulating the exposure of obscene materials to juveniles and unconsenting adults, . . . this Court has never declared these to be the only legitimate state interests permitting regulation of obscene material. . . . "In an unbroken series of cases extending over a long stretch of this Court's history, it has been accepted as a postulate that 'the primary requirements of decency may be enforced against obscene publications.'" . . .

In particular, we hold that there are legitimate state interests at stake in stemming the tide of commercialized obscenity, even assuming it is feasible to enforce effective safeguards against exposure to juveniles and to passersby. Rights and interests "other than those of the advocates are involved." . . . These include the interest of the public in the quality of life and the total community environment, the tone of commerce in the great city centers, and, possibly, the public safety itself. The Hill-Link Minority Report of the Commission on Obscenity and Pornography indicates that there is at least an arguable correlation between obscene material and crime. Quite apart from sex crimes, however, there remains one problem of large proportions aptly described by Professor Bickel:

> It concerns the tone of the society, the mode, or to use terms that have perhaps greater currency, the style and quality of life, now and in the future. A man may be entitled to read an obscene book in his room, or expose himself indecently there. . . . We should protect his privacy. But if he demands a right to obtain the books and pictures he wants in the market, and to foregather in public places—discreet, if you will, but accessible to all—with others who share his tastes, *then to grant him his right is to affect the world about the rest of us, and to impinge on other privacies.* Even supposing that each of us can, if he wishes, effectively avert the eye and stop the ear (which, in truth, we cannot), what is commonly read and seen and heard and done intrudes upon us all, want it or not. . . .

As Mr. Chief Justice Warren stated, there is a "right of the Nation and of the States to maintain a decent society. . . . "

But, it is argued, there are no scientific data which conclusively demonstrate that exposure to obscene material adversely affects men and women or their society. It is urged on behalf of the petitioners that, absent such a demonstration, any kind of state regulation is "impermissible." We reject this argument. It is not for us to resolve empirical uncertainties underlying state legislation, save in the exceptional case where that legislation plainly impinges upon rights protected by the Constitution itself. . . . Although there is no conclusive proof of a connection between antisocial behavior and obscene material, the legislature of Georgia could quite reasonably determine that such a connection does or might exist. . . .

From the beginning of civilized societies, legislators and judges have acted on various unprovable assumptions. Such assumptions underlie much lawful state regulation of commercial and business affairs. . . .

Likewise, when legislatures and administrators act to protect the physical environment from pollution and to preserve our resources of forests, streams, and parks, they must act on such imponderables as the impact of a new highway near or through an existing park or wilderness area. . . . The fact that a congressional directive reflects unprovable assumptions about what is good for the people, including imponderable aesthetic assumptions, is not a sufficient reason to find that statute unconstitutional.

If we accept the unprovable assumption that a complete education requires the reading of certain books, . . . and the well-nigh universal belief that good books, plays, and art lift the spirit, improve the mind, enrich the human personality, and develop character, can we then say that a state legislature may not act on the corollary assumption that commerce in obscene books, or public exhibitions focused on obscene conduct, have a tendency to exert a corrupting and debasing impact leading to antisocial behavior? . . . The sum of experience, including that of the past two decades, affords an ample basis for legislatures to conclude that a sensitive, key relationship of human existence, central to family life, community welfare, and the development of human personality, can be debased and distorted by crass commercial exploitation of sex. Nothing in the Constitution prohibits a State from reaching such a conclusion and acting on it legislatively simply because there is no conclusive evidence or empirical data.

It is argued that individual "free will" must govern, even in activities beyond the protection of the First Amendment and other constitutional guarantees of privacy, and that government cannot legitimately impede an individual's desire to see or acquire obscene plays, movies, and books. We do indeed base our society on certain assumptions that people have the capacity for free choice. Most exercises of individual free choice—those in politics, religion, and expression of ideas—are explicitly protected by the Constitution. Totally unlimited play for free will, however, is not allowed in our or any other society. . . . [N]either the First Amendment nor "free will" precludes States from having "blue sky" laws to regulate what sellers of securities may write or publish about their wares. . . . Such laws are to protect the weak, the uninformed, the unsuspecting, and the gullible from the exercise of their own volition. Nor do modern societies leave disposal of garbage and sewage up to the individual "free will," but impose regulation to protect both public health and the appearance of public places. States are told by some that they must await a "laissez-faire" market solution to the obscenity-pornography problem, paradoxically "by people who have never otherwise had a kind word to say for laissez-faire." . . .

It is asserted, however, that standards for evaluating state commercial regulations are inapposite in the present context, as state regulation of access by consenting adults to obscene material violates the constitutionally protected right to privacy enjoyed by petitioners' customers. . . . [I]t is unavailing to compare a theater open to the public for a fee, with the private home of *Stanley v. Georgia*, . . . and the marital bedroom of *Griswold v. Connecticut*. . . .

Our prior decisions recognizing a right to privacy guaranteed by the Fourteenth Amendment included "only personal rights that can be deemed 'fundamental' or 'implicit' in the concept of ordered liberty." . . . This privacy right encompasses and protects the personal intimacies of the home, the family, marriage, motherhood, procreation, and child rearing. Cf.: *Eisenstadt v. Baird*, . . . *Stanley v. Georgia*, . . . *Loving v. Virginia*, . . . *Griswold v. Connecticut*, . . . Nothing, however, in this Court's decisions intimates that there is any "fundamental" privacy right "implicit in the concept of ordered liberty" to watch obscene movies in places of public accommodation.

If obscene material unprotected by the First Amendment in itself carried with it a "penumbra" of constitutionally protected privacy, this Court would not have found it necessary to decide *Stanley* on the narrow basis of the "privacy of the home," which was hardly more than a reaffirmation that "a man's home is his castle." . . . The idea of a "privacy" right and a place of public accommodation are, in this context, mutually exclusive. Conduct or depictions of conduct that the state police power can prohibit on a public street do not become automatically protected by the Constitution merely because the conduct is moved to a bar or a "live" theater stage, any more than a "live" performance of a man and a woman locked in a sexual embrace at high noon in Times Square is protected by the Constitution because they simultaneously engage in a valid political dialogue. . . .

Finally, petitioners argue that conduct which directly involves "consenting adults" only has, for that sole reason, a special claim to constitutional protection. Our Constitution establishes a broad range of conditions on the exercise of power by the States, but for us to say that our Constitution incorporates the proposition that conduct involving consenting adults only is always beyond state regulation, is a step we are unable to take. Commercial exploitation of depictions, descriptions, or exhibitions of obscene conduct on commercial premises open to the adult public falls within a State's broad power to regulate commerce and protect the public environment. The issue in this context goes beyond whether someone, or even the majority, considers the conduct depicted as "wrong" or "sinful." The States have the power to make a morally neutral judgment that public exhibition of obscene material, or commerce in such material, has a tendency to injure the community as a whole, to endanger the public safety, or to jeopardize, in Mr. Chief Justice Warren's words, the States' "right . . . to maintain a decent society." . . .

MR. JUSTICE BRENNAN, with whom MR. JUSTICE STEWART and MR. JUSTICE MARSHALL join, dissenting. . . .

[I]n *Stanley* we rejected as "wholly inconsistent with the philosophy of the First Amendment" . . . the notion that there is a legitimate state concern in the "control [of] the moral content of a person's thoughts," . . . and we held that a State "cannot constitutionally premise legislation on the desirablity of controlling a person's private thoughts." . . . That is not to say, of course, that a State must remain utterly indifferent to—and take no action bearing on—the morality of the community. The traditional description of state police power does embrace the regulation of morals as well as the health, safety, and general welfare of the citizenry. . . . And much legislation—compulsory public education laws, civil rights laws, even the abolition of capital punishment—is grounded, at least in part, on a concern with the morality of the community. But the State's interest in regulating morality by suppressing obscenity, while often asserted, remains essentially unfocused and ill defined. And, since the attempt to curtail unprotected speech necessarily spills over into the area of protected speech, the effort to serve this speculative interest through the suppression of obscene material must tread heavily on rights protected by the First Amendment.

. . . [T]he effort to suppress obscenity is predicated on unprovable, although strongly held, assumptions about human behavior, morality, sex, and religion. The existence of these assumptions cannot validate the statute that substantially undermines the guarantees of the First Amendment, any more than the existence of similar assumptions on the issue of abortion can validate a statute that infringes the constitutionally protected privacy interests of a pregnant woman. . . .

# C.

# Homosexuality and Privacy

Legal commentators and civil liberties lawyers had argued ever since the *Griswold* decision that the new right of privacy implied a right of adults to control their own sexual activities. The rise of the homosexual rights movement ensured that this idea would be tested by challenges to traditional legal prohibitions of homosexuality. In the following case, a lower federal court rejected such a challenge, with one of the three judges dissenting. On appeal, the Supreme Court affirmed the majority decision summarily, without hearing arguments or even writing an opinion—a treatment the Court typically gives to cases that it thinks do not even raise "substantial" constitutional questions. Three of the Justices (Brennan, Marshall, and Stevens) expressed their view that the Court should have given the case a full hearing.

Following the opinions in *Doe v. Commonwealth's Attorney* is an excerpt from a law review article by David Richards that spells out in some detail the argument for a constitutional right of sexual freedom for homosexuals.

In reading these excerpts, consider the following questions:

(1) In his dissenting opinion in *Doe*, how does Judge Merhige avoid the force of the explicit approving references to laws prohibiting homosexuality in the *Griswold* opinions?

(2) Does *Eisenstadt*, in protecting the constitutional right of unmarried persons to have access to contraceptives, necessarily imply that they have a constitutional right to have the sexual relations in which those contraceptives would be used?

(3) If heterosexual intercourse outside marriage were held to be constitutionally protected by the right of privacy, could the Court consistently decide that the right does not extend to homosexual intercourse? Is any connection between lawful intercourse and procreation decisively broken by *Griswold*, as Richards argues?

(4) Is it Richards's thesis that all sexual practices not involving coercion or children are constitutionally protected? If his argument were accepted, would laws prohibiting sexual practices with animals and with dead bodies be unconstitutional?

## 1. *Doe v. Commonwealth's Attorney for City of Richmond**

BRYAN, Senior Circuit Judge:

Virginia's statute making sodomy a crime is unconstitutional, each of the male plaintiffs aver, when it is applied to his active and regular homosexual relations with another *adult male, consensually and in private.* . . .

So far as relevant, the Code of Virginia, 1950, as amended, provides:

> § 18.1-212. Crimes against nature. —If any person shall carnally know in any manner any brute animal, or carnally know any male or female person by the anus or by or with the mouth, or voluntarily submit to such carnal knowledge, he or she shall be guilty of a felony and shall be confined in the penitentiary not less than one year nor more than three years.

Our decision is that on its face and in the circumstances here it is not unconstitutional. No judgment is made upon the wisdom or policy of the statute. It is simply that we cannot say that the statute

* 403 F. Supp. 1199 (1975).

offends the Bill of Rights or any other of the Amendments and the wisdom or policy is a matter for the State's resolve.

I.  Precedents cited to us as *contra* rest exclusively on the precept that the Constitution condemns State legislation that trespasses upon the privacy of the incidents of marriage, upon the sanctity of the home, or upon the nurture of family life. This and only this concern has been the justification for nullification of State regulation in this area. Review of plantiffs' authorities will reveal these as the principles underlying the referenced decisions.

In *Griswold v. Connecticut* . . . (1965), plaintiffs' chief reliance, the Court has most recently announced its views on the question here. Striking down a State statute forbidding the use of contraceptives, the ruling was put on the right of marital privacy—held to be one of the specific guarantees of the Bill of Rights—and was also put on the sanctity of the home and family. . . .

That *Griswold* is premised on the right of privacy and that homosexual intimacy is denunciable by the State is unequivocally demonstrated by Mr. Justice Goldberg in his concurrence . . . in his adoption of Mr. Justice Harlan's dissenting statement in *Poe v. Ullman.* . . .

> Adultery, *homosexuality* and the like are sexual intimacies *which the State forbids* . . . but the intimacy of husband and wife is necessarily an essential and accepted feature of the institution of marriage, an institution which the State not only must allow, but which always and in every age it has fostered and protected. *It is one thing when the State exerts its power either to forbid extramarital sexuality* . . . or to say who may marry, but it is quite another when, having acknowledged a marriage and the intimacies inherent in it, it undertakes to regulate by means of the criminal law the details of the intimacy. (Emphasis added.)

Equally forceful is the succeeding paragraph of Justice Harlan:

> In sum, even though the State has determined that the use of contraceptives is as iniquitous as any act of extramarital sexual immorality, the intrusion of the whole machinery of the criminal law into the very heart of marital privacy, requiring husband and wife to render account before a criminal tribunal of their uses of that intimacy is surely *a very different thing indeed from punishing those who establish intimacies which the law has always forbidden and which can have no claim to social protection.*

. . . On the plaintiffs' effort presently to shield the practice of homosexuality from State incrimination by according it immunity when committed in private as against public exercise, the Justice said this:

> Indeed to attempt a line between public behavior and that which is purely consensual or solitary would be to withdraw from community concern a range of subjects with which every society in civilized times has found it necessary to deal. The laws regarding marriage which provide both when the sexual powers may be used and the legal and societal context in which children are born and brought up, as well as *laws forbidding adultery, fornication and homosexual practices which express the negative of the proposition*, confining sexuality to lawful marriage, form a pattern so deeply pressed into the substance of our social life that any Constitutional doctrine in this area must build upon that basis. . . .

Again:

> Thus, I would not suggest that *adultery, homosexuality, fornication and incest are immune* from criminal enquiry, *however privately practiced*. So much has been explicitly recognized in acknowledging the State's rightful concern for its people's moral welfare. . . . But not to discriminate between what is involved in this case and either the traditional offenses against good morals or crimes which, though they may be committed anywhere, happen to have been committed or concealed in the home, would entirely misconceive the argument that is being made.

Many states have long had, and still have, statutes and decisional law criminalizing conduct depicted in the Virginia legislation. . . .

II. With no authoritative judicial bar to the proscription of homosexuality—since it is obviously no portion of marriage, home or family life—the next question is whether there is any ground for barring Virginia from branding it as criminal. If a State determines that punishment therefor, even when committed in the home, is appropriate in the promotion of morality and decency, it is not for the courts to say that the State is not free to do so. . . . In short, it is an inquiry addressable only to the State's Legislature. . . .

Although a questionable law is not removed from question by the lapse of any prescriptive period, the longevity of the Virginia statute does testify to the State's interest and its legitimacy. It is not an upstart notion; it has ancestry going back to Judaic and Christian law. . . .

MERHIGE, District Judge (dissenting).

. . . In my view, in the absence of any legitimate interest or rational basis to support the statute's application, we must, without regard to our own proclivities and reluctance to judicially bar the state proscription of homosexuality, hold the statute as it applies to the plaintiffs to be violative of their rights under the Due Process Clause of the Fourteenth Amendment to the Constitution of the United States. The Supreme Court decision in *Griswold v. Connecticut* . . . is, as the majority points out, premised on the right of privacy, but I fear my brothers have misapplied its precedential value through an apparent over-adherence to its factual circumstances.

The Supreme Court has consistently held that the Due Process Clause of the Fourteenth Amendment protects the right of individuals to make personal choices, unfettered by arbitrary and purposeless restraints, in the private matters of marriage and procreation. *Roe v. Wade* . . . I view those cases as standing for the principle that every individual has a right to be free from unwarranted governmental intrusion into one's decisions on private matters of intimate concern. A mature individual's choice of an adult sexual partner, in the privacy of his or her own home, would appear to me to be a decision of the utmost private and intimate concern. Private consensual sex acts between adults are matters, absent evidence that they are harmful, in which the state has no legitimate interest.

To say, as the majority does, that the right of privacy, which every citizen has, is limited to matters of marital, home or family life is unwarranted under the law. Such a contention places a distinction in marital-nonmarital matters which is inconsistent with current Supreme Court opinions and is unsupportable.

In my view, the reliance of the majority on Mr. Justice Harlan's dissenting statement in *Poe v. Ullman* . . . is misplaced. An analysis of the cases indicates that in 1965 when *Griswold*, which invalidated a statute prohibiting the use of contraceptives by married couples, was decided, at least three of the Court, relying primarily on Mr. Justice Harlan's dissent in *Poe v. Ullman*, and Mr. Justice Harlan himself, would not have been willing to attach the right of privacy to homosexual conduct. In my view, *Griswold* applied the right of privacy to its particular factual situation. That the right of privacy is not limited to the facts of *Griswold*, is demonstrated by later Supreme Court decisions. After *Griswold*, by virtue of *Eisenstadt v. Baird* . . . the legal viability of a marital-nonmarital distinction in private sexual acts if not eliminated, was at the very least seriously impaired. In *Eisenstadt* . . . the Court declined to restrict the right of privacy in sexual matters to married couples:

> Yet the marital couple is not an independent entity with a mind and heart of its own, but an association of two individuals each with a separate intellectual and emotional makeup. If the right of privacy means any-thing, it is the right of the *individual*, married or single, to be free from unwarranted governmental intrusion into matters so fundamentally af-fecting a person as the decision whether to bear or beget a child. . . .

In significantly diminishing the importance of the marital-non-marital distinction, the Court to a great extent vitiated any implica-tion that the state can, as suggested by Mr. Justice Harlan in *Poe v. Ullman*, forbid extra-marital sexuality, and such implications are no longer fully accurate.

> It is one thing when the State exerts its power either to forbid extra-marital sexuality altogether, or to say who may marry, but it is quite another when, having acknowledged a marriage and the intimacies inherent in it, it undertakes to regulate by means of the criminal law the details of the intimacy. . . .

*Griswold* . . . in its context, applied the right of privacy in sexual matters to the marital relationship. *Eisenstadt* . . . however, clearly demonstrates that the right to privacy in sexual relationships is not limited to the marital relationship. Both *Roe* . . . and *Eisenstadt* . . . cogently demonstrate that intimate personal decisions or private matters of substantial importance to the well-being of the individuals involved are protected by the Due Process Clause. The right to select consenting adult sexual partners must be considered within this category. The exercise of that right, whether heterosexual or homo-sexual, should not be proscribed by state regulation absent compel-ling justification.

This approach does not unqualifiedly sanction personal whim. If the activity in question involves more than one participant, as in the instant case, each must be capable of consenting, and each must in fact consent to the conduct for the right of privacy to attach. For example, if one of the participants in homosexual contact is a minor, or force is used to coerce one of the participants to yield, the right will not attach. . . . Similarly, the right of privacy cannot be extended to protect conduct that takes place in publicly frequented areas. . . . However, if the right of privacy does apply to specific courses of conduct, legitimate state restriction on personal autonomy may be justified only under the compelling state interest test. See *Roe v. Wade*. . . .

Plaintiffs are adults seeking protection from the effects of the statute under attack in order to engage in homosexual relations in private. Viewing the issue as we are bound to, as Mr. Justice Blackmun stated in *Roe v. Wade* . . . "by constitutional measurement, free of emotion and predilection," it is my view that they are entitled to be protected in their right to privacy by the Due Process Clause.

The defendants, represented by the highest legal officer of the state, made no tender of any evidence which even impliedly demonstrated that homosexuality causes society any significant harm. No effort was made by the defendants to establish either a rational basis or a compelling state interest so as to justify the proscription of § 8.1-212 of the Code of Virginia, presently under attack. To suggest, as defendants do, that the prohibition of homosexual conduct will in some manner encourage new heterosexual marriages and prevent the dissolution of existing ones is unworthy of judicial response. In any event, what we know as men is not forgotten as judges—it is difficult to envision any substantial number of heterosexual marriages being in danger of dissolution because of the private sexual activities of homosexuals.

On the basis of this record one can only conclude that the sole basis of the proscription of homosexuality was what the majority refers to as the promotion of morality and decency. As salutary a legislative goal as this may be, I can find no authority for intrusion by the state into the private dwelling of a citizen. *Stanley v. Georgia* . . . teaches us that socially condemned activity, excepting that of demonstrable external effect, is and was intended by the Constitution to be beyond the scope of state regulation when conducted within the privacy of the home, . . . Whether the guarantee of personal privacy springs from the First, Fourth, Fifth, Ninth, the penumbra of the Bill of Rights, or, as I believe, in the concept of liberty guaranteed by the first section of the Fourteenth Amendment, the Supreme Court has made it clear that fundamental rights of such an intimate facet of an individual's life as sex, absent circumstances warranting intrusion by the state, are to be respected. My brothers, I respectfully suggest, have by today's ruling misinterpreted the issue—the issue centers not around morality or decency, but the constitutional right of privacy. I respectfully note my dissent.

**2.** *David Richards, "Sexual Auton-* ═══════════
*omy and the Constitutional Right to Privacy: A Case Study in Human Rights and the Unwritten Constitution"** *

From its recognition in *Griswold v. Connecticut*, the constitutional right to privacy commonly has been attacked as expressing subjective judicial ideology, as lacking a constitutionally neutral principle, and as being, in substance, a form of legislative policy not properly pursued by the courts. In particular, critics, both on and off the Supreme Court, have questioned the methodology of the Court in inferring an independent constitutional right to privacy that is not within the contours of the rights expressly guaranteed by the Constitution; in brief, how can the Court legitimately appeal to an unwritten constitution when the *point* of the constitutional design was to limit governmental power by a written text?

The summary affirmance in *Doe v. Commonwealth's Attorney for Richmond*, which could be read as excluding homosexual acts between consenting adults from the scope of the constitutional right to privacy, may give compelling force to these kinds of objections. The Court may have summarily limited the right to privacy in a way that suggests fiat, not articulated principle, for how can the Court in a principled way sustain the constitutional right to privacy of married and unmarried people to use contraceptives or to have abortions or to use pornography in the privacy of one's home, and not sustain the rights of consenting adult homosexuals to engage in the form of sex they find natural? . . .

The understanding of *Griswold* and its progeny begins with repudiation of the procreational model of sexual love which was given its classic formulation by St. Augustine. For Augustine, sexuality was a natural object of continuing shame because it involved loss of control. Accordingly, the only proper form of sex was that which was done with the controlled intention to procreate;

---

* David A. J. Richards, *Sexual Autonomy and the Constitutional Right to Privacy: A Case Study in Human Rights and the Unwritten Constitution*, 30 *Hastings Law Journal* 957 (1979) (© 1979 Hastings College of the Law).

sexuality without procreation or independent of such intentions was, for Augustine, intrinsically degrading. It follows from this view that certain rigidly defined kinds of intercourse in conventional marriage, always with the intention to procreate, are alone moral; contraception, whether within or outside marriage, extramarital and, of course, homosexual intercourse are forbidden since these do not involve intent to procreate.

Augustine's argument rests on a rather remarkable fallacy. Augustine starts with two anthropological points about human sexual experience: first, humans universally insist on having sex alone and unobserved by others; and second, humans universally cover their genitals in public. Augustine argues that the only plausible explanation for these two empirical facts about human sexuality is that humans experience sex as intrinsically degrading because it involves the loss of control; this perception of shame, in turn, must rest on the fact that the only proper form of sex is having it with the controlled intention to procreate; sexuality is intrinsically degrading because we tend to experience it without or independent of the one intention that alone can validate it. Assuming, *arguendo*, the truth of Augustine's anthropological assumptions, it does not follow that humans must find sex intrinsically shameful. These facts are equally well explained by the fact that people experience embarrassment in certain forms of publicity of their sexuality, not shame in the experience of sex itself. Shame is conceptually distinguishable from embarrassment in that its natural object is a failure of personally esteemed competent self-control, whether the failure is public or private; embarrassment, in contrast, is experienced when a matter is made public that properly is regarded as private. The twin facts adduced by Augustine are, indeed, better explained by the hypothesis of embarrassment, not shame. Surely many people experience no negative self-evaluation when they engage in sex in private, which is what the hypothesis of embarrassment, not shame, would lead us to expect. For example, people may experience pride in knowing that other young people know or believe that they are having sex (the recently married young couple). There is no shame here, but there would be severe embarrassment if the sex act were actually observed. That people would experience such embarrassment reveals something important about human sexual experience, but it is not Augustine's contempt for the loss of control of sexual passion. Sexual experience is, for human beings, a profoundly personal, spontaneous, and absorbing experience in which they express intimate fantasies and vulnerabilities which typically cannot brook the sense of an external, critical observer. That humans require privacy for sex relates to the nature of the experience; there is no suggestion that the experience is, *pace* Augustine, intrinsically degrading.

The consequence of Augustine's fallacy is to misdescribe and misidentify natural features of healthy sexual experience, namely, the privacy required to express intimate sensual vulnerabilities, in terms of putatively degrading properties of sexual experience per se. In fact, this latter conception of sexuality relies on and expresses an overdeveloped willfulness that fears passion itself as a form of loss of control, as though humans cannot with self-esteem indulge emotional spontaneity outside the rule of the iron procreational will. Such a conception both underestimates the distinctly human capacity for self-control and overestimates the force of sexuality as a dark, unreasoning, Bacchic possession whose demands inexorably undermine the rational will. It also fails to fit the empirical facts, indeed contradicts them. Human, as opposed to animal, sexuality is crucially marked by its control by higher cortical functions and thus its involvement with the human symbolic imagination, so that sexual propensities and experience are largely independent of the reproductive cycle. Consequently, humans use sexuality for diverse purposes—to express love, for recreation, or for procreation. No one purpose necessarily dominates; rather, human self-control chooses among the purposes depending on context and person.

The constitutional right to privacy was developed in *Griswold* and its progeny because the procreational model of sexuality could no longer be sustained by sound empirical or conceptual argument. Lacking such support, the procreational model could no longer be legally enforced on the grounds of the "public morality," for it failed to satisfy the postulate of constitutional morality that legally enforceable moral ideas be grounded on equal concern and respect for autonomy and demonstrated by facts capable of empirical validation. Accordingly, since anticontraceptive laws are based on the concept that nonprocreational sex is unnatural, the *Griswold* court properly invoked the right of privacy to invalidate the Connecticut statute. . . .

If the right to privacy extends to sex among unmarried couples or even to autoeroticism in the home, it is difficult to understand how in a principled way the Court could decline to consider fully the application of this right to private, consensual, deviant sex acts. The Court might distinguish between heterosexual and homosexual forms of sexual activity; but could this distinction be defended rationally? At bottom, such a view must rest on the belief that homosexual or deviant sex is unnatural. . . .

The use of so imprecise a notion as "unnatural" to distinguish between those acts not protected by the constitutional right to privacy and those which are so protected is clearly unacceptable. The case where the constitutional right to privacy had its origin was one involving contraception—a practice which the Augustinian view would deem unnatural. Yet, the Court has apparently concluded that the "unnaturalness" of contraception or abortion is constitutionally inadmissible and cannot limit the scope of the right to privacy. . . .

For the same reasons that notions of the unnatural are constitutionally impermissible in decisions involving contraception, abortion, and the use of pornography in the home, these ideas are also impermissible in the constitutional assessment of laws prohibiting private forms of sexual deviance between consenting adults. No empirical evidence compels a finding that homosexuality is unnatural. Indeed, there have been cultures that possessed normative assumptions of what is natural that nevertheless did not regard homosexuality as unnatural. Indeed, societies (including ancient Greece) have included or include homosexuality among legitimate sexual conduct, and some prescribe it in the form of institutional pederasty. Individuals within our own culture have assailed the view that homosexuality is unnatural by adducing various facts which traditionalists either did not know or did not understand. For example, it is now known that homosexual behavior takes place in the animal world, suggesting that homosexuality is part of our mammalian heritage of sexual responsiveness.

Some have attempted to distinguish between individuals who are exclusively homosexual and the general population based on symptoms of mental illness or measures of self-esteem and self-acceptance. In general, however, apart from their sexual preference, exclusive homosexuals are psychologically indistinguishable from the general population.

The view sometimes expressed that male homosexuality necessarily involves the loss of desirable character traits probably rests on the idea that sexual relations between males involve the degradation of one or both parties to the status of a woman. This view, however, rests on intellectual confusion and unacceptable moral premises since it confuses sexual preference with gender identity, whereas, in fact, no such correlation exists. Male homosexuals or lesbians may be quite insistent about their respective gender identities and have quite typical "masculine" or "feminine" personalities. Their homosexuality is defined only by their erotic preference for members of the same gender. The notion that the status of woman is a degradation is morally repugnant to contemporary jurisprudence and morality. If such crude and unjust sexual stereotypes lie at the bottom of the antihomosexuality laws, they should be uprooted, as is being done elsewhere in modern life.

Finally, homosexual preference appears to be an adaption of natural human propensities to very early social circumstances of certain kinds, so that the preference is settled, largely irreversibly, at a quite early age.

# D.
# Homosexual Marriage

The modern debate over Mill's principle has focused on the use of the criminal law to enforce sexual morality. Actually the criminal law is only very rarely applied today to adult consensual sexual activity. Most legal enforcement of sexual morality is imposed through civil disabilities and remedies. This section and sections E and F that follow explore the extent to which the problems of sexual morals enforcement vary in three different civil contexts—marriage, employment, and child custody.

In reading the following case and law review note on the question of whether the Constitution requires that homosexuals be allowed to marry, consider these questions:

(1) The author of the law review note criticizes the argument that marriage is "by definition" between members of opposite sexes as question-begging. Is the law's traditional association of marriage with sexual relations likewise arbitrary? Should friends not in a sexual relation to each other be allowed to marry, with the tax, property, and other consequences the status brings—or is the appropriate response that marriage is "by definition" the legal solemnization of a sexual relationship?

(2) If homosexual marriage must be recognized, must plural marriage? Incestuous marriage?

(3) Can you articulate any ground why homosexual marriage should not be permitted that does not equally apply to a heterosexual couple that is physically incapable of having children?

## 1. *Baker v. Nelson**

PETERSON, Justice.

The questions for decision are whether a marriage of two persons of the same sex is authorized by state statutes and, if not, whether state authorization is constitutionally compelled.

Petitioners, Richard John Baker and James Michael McConnell, both adult male persons, made application to respondent, Gerald R. Nelson, clerk of Hennepin County District Court, for a marriage license pursuant to Minn. St. 517.08. Respondent declined to issue the license on the sole ground that petitioners were of the same sex, it being undisputed that there were otherwise no statutory impediments to heterosexual marriage by either petitioner.

The trial court . . . ruled that respondent was not required to issue a marriage license to petitioners and specifically directed that a marriage license not be issued to them. This appeal is from those orders. We affirm.

Petitioners contend, first, that the absence of an express statutory prohibition against same-sex marriages evinces a legislative intent to authorize such marriages. We think, however, that a sensible reading of the statute discloses a contrary intent.

Minn. St. c. 517, which governs "marriage," employs that term as one of common usage, meaning the state of union between persons of the opposite sex.† It is unrealistic to think that the original draftsmen of our marriage statutes, which date from territorial days, would have used the term in any different sense. The term is of contemporary

---

* 191 N.W. 2d 185 (1971) (Supreme Court of Minnesota).
† *Webster's Third New International Dictionary* (1966) p. 1384 gives this primary meaning to marriage: "1 a: the state of being united to a person of the opposite sex as husband or wife."

Black, *Law Dictionary* (4 ed.) p. 1123 states this definition: Marriage . . . is the civil status, condition, or relation of one man and one woman united in law for life, for the discharge to each other and the community of the duties legally incumbent on those whose association is founded on the distinction of sex."

significance as well, for the present statute is replete with words of heterosexual import such as "husband and wife" and "bride and groom." . . .

We hold, therefore, that Minn. St. c. 517 does not authorize marriage between persons of the same sex and that such marriages are accordingly prohibited.

Petitioners contend, second, that Minn. St. c. 517, so interpreted, is unconstitutional. There is a dual aspect to this contention: The prohibition of a same-sex marriage denies petitioners a fundamental right guaranteed by the Ninth Amendment to the United States Constitution, arguably made applicable to the states by the Fourteenth Amendment, and petitioners are deprived of liberty and property without due process and are denied the equal protection of the laws, both guaranteed by the Fourteenth Amendment.

These constitutional challenges have in common the assertion that the right to marry without regard to the sex of all persons and that restricting marriage to only couples of the opposite sex is irrational and invidiously discriminatory. We are not independently persuaded by these contentions and do not find support for them in any decisions of the United States Supreme Court.

The institution of marriage as a union of man and woman, uniquely involving the procreation and rearing of children within a family, is as old as the book of Genesis. *Skinner v. Oklahoma ex rel. Williamson,* 316 U.S. 535 . . . which invalidated Oklahoma's Habitual Criminal Sterilization Act on equal protection grounds, stated in part: "Marriage and procreation are fundamental to the very existence and survival of the race." This historic institution manifestly is more deeply founded than the asserted contemporary concept of marriage and societal interests for which petitioners contend. The due process clause of the Fourteenth Amendment is not a charter for restructuring society by judicial legislation.

*Griswold v. Connecticut* . . . upon which petitioners rely, does not support a contrary conclusion. A Connecticut criminal statute prohibiting the use of contraceptives by married couples was held invalid, as violating the due process clause of the Fourteenth Amendment. The basic premise of that decision, however, was that the state, having authorized marriage, was without power to intrude upon the right of privacy inherent in the marital relationship. Mr. Justice Douglas, author of the majority opinion, wrote that this criminal statute "operates directly on an intimate relation of husband

and wife," . . . and that the very idea of its enforcement by police search of "the sacred precincts of marital bedrooms for telltale signs of the use of contraceptives . . . is repulsive to the notions of privacy surrounding the marriage relationship," . . . In a separate opinion for three justices, Mr. Justice Goldberg similarly abhorred this state disruption of "the traditional relation of the family—a relation as old and as fundamental as our entire civilization." . . .

The equal protection clause of the Fourteenth Amendment, like the due process clause, is not offended by the state's classification of persons authorized to marry. There is no irrational or invidious discrimination. Petitioners note that the state does not impose upon heterosexual married couples a condition that they have a proved capacity or declared willingness to procreate, posing a rhetorical demand that this court must read such condition into the statute if same-sex marriages are to be prohibited. Even assuming that such a condition would be neither unrealistic nor offensive under the *Griswold* rationale, the classification is no more than theoretically imperfect. We are reminded, however, that "abstract symmetry" is not demanded by the Fourteenth Amendment.

*Loving v. Virginia* . . . upon which petitioners additionally rely, does not militate against this conclusion. Virginia's antimiscegenation statute, prohibiting interracial marriages, was invalidated solely on the grounds of its patent racial discrimination. As Mr. Chief Justice Warren wrote for the court . . . .

> Marriage is one of the "basic civil rights of man," fundamental to our very existence and survival. *Skinner v. Oklahoma.* . . . To deny this fundamental freedom on so unsupportable a basis as the racial classifications embodied in these statutes, classifications so directly subversive of the principle of equality at the heart of the Fourteenth Amendment, is surely to deprive all the State's citizens of liberty without due process of law. The Fourteenth Amendment requires that the freedom of choice to marry not be restricted by invidious racial discriminations.

*Loving* does indicate that not all state restrictions upon the right to marry are beyond reach of the Fourteenth Amendment. But in common sense and in constitutional sense, there is a clear distinction between a marital restriction based merely upon race and one based upon the fundamental differences in sex. . . .

## 2. Note, "The Legality of Homosexual Marriage"*

Two men recently petitioned the Minnesota Supreme Court to compel the state to grant them a marriage license. The court rejected their application for mandamus, and their appeal was subsequently dismissed by the United States Supreme Court. But the claim was far from frivolous. A credible case can be made for the contention that the denial of marriage licenses to all homosexual couples violates the Equal Protection Clause of the Fourteenth Amendment. . . .

It is by now well established that the Supreme Court varies the degree of scrutiny to which it subjects legislative classifications according to the groups and interests affected by any given classification. The so-called "strict scrutiny" standard is usually triggered by legislation which either contains a classification that is suspect because of the nature of the group disadvantaged, or threatens a "basic civil right of man." When this standard is employed, the government is required to prove the presence of a "pressing public necessity" to justify such classification.

In actual practice, the Court has applied the full strict scrutiny standard only rarely outside the context of racial discrimination. In cases involving non-racial classifications, the Court's approach can more realistically be viewed as a balancing process, perhaps best articulated by Justice Marshall in his dissenting opinion in *Dandridge v. Williams.*

> In my view equal protection analysis of this case is not appreciably advanced by the *a priori* definition of a "right," fundamental or otherwise. Rather, concentration must be placed upon the character of the classification in question, the relative importance to individuals in the class discriminated against of the governmental benefits that they do not receive, and the asserted state interests in support of the classification.

There are thus three basic factors to be balanced: the degree to which legislative classifications disfavoring homosexuals should be "suspect," because of legislative motivation; the importance of obtaining marriage licenses to homosexuals as a class; and the

* 82 Yale L.J. 573 (1973). Reprinted by permission of The Yale Law Journal Company and Fred B. Rothman & Company from *The Yale Law Journal,* Vol. 82, pp. 573 ff.

interests of the government in denying such licenses to all same-sex couples.

The Supreme Court has never explicated its grounds for declaring certain classifications to be inherently suspect. However, examination of the classifications thus far held to be suspect does reveal certain common denominators which may have motivated the Court in so designating them.

Judge J. Skelly Wright expressly articulated one relevant criterion when he observed that classifications disfavoring "a politically voiceless and invisible minority" should be subjected to "closer judicial surveillance and review." Homosexuals as a group would appear to have no more political influence than the black and poor minorities with which Judge Wright was dealing.

Classifications have also been found suspect when they are based on attributes which are inherent in the individual and wholly, or largely, beyond his control. Whatever the causes of homosexuality, the orientation itself does not appear to be one that is freely chosen, nor in most instances can it be changed. Groups which are subjects of derogatory myths or stereotypes are among those which have been accorded the protection of the strict scrutiny standard, perhaps in part to insure that such stereotypes do not become the bases for legislative classification. Certainly disparaging misconceptions about homosexuals are endemic in Western society.

Perhaps most importantly, a history of discrimination, both public and private, seems to characterize the groups granted this special judicial status. Discrimination against homosexuals represents a cultural theme in Western society which dates back to Biblical days. Such discrimination arguably has been at least as burdensome as that which has afflicted several of the minorities (including aliens and the poor) which have been shielded on occasion by the stricter judicial standard of review. However, the Court might reasonably find that discrimination against homosexuals has not been as burdensome as that affecting other minority groups, particularly blacks.

With respect to the second element in the balance—the importance of marriage licenses to homosexuals . . . the Court has stated that the right to marry is "one of the vital personal rights essential to the orderly pursuit of happiness by free men . . . one of the 'basic civil rights of man,' fundamental to our very existence." This fact was found to be crucial to the Court's conclusion that antimiscegenation statutes deprive interracial couples of due process of law. The Court's plurality opinion in *Griswold v. Connecticut* again stressed the fundamental nature of the marriage relationship, noting that it draws special protection from a variety of constitutional safeguards, including the right of association. Most importantly, in *Skinner v. Oklahoma*, the progenitor of strict scrutiny cases, the Court held that the state's sterilization statute required use of that more stringent standard in an equal protection context because of the fundamentality of "[m]arriage and procreation."

However, even explicit judicial recognition of marriage as a fundamental interest to a heterosexual couple would not prove *a fortiori* that homosexuals have interests of a comparable magnitude in being permitted to obtain marriage licenses. *Skinner* is not alone among Supreme Court cases in linking marriage with procreation when considering the importance of those rights. It is unlikely, in light of Court dicta and of the evolving attitudes toward marriage in our society, that constitutional protections surrounding the institution of marriage would be made dependent on the ability or willingness to bear children. But it is still true that part of the importance of the marriage license to heterosexual couples derives from the social acceptance and legal protection which it guarantees for their natural children. Such considerations would not apply to a same-sex pair.

On the other hand, state sanctioning of the marriage relationship brings with it numerous other legal, social and even psychic benefits which are of undiminished importance to homosexuals. Married individuals enjoy substantial tax benefits, tort recovery for wrongful death, intestate succession, and a host of other statutory and common law privileges. They also incur special liabilities, such as the responsibility for support and maintenance during marriage and for similar provision after divorce, which may on balance be viewed as beneficial by a couple regardless of sexual orientation. Beyond these strictly legal benefits, the formal status of marriage might reasonably be viewed as enhancing the stability, respectability, and emotional depth of any relationship between two individuals, regardless of whether the relationship is homosexual or heterosexual.

Against the interests of homosexuals and the suspect nature of classifications disfavoring them must be placed the interests of the government in uniformly denying marriage licenses to same-sex couples. . . .

The vast majority of Americans view marriage to be *by definition* a union of man and woman; a scarcely smaller number see homosexuality as "unnatural" and morally reprehensible. The easy answer to these propositions is that the Fourteenth Amendment was passed for the express purpose of preventing the enforcement of exclusionary classifications based upon deeply felt beliefs which are not grounded on objective, rational distinctions. Not long before the passage of that Amendment, thousands of Americans sincerely believed that a voter was "by definition" a white, male, property owner, and that interracial marriages were immoral. Despite this argument, however, society's basic institutional conceptions must inevitably carry some weight in the balance of interests, even though they may not suffice alone to justify the denial of concrete legal benefits to those whose conceptions differ. . . .

# E.

# Employment and Sexual Freedom

Sexual morality is probably most pervasively enforced against adults through their jobs. This is perhaps most true for schoolteachers, who are thought to serve as particularly important moral examples to the young. In recent years the courts have moved away from the traditional view that public employment was a privilege that could be granted and withdrawn at will and have placed some constitutional restraints on the grounds for dismissing public employees. It remains an open question how closely dismissal from a job or revocation of a professional license is to be analogized to criminal punishment for purposes of constitutional analysis. The following case raises that question with respect to a schoolteacher. In reading it, consider these questions:

(1) Oral copulation is no longer a crime in California. If the case arose now, would it be treated differently? Is the main argument that Mrs. Pettit has not respected the law, or is it that she has not respected society's sexual mores? You might ask yourself how the court might respond if her license were revoked on the grounds that she had accumulated a large number of unpaid parking tickets. What if she were convicted of income tax evasion?

(2) What if Mrs. Pettit went on the radio talk show to discuss her "swinging" activities without any effort to disguise herself? What if

she spoke of those activities openly in class, in the context of a discussion of the limits of tolerance of different lifestyles—would that provide stronger grounds for taking away her license?

## 1. Pettit v. State Board of Education*

BURKE, Justice.

Plaintiff is an elementary school teacher, having held a California teaching credential since 1957. According to the record, in November 1967 plaintiff (then 48 years old) and her husband applied for membership in "The Swingers," a private club in Los Angeles evidently devoted primarily to promoting diverse sexual activities between members at club parties. Sergeant Berk, an undercover officer working for the Los Angeles Police Department, investigated the club, was accepted for membership, and, on December 2, 1967, attended a party at a private residence during which he observed the incidents in question. . . . In a one-hour period, Berk observed plaintiff commit three separate acts of oral copulation with three different men at the party. When these acts took place, the participants were undressed, and there were other persons looking on.

Plaintiff was subsequently arrested and charged with violating Penal Code section 288a (oral copulation). Evidently a plea bargain was arranged and plaintiff pleaded guilty to Penal Code section 650-1/2 (outraging public decency), a misdemeanor. Plaintiff was fined and placed on probation; upon payment of the fine probation was terminated and the criminal proceedings dismissed.

Subsequently, in February 1970, the disciplinary proceedings now before us were initiated to revoke plaintiff's teaching credential on the grounds (among others) that her conduct involved moral turpitude and demonstrated her unfitness to teach. . . . [T]hree elementary school superintendents testified that in their opinion plaintiff's conduct disclosed her unfitness to teach.† Plaintiff did not testify at

---

* 10 Cal. 3d 29 (1973).
† William B. Calton, Superintendent of the Cypress School District which employed plaintiff, testified that a person who committed the sexual acts performed by plaintiff would be unfit to teach in an elementary school. In Calton's opinion, a teacher has the responsibility to practice as well as teach moral values; one who failed to practice morality would have difficulty teaching it. Since pupils look to their teacher for moral guidance, plaintiff would lose her effectiveness and ability as a teacher and might even inject her ideas regarding sexual morals into the classroom.

the hearing. . . . Mr. Pettit . . . testified that he and plaintiff had, in 1966, appeared on the Joe Pyne television show and also another similar show a few weeks later, and had on both occasions discussed "nonconventional sexual life styles." Mr. Pettit recalled that the subjects of adultery and "wife swapping" were discussed and that "probably" the Pettits expressed a "philosophic" attitude on those subjects since they were not "uptight" about them. Although plaintiff and her husband wore a mask and false beard respectively on these shows, Superintendent Calton testified that one of plaintiff's fellow teachers had discussed plaintiff's televised statement with him and with other teachers. . . .

At the conclusion of the hearing, the hearing examiner found that plaintiff has engaged in acts of sexual intercourse and oral copulation with men other than her husband; that plaintiff appeared on television programs while facially disguised and discussed nonconventional sexual behavior, including wife swapping; that although plaintiff's services as a teacher have been "satisfactory," and although she is unlikely to repeat the sexual misconduct, nevertheless she has engaged in immoral and unprofessional conduct, in acts involving moral turpitude, and in acts evidencing her unfitness for service. Accordingly, the hearing examiner concluded that cause exists for the revocation of her life diploma. The board adopted the findings and conclusions of its hearing officer in toto. . . . Plaintiff appeals.

The Education Code contains the provisions governing revocation of a teacher's life diploma or credential. Section 13202 provides in pertinent part that the board "shall revoke or suspend for immoral or unprofessional conduct . . . or for any cause which would have warranted the denial of an application for a certification document or the renewal thereof, or for evident unfitness for service. . . ." Among the various statutory grounds for denial of an application for a credential or life diploma, or renewal thereof, are the commission of an act involving moral turpitude and the failure to furnish reasonable evidence of good moral character. . . .

In *Morrision v. State Board of Education* . . . [1969] this court was faced with the problem whether certain homosexual conduct by a public school teacher justified revocation under the above statutory language. A majority of the court concluded that, in order to save the statute from attack on vagueness grounds, a teacher's actions could not constitute "immoral or unprofessional conduct" or "moral turpitude" unless that conduct indicated an unfitness to teach. In view of the total lack of evidence in the record demonstrating

Morrison's unfitness to teach, the court reversed the superior court's judgment denying mandate. We made it clear, however, that in future cases revocation will be upheld if the evidence discloses that the teacher's retention within the school system "poses a significant danger of harm to either students, school employees, or others who might be affected by his action as a teacher." . . .

Plaintiff contends that *Morrison* controls here and that the record contains no substantial evidence of her unfitness to teach. We disagree. Initially, we note several important factors which would distinguish *Morrison* from the instant case. In *Morrison*, the unspecified conduct at issue was noncriminal in nature, and the court was careful to point out that oral copulation was not involved. . . .

A second distinguishing feature between *Morrison* and the instant case is, of course, that in *Morrison* the conduct at issue occurred entirely *in private* and involved only two persons, whereas plaintiff's indiscretions involved three different "partners," were witnessed by several strangers, and took place in the semi-public atmosphere of a club party. Plaintiff's performance clearly reflected a total lack of concern for privacy, decorum or preservation of her dignity and reputation. Even without expert testimony, the board was entitled to conclude that plaintiff's flagrant display indicated a serious defect of moral character, normal prudence and good common sense. A further indication that plaintiff lacked that minimum degree of discretion and regard for propriety expected of a public school teacher is disclosed by her television appearances, giving notoriety to her unorthodox views regarding sexual morals. As noted above, apparently plaintiff's disguise was not wholly effective for she was recognized by at least one teacher at plaintiff's school.

Finally, in *Morrison* the board acted without sufficient evidence of unfitness to teach. In the instant case, in addition to the evidence of plaintiff's misconduct itself and its criminal and semi-public nature, the board heard expert testimony asserting plaintiff's unfitness to teach. . . . In general, these witnesses expressed concern that plaintiff might attempt to inject her views regarding sexual morality into the classroom or into her private discussions with her pupils, and that plaintiff would be unable effectively to act as a moral example for the children she taught. Plaintiff attacks this testimony as reflecting only the personal opinions of the witnesses regarding unorthodox sexual mores, yet the testimony goes further and calls into question plaintiff's fitness to teach moral principles. Expert testimony is necessarily based to an extent upon the personal opinion of the witness, supported by his special education and experience. We see no reason for discrediting the opinion of a school superintendent regarding the fitness of teachers to teach merely because that opinion is based in part upon personal moral views. . . .

[I]t is the statutory duty of a teacher to "endeavor to impress upon the minds of the pupils the principles of morality . . . and to instruct them in manners and morals. . . ." Accordingly . . . several cases have held that the inability of a teacher to obey the laws of this state or otherwise act in accordance with traditional moral principles may constitute sufficient ground for revocation or dismissal. . . .

. . . Mrs. Pettit's illicit and indiscreet actions disclosed her unfitness to teach in public elementary schools.

TOBRINER, Justice (dissenting).

For the past 13 years plaintiff has taught mentally retarded elementary school children, a task requiring exceptional skill and patience. Throughout her career her competence has been unquestioned; not a scintilla of evidence suggests that she has ever failed properly to perform her professional responsibilities. One can ask for no better proof of fitness to teach than this record of consistent, capable performance.

Yet in the face of this record, the State Board of Education, branding plaintiff "unfit," revokes her elementary school life diploma—a ruling that will not only force her discharge from her present employment, but, regardless of the need for a teacher of her experience and qualifications, will also bar any school district in California from hiring her. . . .

The board in the instant case has been driven to exhume an old and admitted indiscretion in order to lay the basis for the revocation of plaintiff's teaching credential. The challenged act was committed on December 2 1967; the criminal proceedings were thereafter dismissed; subsequently, in February 1970—years later—the disciplinary proceedings were initiated. I am hard put to understand the motivation of the board in bringing charges on a matter which plaintiff now recognizes as an indiscretion and for which she has paid the penalty—charges brought despite the fact that plaintiff has devoted 13 years to the exemplary and humane teaching of retarded elementary school children—charges designed to bar her permanently from teaching.

The kind of wastefulness of needed human resources that this procedure threatens becomes the more dangerous when we examine it in the context of other professions. If a highly proficient attorney commits an unorthodox sex act and thereafter suffers a misdemeanor conviction that is subsequently dismissed, may he then, years later, be disbarred because he admittedly committed the act and hence was guilty of "immoral" and "unprofessional" conduct? Should the skilled surgeon involved in a parallel situation suffer the same tragedy? The university professor? The danger of the majority's doctrine becomes especially onerous when we know that a large proportion of the younger generation do engage in unorthodox sexual activities deemed anathema by some members of the older generation. To what extent will we frustrate highly productive careers of younger persons in order to castigate conduct that is widely practiced by some but regarded by others as abominable? Is the legal standard to be no more definite or precise than that the involved practice is regarded as "immoral" or "unprofessional" or "tasteless" by judges? . . .

The principle that a criminal conviction is not *ipso facto* the basis for revocation of a certificate on the grounds of immoral or unprofessional conduct becomes clear when tested against specific acts of unlawful conduct. Obviously the commission of a misdemeanor, such as a traffic offense, could not seriously be urged as an automatic ground for revocation of a certificate. Convictions of other technical and legal offenses common in the society do not intrinsically constitute "immoral" or "unprofessional" conduct. Hence, in order to resolve the issue, we must examine the nature of the conduct and its relation, if any, to the role and functions of the teacher.

In the instant case the conduct involved consensual sexual behavior which deviated from traditional norms. Yet recognized authority tells us the practice pursued here is, indeed, quite common. An estimated "95% of adult American men and a large percentage of American women have experienced orgasm in an illegal manner" (McCary, *Human Sexuality* (2d ed. 1973) p. 460). The 1953 Kinsey report, *Sexual Behavior in the Human Female*, at page 399 indicates that 62 percent of the adult women of plaintiff's educational level and age range engage in oral copulation; more recently, the report's co-authors have stated that newer studies suggest the figure now lies around 75 to 80 percent.

The consensual and, as I shall explain, private act did not affect, and could not have affected, plaintiff's teaching ability. The whole matter would have been forgotten and lost in the limbo of the privacy of its occurrence if it had not been clandestinely observed by means of a surreptitious intrusion which reminds one of the surveillance of restrooms which this court has condemned. . . . The commission of a sex act, surreptitiously observed, not disclosed to fellow teachers or to pupils, not remotely adversely affecting plaintiff's teaching ability, must fail to support revocation of the certificate even though the act is labelled "criminal" on the books.

I am at somewhat of a loss to understand the majority's second ground for distinguishing *Morrison*: that plaintiff's acts in the instant case took place in the "semi-public atmosphere of a club party." . . .

Plaintiff's acts occurred in the bedroom of a private home. The only persons witness to the conduct were members of "The Swingers," a private club limited to persons who expressly attested their desire to view or engage in diverse sexual activity. Consequently, I conclude that plaintiff's acts occurred in a private place, not a public one or one open to public view.

. . . [P]laintiff took reasonable precautions to assure that she was viewed only by persons who would not be offended by her conduct; many would argue that under such circumstances her behavior was neither imprudent nor immoral. In essence, the majority are saying that even though her fellow "swingers" were not offended, they—the majority—find plaintiff's behavior shocking and embarrassing. Yet this important issue of plaintiff's right to teach should not turn on the personal distaste of judges; the test, as this court has announced in the cases, is the rational one of the effect of the conduct, if any, on the teacher's fitness to teach. . . .

The unproven premise of both the expert testimony and the majority opinion is that the fact of plaintiff's sexual acts at the "swingers'" party in itself demonstrates that she would be unable to set a proper example for her pupils or to teach them moral principles; this inability in turn demonstrates her unfitness to teach. This reasoning rests on factual assumptions concerning the relationship of consensual adult sexual behavior to classroom teaching which have absolutely no support in the evidence. If "immoral conduct" ipso facto shows inability to model or teach morals, and this in turn shows unfitness to teach, then we are left with the proposition that proof of "immoral conduct," whatever it may be, will always justify revocation of a teaching credential. . . .

In conclusion, I submit that the majority opinion is blind to the reality of sexual behavior. Its view that teachers in their private lives should exemplify Victorian principles of sexual morality, and in the classroom should subliminally indoctrinate the pupils in such principles, is hopelessly unrealistic and atavistic. The children of California are entitled to competent and dedicated teachers; when, as in this case, such a teacher is forced to abandon her lifetime profession, the children are the losers. . . .

# F.

# Child Custody and Sexual Freedom

There has long been pervasive indirect legal enforcement of sexual morality through the operation of child custody laws. The legal standard for the award and continuation of child custody has typically been "the best interests of the child." The vagueness of this standard has meant that many parents (in practice mostly mothers) who have deviated from traditional sexual norms have lost custody of their children to their former spouses, as in the following case. In reading it, consider these questions:

(1) To what extent does the majority's argument rest on the Illinois criminal statute prohibiting "open and notorious cohabitation"? Would the case be different if (as in many states) Mrs. Jarrett's living arrangement violated no criminal statute? Is it relevant that the cohabitation statute is never enforced by criminal prosecution? Given the absence of prosecution, is it still right to say that the statute really reflects the contemporary legislative attitude toward living together without marriage?

(2) If it were held that Mrs. Jarrett and Hammon were protected against criminal prosecution for cohabitation by the constitutional right to privacy, would that necessarily alter the outcome of the case? Would it be constitutional to award custody to one parent on the ground that the other parent was teaching the children the doctrines of Naziism? Suppose a parent's unpopular but constitutionally protected views or living arrangements exposed the children to constant abuse and harassment by their peers—would it be unconstitutional to shift custody to the other parent on that account?

(3) Mill's principle allows state intervention only where there may be "harm to others." Is it reasonable to say that the principle can *never* apply to limit the grounds of state intervention into child custody, because the effects of a parent's conduct or way of life *always* directly affect a child living with him or her?

## 1. *Jarrett v. Jarrett**

UNDERWOOD, Justice:

On December 6, 1976, Jacqueline Jarrett received a divorce from Walter Jarrett in the circuit court of Cook County on grounds of extreme and repeated mental cruelty. The divorce decree, by agreement, also awarded Jacqueline custody of the three Jarrett children subject to the father's right of visitation at reasonable times. Seven months later, alleging changed conditions, Walter petitioned the circuit court to modify the divorce decree and award him custody of the children. . . .

During their marriage, Walter and Jacqueline had three daughters, who, at the time of the divorce, were 12, 10, and 7 years old. In addition to custody of the children, the divorce decree also awarded Jacqueline the use of the family home, and child support; Walter received visitation rights at all reasonable times and usually had the children from Saturday evening to Sunday evening. In April 1977, five months after the divorce, Jacqueline informed Walter that she planned to have her boyfriend, Wayne Hammon, move into the family home with her. Walter protested, but Hammon moved in on May 1, 1977. Jacqueline and Hammon thereafter cohabited in the Jarrett home but did not marry.

The children, who were not "overly enthused" when they first learned that Hammon would move into the family home with them, asked Jacqueline if she intended to marry Hammon, but Jacqueline responded that she did not know. At the modification hearing Jacqueline testified that she did not want to remarry because it was too soon after her divorce; because she did not believe that a marriage license makes a relationship; and because the divorce decree required her to sell the family home within six months after remarriage. She did not want to sell the house because the children did not want to move and she could not afford to do so. Jacqueline

* 400 N.E. 2d 421 (1979) (Illinois Supreme Court).

explained to the children that some people thought it was wrong for an unmarried man and woman to live together but she thought that what mattered was that they loved each other. Jacqueline testified that she told some neighbors that Hammon would move in with her but that she had not received any adverse comments. Jacqueline further testified that the children seemed to develop an affectionate relationship with Hammon, who played with them, helped them with their homework, and verbally disciplined them. Both Jacqueline and Hammon testified at the hearing that they did not at that time have any plans to marry. In oral argument before this court Jacqueline's counsel conceded that she and Hammon were still living together unmarried.

Walter Jarrett testified that he thought Jacqueline's living arrangements created a moral environment which was not a proper one in which to raise three young girls. He also testified that the children were always clean, healthy, well dressed and well nourished when he picked them up, and that when he talked with his oldest daughter, Kathleen, she did not object to Jacqueline's living arrangement.

The circuit court found that it was "necessary for the moral and spiritual well-being and development" of the children that Walter receive custody. In reversing, the appellate court reasoned that the record did not reveal any negative effects on the children caused by Jacqueline's cohabitation with Hammon, and that the circuit court had not found Jacqueline unfit. It declined to consider potential future harmful effects of the cohabitation of the children. . . .

The chief issue in this case is whether a change of custody predicated upon the open and continuing cohabitation of the custodial parent with a member of the opposite sex is contrary to the manifest weight of the evidence in the absence of any tangible evidence of contemporaneous adverse effect upon the minor children.

[We] conclude that under the facts in this case the trial court properly transferred custody of the Jarrett children from Jacqueline to Walter Jarrett.

The relevant standards of conduct are expressed in the statutes of this State: Section 11-8 of the Criminal Code of 1961 . . . provides that "[a]ny person who cohabits or has sexual intercourse with another not his spouse commits fornication if the behavior is open and notorious." . . .

Jacqueline argues . . . that her conduct does not affront public morality because such conduct is now widely accepted, and cites 1978 Census Bureau statistics that show 1.1 million households composed of an unmarried man and woman, close to a quarter of which also include at least one child. . . . The number of people living in such households forms only a small percentage of the adult population, but more to the point, the statutory interpretation urged upon us by Jacqueline simply nullifies the fornication statute. The logical conclusion of her argument is that the statutory prohibitions are void as to those who believe the proscribed acts are not immoral, or, for one reason or another, need not be heeded. So stated, of course, the argument defeats itself. The rules which our society enacts for the governance of its members are not limited to those who agree with those rules—they are equally binding on the dissenters. The fornication statute and the Illinois Marriage and Dissolution of Marriage Act evidence the relevant moral standards of this State, as declared by our legislature. The "open and notorious" limitation on the former's prohibitions reflects both a disinclination to criminalize purely private relationships and a recognition that open fornication represents a graver threat to public morality than private violations. Conduct of that nature, when it is open, not only violates the statutorily expressed moral standards of the State, but also encourages others to violate those standards, and debases public morality. While we agree that the statute does not penalize conduct which is essentially private and discreet . . . Jacqueline's conduct has been neither, for she has discussed this relationship and her rationalization of it with at least her children, her former husband and her neighbors. It is, in our judgment, clear that her conduct offends prevailing public policy. . . .

Jacqueline's disregard for existing standards of conduct instructs her children, by example, that they, too, may ignore them . . . and could well encourage the children to engage in similar activity in the future. That factor, of course, supports the trial court's conclusion that their daily presence in that environment was injurious to the moral well-being and development of the children.

It is true that, as Jacqueline argues, the courts have not denied custody to every parent who has violated the community's moral standards, nor do we now intimate a different rule. Rather than mechanically denying custody in every such instance, the courts of this State appraise the moral example currently provided and the example which may be expected by the parent in the future. We held in *Nye v. Nye* (1952) . . . that past moral indiscretions of a parent are not sufficient grounds for denying custody if the parent's present conduct establishes the improbability of such lapses in the future. This rule focuses the trial court's attention on the moral values which the parent is actually demonstrating to the children. . . .

At the time of this hearing, however, and even when this case was argued orally to this court, Jacqueline continued to cohabit with Wayne Hammon and had done nothing to indicate that this relationship would not continue in the future. Thus the moral values which Jacqueline currently represents to her children, and those which she may be expected to portray to them in the future, contravene statutorily declared standards of conduct and endanger the children's moral development. . . .

While our comments have focused upon the moral hazards, we are not convinced that open cohabitation does not also affect the mental and emotional health of the children. . . . It is difficult to predict what psychological effects or problems may later develop from their efforts to overcome the disparity between their concepts of propriety and their mother's conduct. . . . If the Jarrett children remained in that situation, they might well be compelled to try to explain Hammon's presence to their friends and, perhaps, to endure their taunts and jibes. In a case such as this the trial judge must also weigh these imponderables, and he is not limited to examining the children for current physical manifestations of emotional or mental difficulties.

GOLDENHERSH, Chief Justice, with whom THOMAS J. MORAN, Justice, joins, dissenting:

[T]he effect of the decision is that the plaintiff's cohabitation with Hammon *per se* was sufficient grounds for changing the custody order previously entered. This record shows clearly that the children were healthy, well adjusted, and well cared for, and it should be noted that both the circuit and appellate courts made no finding that plaintiff was an unfit mother. The majority, too, makes no such finding and based its decision on a nebulous concept of injury to the children's "moral well-being and development." . . . I question that any competent sociologist would attribute the increase of "live in" unmarried couples to parental example.

The fragililty of its conclusion concerning "prevailing public policy" is demonstrated by the majority's reliance on cases decided by this court in 1852 . . . and an appellate court decision . . . which, rather than "prevailing public policy," more clearly indicates the prejudice extant in that period against interracial sexual relations.

As the appellate court pointed out, the courts should not impose the personal preferences and standards of the judiciary in the decision of this case. Courts are uniquely equipped to decide legal issues and are well advised to leave to the theologians the question of the morality of the living arrangement into which the plaintiff had entered.

As a legal matter, simply stated, the majority has held that on the basis of her presumptive guilt of fornication, a Class B misdemeanor, plaintiff, although not declared to be an unfit mother, has forfeited the right to have the custody of her children. This finding flies in the face of the established rule that, in order to modify or amend an award of custody, the evidence must show that the parent to whom custody of the children was originally awarded is unfit to retain custody, or that a change of conditions makes a change of custody in their best interests. This record fails to show either. Mr. Justice Moran and I dissent and would affirm the decision of the appellate court.

# G.

## Constitutional Privacy and Sexual Freedom: An Alternative View

The dominant view of the privacy cases among legal commentators is that they represent a partial infusion of Mill's principle into constitutional law. On this view, cases like *Paris Adult Theater* and *Doe v. Commonwealth's Attorney* are reactionary deviations from the natural development of the law toward a right of sexual freedom for consenting adults.

The following excerpt suggests a different interpretation of the constitutional right of privacy, one that takes seriously the Court's invocation of traditional conservative familial values. Despite the different analysis, the excerpt concludes with a prediction that the Court will soon establish a limited right of sexual freedom, but one responding to the demands of influential groups rather than the rights of individuals. Consider whether this analysis has any implications for the normative question whether Mill's principle *should* be embodied in constitutional law.

## 1. Thomas C. Grey, "Eros, Civilization and the Burger Court"*

[Perhaps] the Court meant what it said in *Griswold*: that the right of privacy protects only the historically sanctified institutions of marriage and the family, and has no implication for laws regulating sexual expression outside of traditional marriage. . . . [On this interpretation] the contraception and abortion cases are simply family planning cases. They represent two standard conservative views: that social stability is threatened by excessive population growth; and that family stability is threatened by unwanted pregnancies, with their accompanying fragile marriages, single parent families, irresponsible youthful parents, and abandoned and neglected children. . . .

The Court has [then] consistently protected traditional familial institutions, bonds, and authority against the centrifugal forces of an anomic modern society. Where less traditional values have been directly protected, conspicuously in the cases involving contraception and abortion, the decisions reflect not any Millian glorification of diverse individuality, but the stability-centered concerns of Planned Parenthood. . . .

On my interpretation, the Supreme Court's attitude toward sexual freedom is quite different from that of the liberal academic supporters of modern Millianism. But the Court itself reflects a characteristic attitude in modern times, and one not really adequately captured by terms such as "Victorian" or "puritan," insofar as these terms imply simply a devaluation of sexuality. Indeed, the Court's view of sex might be seen as a very exalted one, one that takes sex more seriously than do its opponents, the liberals.

Consider a familiar passage in the Court's first obscenity decision. The Court said that obscenity is "utterly without redeeming social importance," so that any benefit that might flow from it was "clearly outweighed by the social interest in order and morality. . . ." But, the Court made clear, not all explicit discussion of sex was unprotected. Why? Because "sex, a great and mysterious motive force

* 43 Law & Contemporary Problems 87 (1980).

in human life, has indisputably been a subject of absorbing interest to mankind through the ages. . . ."

Sex is, then, not something trivial, but a "great and mysterious . . . force." Obscenity, writing designed to arouse as directly as possible this great and mysterious force, is then not utterly unimportant; it is rather utterly without "redeeming *social* importance," and it may be suppressed in the name of "the *social* interest in order. . . ." To paraphrase a bit, obscenity unleashes a great and mysterious *anti-social* force, the force of sexuality.

The viewpoint implicit here is not an abstruse or unfamiliar one; indeed it is a view that has been central to modern thought, and far more widely accepted in our time than contemporary versions of the liberalism of John Stuart Mill. This is the view, most closely identified with Freud, but also to be found both among many left-wing theorists and in the Weberian sociological tradition, that modern civilization is built upon repression, particularly the repression of sexual drives.

One of Freud's central themes was that communal life, whether in the family or the larger society, depends directly on sexual repression. First, the family was based on the incest taboo, "the most drastic mutilation which man's erotic life has in all time experienced." Beyond this, civilization exacted further repressions, increasing with the complexity of the society, since "a large part of the psychical energy which it uses for its own purposes has to be drawn from sexuality." In the process of bottling up sex and withdrawing the stored energy for social use as work and achievement, Western European civilization has reached a high-water mark in repressiveness, accepting as it does only heterosexual, genital, monogamous sexuality as legitimate. Though of course very imperfectly enforced, still this narrow channel of sexual legitimacy "cuts off a fair number of people from sexual enjoyment, and so becomes the source of serious injustice." To defend its draconian restrictions, "civilization behaves toward sexuality as a people or a stratum of its population does which has subjected another one to its exploitation. Fear of a revolt by the suppressed elements drives it to stricter precautionary measures."

These restraints are necessary not only so that energy may be deflected to work and creative achievement. The larger community requires that its members be bound to each other by common sympathy; the energy for these bonds can only come from "aim-inhibited libido," erotic energy deflected from sex to desexualized social ties. These bonds are necessary to counter the power of Eros' ancient enemy, Thanatos, the death instinct, which takes the form of aggressiveness when turned outward.

> Men are not gentle creatures who want to be loved . . . they are, on the contrary, creatures among whose instinctual endowments is to be reckoned a powerful share of aggressiveness. As a result, their neighbor is for them not only a potential helper or sexual object, but someone who tempts them to satisfy their aggressiveness on him, to exploit his capacity for work without compensation, to use him sexually without his consent, to seize his possessions, to humiliate him, to cause him pain, to torture and to kill him.

. . . With this somber view, it is not surprising that Freud placed no very high priority on relieving the "injustices" that attend sexual repression. He saw the history of the world as "essentially a series of race murders"; "we spring from an endless ancestry of murderers, with whom the lust for killing was in the blood." If man's sexual life was mutilated by civilization, civilization was worth the price.

No other social theorist has placed quite such high a stake on the sexual repressions of modern civilization as did Freud. But every thinker of the great central tradition of the last century's social thought has seen repressed sexuality and the authoritarian family structure as close to the core of our civilization. Conservative theorists have defended repression as necessary; revolutionaries have urged that society would have to be overthrown to free us from its tyranny.

Weber, it will be recalled, located much of the motive power behind the creation of capitalism in the coming of Protestant, and particularly Calvinist, religion to Europe. The effect was twofold: first, work was infused with religious significance, and so became a calling; second, Protestant asceticism "turned with all its force against one thing: the spontaneous enjoyment of life and all it had to offer"—this because "impulsive enjoyment of life, which leads away both from work as a calling and from religion, was as such the enemy of rational asceticism. . . ." The Puritans strove toward the "strict exclusion of the erotic . . . from the realm of toleration." And Weber argued that the "powerful tendency toward uniformity of life, which today so immensely aids the capitalistic interest in the standardization of production, had its ideal foundations in the repudiation of all idolatry of the flesh."

. . . On the other side, the enemies of bourgeois society, the Marxists, have preached a similar message from a different perspective. Engels wrote of the close ties between the patriarchal family, sexual possessiveness and parental authority on the one hand, and the capitalist economy on the other. His ideas form the basis for a strong strand in Western Marxist thought, particularly when combined with later Freudian ideas, as in the writings of Herbert Marcuse and the early Wilhelm Reich. These writers have argued that the desirable goal of sexual liberation could only come with the destruction of capitalism—a view that must fortify the association of traditional sexual restrictions with existing political and economic institutions in the minds of more conservative thinkers.

Another strand in left-wing thought on family and sexuality runs contrary to the standard simple equation of capitalism with repression. On this view, early capitalism does indeed require and hence generate the traditional bourgeois family. But that bourgeois family, close-knit, loving and emotion-laden, albeit authoritarian and repressive, ultimately comes into contradiction with the development of capitalism in its later phases. Late capitalism requires not hard-working inner-directed Puritans, but rootless compulsive consumers, with no emotional ties except to their own narcissistic pleasures. Against this social demand, the traditional family provides a model of a human group founded on non-market altruistic loving relationships, and hence generates serious dissatisfaction with the soulless late-capitalist marketplace. On this view, associated in this country with the writings of Christopher Lasch, it is the very sexual repressiveness of the family, with its Oedipal rivalries, incest taboos, and castration anxieties, that generates the emotional intensity which sustains the family as a "haven in a heartless world." This strongly Freud-influenced view, then, sees the sexual revolution as an ideological manifestation of late capitalism, but shares the Weberian view that this development will lead to social disintegration. . . .

[Paradoxically, this very analysis of the ideology behind the privacy cases leads me to] expect that within a few years fornication and sodomy laws will be found unconstitutional, on something like the very dogma of the rights of consenting adults to control their own sex lives that the Court has until now so rigorously avoided. But the real reasons for the decisions will have little to do with any notion in the Justices' minds that sexual freedom is essential to the pursuit of happiness.

Rather the decisions will respond to the same demands of order and social stability that have produced the contraception and abortion decisions. Thousands of couples are living together today outside of marriage. The fornication laws, otherwise empty formalities as they are, stand in the way of providing a stabilizing legal framework for these unions, for governing custody and rearing of children born in them, for distributing property acquired while they exist. For this reason those laws will be struck down in the jurisdictions which have not legislatively repealed them first.

Similarly, the homosexual community is becoming an increasingly public sector of our society. For that community to be governed effectively, it must be recognized as a legitimate as well as a visible subculture. Perhaps something like marriage will have to be recognized for homosexual couples, not because *they* need it for their happiness (though they may), but because *society* needs it to avoid the sense of insecurity and instability generated by the existence in its midst of a permanent and influential subculture outside the law. Effective regulation of the family and community life of gay people will require that the laws which symbolically proclaim their sexual identity illegitimate in the eyes of the larger society must be eliminated. Some of the fierce conservatives in our midst will not see this conservative necessity, and their views will prevail in the legislatures of a few jurisdictions. The Supreme Court will then step in and play its traditional role as enlightened conservator of the social interest in ordered stability, and will strike down those laws, in the glorious name of the individual.

# THE TREATMENT OF THE DEAD

All societies of which there is any record have had customs concerning the treatment of the bodies of the dead. In some cases these customs have been central to basic values and symbols of a culture; for example, the burial customs of ancient Egypt have left to us the pyramids, the mummies, and the Book of the Dead. A basic document of Western civilization is Sophocles' *Antigone*, in which the center of the drama is the heroine's refusal to obey the king's command that her brother's body be left unburied. Such a command could not be lawful, she says; it would violate "the gods' unwritten and unfailing laws."

Our own culture has its own rules about the treatment of human remains, and many of these rules are enforced by law. The law governing the treatment of human remains rests on widespread horror at corpse desecration. Are these restrictions different in kind from the prohibitions of the culturally deviant sexual practices that have traditionally been called perverted and unnatural? Lord Devlin argued that sexual prohibitions have had and need no better justification than that they are supported by widespread "indignation, intolerance and disgust" and the prohibited acts. His critics have urged that irrational emotion, however intense, cannot support coercive law. Do the contemporary and historical restrictions on the use of cadavers that follow depend upon a Devlinite justification?

# A.

# The Law of Cadavers: Introduction and Historical Background

## 1. N. Wade, "The Quick, the Dead, and the Cadaver Population"*

*After reading this report, imagine that you work for Congressman Moss and try to state why this use of cadavers is morally offensive, while using them for dissection in anatomy classes is not.*

The Department of Transportation has issued a stop-work order

* "The Quick, the Dead, and the Cadaver Population," by N Wade, reprinted from *Science*, Vol. 199, 1420–1421, 31 March 1978. Copyright 1978 by the American Association for the Advancement of Science. Reprinted by permission.

putting all work with the cadaver population into suspended animation.

The Department has been prompted to this exercise of its powers by Congressman John E. Moss of California. During the recent debate on air bags, Moss learned that dead bodies had been used to assess the protection afforded by the devices to passengers in car crashes.

He wrote to the Secretary of Transportation saying, in effect, that the Department had better have good reason for its use of cadavers because many would find such research morally offensive. Moss is chairman of the House sub-commitee on oversight and investigations, and his opinions are of interest to the Department of Transportation.

Department officials soon ascertained that Moss himself was among those who found such research morally offensive. It was explained to Moss that almost all the cadavers so used come from the "willed body program," and that family permission is secured whenever possible. Crash testing requires an insignificant number of bodies compared with other uses, such as in medical schools. The information gained from cadavers is regarded as critical to the design of better dummies, and the present research program will be completed by 1980.

In full understanding of all these reasons, Moss replied to Secretary Brock Adams on 6 January, he nevertheless adhered to the view "that the use of human cadavers for vehicle safety research crudely violates fundamental notions of morality and human dignity, and must therefore permanently be stopped."

The Department issued 90-day stop-work orders to its six contractors in mid-November, and the ban is being continued by mutual agreement until 1 July, when a review of policy will have been completed. Some observers believe the Department may just be trying to wait Moss out—he has announced that he is retiring at the end of this session—but others say that Joan Claybrook, the new head of the National Highway Traffic Safety Administration, is interested in a serious review. The issue is not likely to become a political bandwagon: most congressmen seem interested in keeping as far away from it as they can.

One research contractor is at Wayne State University. Asked what he will use instead of cadavers in crash tests, chairman Albert I. King says "Living volunteers—but at lower g's." Wayne

State uses about 10 to 20 cadavers a year in its crash test program.

Moss's inquiries elicited from the Department of Transportation the following official account of how cadaver crash testing came into being. Originally, it seems, crash studies were performed on "a dummy representing a 50th percentile male." Unfortunately a court "found the dummy insufficiently objective as a test device." After further test and development, "the Hybrid II dummy was adopted . . . as the official measuring instrument." One feature lacked by the Hybrid II dummy was the characteristic known as "bio-fidelity." It behaved well in frontal crashes but failed to mimic human kinematics in side and rear crashes as well as in pedestrian impacts.

The search began for an advanced dummy. But design of a better dummy required comparison with the real thing. "Of all available surrogates for the human body, the cadaver possesses by far the greatest mechanical and geometrical similarity with the living person," the Department of Transportation explained to Moss. True, cadavers were of different shapes and sizes, but "the variability of the cadaver population accurately reflects the variability of the population of living humans which the safety standards are designed to protect." Not that cadavers are perfect: "It is generally recognized that a number of limitations surround using the cadaver as a surrogate for a living human being." Nonetheless, a prohibition of cadaver use for trauma research would set back progress toward these important ends many years into the future, the Department of Transportation concluded.

Moss read this document, but was not persuaded to the opposite view.

## 2. *Rex v. Lynn**

*The conflict between the use of human remains for the advancement of science and medicine, and the protection of their sacred repose, is an old one, as the following excerpt—the first important English case on the subject—suggests.*

The defendant having been convicted on an indictment charging him with entering a certain burying ground, and taking a coffin out of

* 100 Eng. Rep. 394 (1788).

the earth, from which he took a dead body, and carried it away for the purpose of dissecting it.

[His lawyer argued:] The crime imputed to the defendant is not made penal by any statute: the only Act of Parliament which has any relation to this subject, is that which makes it felony to steal dead bodies for the purposes of witchcraft; but that clearly cannot affect the present question. . . . And all the writers on this subject have considered the injury which is done to the executors of the deceased by taking the shroud, and the trespass in digging the soil; taking it for granted that the act of carrying away a dead body was not criminal.

The Court said that common decency required that the practice should be put a stop to. That the offence was cognizable in a Criminal Court, as being highly indecent, and contra bonos mores[†]; at the bare idea alone of which nature revolted. That the purpose of taking up the body for dissection did not make it less an indictable offence. . . . But inasmuch as this defendant might have committed the crime merely from ignorance, no person having been before punished in this Court for this offence, they only fined him five marks.

## 3. *M. J. Durey, "Bodysnatchers and Benthamites"** ========

*Rex v. Lynn made it a crime to desecrate a grave in order to remove the corpse for purposes of dissection. The following excerpt describes the consequent struggle between the demands of medical science and those of popular feeling. Does the alliance of working-class radicals and traditional conservatives who opposed the liberals supporting medical access to cadavers have implications for controversies on similar subjects in our time?*

The revolution in medical science and training which radiated from the universities of Leyden and Edinburgh in the eighteenth century relied heavily on the empirical study of the human body. In London its influence was most clearly demonstrated by the emergence from about the middle of the century of the independent medical schools at which surgeons gave private lectures on anatomical science using dead bodies for demonstration purposes.

The human body provided the raw material for the new empirical

---

† Against sound customs.
* M.J. Durey, 22 *The London Journal* 200 (1976). Reprinted from *The London Journal* by permission of the Trustees of London Journal Trust.

teaching methods. Each student ideally required three bodies on which to practise during his sixteen-month course in surgery and anatomy. Thus, in the late 1820s more than two thousand bodies per annum were needed in London alone. But there was no legal provision for the supply of bodies to the schools on this scale. The Murder Act of 1752, which ordered either public dissection or hanging in chains for executed murderers, did provide some corpses, but never in sufficient quantity to satisfy the schools' needs.

The surgeon-teachers had, therefore, to rely on their own ingenuity to obtain the materials of their trade. Before the 1790s this usually resulted in small bands of students exhuming newly buried corpses from cemeteries in the dead of night.*

Better protection for the newly buried resulted in a serious shortfall in the body supply to the schools. The price of bodies had always fluctuated according to demand and in difficult times many of the schools had suffered serious financial embarrassment. But in the 1820s students forsook London for Paris because of the uncertainty surrounding the supply of subjects for dissection. Between 1823 and 1828 the number of students in London fell from one thousand to eight hundred.

. . . In the first few months of 1828, two judicial decisions suddenly put the medical profession outside the law. At two separate trials in Lancashire, William Gill—a very reputable Liverpool surgeon—and a medical student called Davies were found guilty of receiving a body for dissection, knowing it to have been disinterred. As the law was interpreted in their cases, it was now an offence for a medical man to have possession of a dead body, if it could be shown that he knew how the body had been obtained. The supplied had become as guilty as the suppliers and were liable to be charged with the common law offence of offending public decency. The medical profession was in a completely untenable position. If a practitioner obtained a body on which to practise, he was committing a common law offence; if he made an error whilst operating on a patient (increasingly likely in the future if he had not been adequately trained), he could be sued by civil action. Without fully appreciating it, two Lancashire judges had jeopardised the future development of modern medical science.

The London medical profession responded by sending petitions to

* It was this practice that was declared a crime in *Rex v. Lynn*.

Parliament and in April 1828, at the request of Henry Warburton, a Select Committee of Inquiry into Anatomy was established. Warburton's subsequent role was to be crucial, for he not only represented the interests of the reforming medical profession, but he was also a spokesman for that looseknit group of political economists who adhered to the ideas and philosophy of Jeremy Bentham.

Predictably, the select committee recommended that the bodies of those who during life had been maintained at public charge, and who had died in workhouses, hospitals or other charitable institutions, should—if not claimed by next of kin within a certain time of death—be given to an anatomist. In a classical espousal of the theory of utility the members of the committee justified themselves by claiming that the misery of those related to the exhumed dead could only be diminished "by giving up for dissection a certain portion of the whole, in order to preserve the remainder from disturbance." The Report ended: "To neglect the practice of dissection, would lead to the greatest aggravation of human misery; since anatomy, if not learned by that practice, must be learned by mangling the living."

These were prophetic words indeed, for only four months later the Burke and Hare outrages in Edinburgh were discovered. Between December 1827 and October 1828 Burke and Hare had murdered at least sixteen people and sold the bodies to Robert Knox of the independent medical school in Edinburgh. Popular feeling against bodysnatching and anatomical research was already high, but it now reached a new peak of intensity. The medical profession collected its fair share of this popular hatred. Although it is true that teachers of anatomy were forced to rely on the criminal classes against their wishes, it is also true that in some instances they deserved their bad reputation. For example, very little attention was paid to the remains of a body after use. Much of the distaste for anatomy came from a knowledge of the pranks which medical students were notoriously liable to play. In one case in London a riot ensued after a student climbed onto the roof of a house and dropped an amputated leg down the chimney. It fell into a pot of stew and gave a chimneysweep's wife hysterics. Such activities (and more could be instanced) displayed a lack of common humanity which alienated the poor from the medical profession.

Ironically, Henry Warburton introduced his Anatomy Bill (the result of the select committee's findings) into parliament on the very day Burke was hanged in Edinburgh. It was an inauspicious omen. The Bill was extremely unpopular and soon became known as the Dead Body Bill. . . . The Bill passed the House of Commons but was not permitted to go to committee by the House of Lords.

[When a revised version of the Bill was introduced two years later, those in opposition to it] although holding widely varying political positions, . . . were united in their common humanitarianism and their detestation of political economy. They appreciated that the Bill was aimed against the poor, for it was that class which was to be sacrificed on the altar of Utility. Sir Richard Vyvyan believed that "those who died in the poor-house were as much entitled to the protection of the law as those who died in palaces." At the other political extreme Henry Hunt felt the Bill would tempt the poor to neglect and ill-treat their aged and infirm relatives. Sadler argued that dislike of dissection was not a prejudice but a natural feeling which could only be destroyed at the expense of some of the best feelings of human nature. The Bill would lead the lower classes, "whose crime was poverty and whose fault was prejudice," to avoid the hospitals and die unattended in the streets.

While Vyvyan, Hunt and Sadler invoked a mixture of paternalism and social concern to defend the poor, Warburton and his associates defended the Bill from the impregnable heights of strict social utility. When introducing the Bill, Warburton argued that public opinion, which he conceded was hostile, should in some circumstances be overridden by the needs of the state. This was just such a time. Macaulay thought likewise. "If [the Bill] is unpopular," he said, "I am sorry for it. But I shall cheerfully take my share of its unpopularity. . . Such I am convinced ought to be the conduct of one whose object it is, not to flatter the people but to serve them."

In August 1832 the Anatomy Bill became law, after Warburton had accepted certain additions to it. It was a clear victory for philosophic radicalism and the theories of social utility, foreshadowing the class legislation of the Poor Law Amendment Act. The middle class's fears were assuaged but at the expense of further degrading the poor, who continued to pay their debt to society even after death. It is noteworthy that Bentham's attempt to influence public opinion by bequeathing his body for research was a complete failure. Few followed his example. . . .

## 4. *State v. Bradbury**

*The history of the law of burial has been shaped by threats to sacred repose other than those posed by science. Consider, in the following case, the court's statement that cremation is a crime only if it is* indecent. *What made the burning of the corpse in this case indecent? Was it that Bradbury dragged his sister's body with a rope? That his furnace was not big enough to receive her body all at once? That the burning gave off a disagreeable odor? Or just that the cremation was carried out at home, depriving the local undertaker of business?*

*Note the quotation of Holmes's famous remark that "the law should correspond with the actual feelings and demands of the community, whether right or wrong." Does the decision violate Mill's principle?*

THAXTER, Justice.

The respondent, Frank E. Bradbury, lived with an unmarried sister, Harriet, in a two and a half story building situated on Main Street in the City of Saco. They were old people and the last survivors of their family. In June 1938 Harriet was in failing health. She appeared to have suffered some injury from a fall and during the night of June 9th she remained in a reclining chair in the front room of their home. About four o'clock in the morning of June 10th she died. The respondent thereupon built a hot fire in the furnace in the basement of the house, tied a rope around the legs of his sister's body, dragged it down the cellar stairs, shoved it into the furnace and burned it. It was impossible to get it all into the fire box at once, but as the head and shoulders were consumed, he forced it farther and farther until he was able to close the furnace door. Reverend Ward R. Clark, who lived in the house next door, testified that during the morning of June 10th a heavy, dark smoke, with a very disagreeable odor poured from the chimney of the house. The next day an investigation was made by the authorities, who asked the respondent to show them the remains of his sister. Going to the basement of the house, he took down the crank used for shaking down the furnace, turned over the grates, shovelled out the ashes and said: "If you want to see her, there she is." A few bones were found; the rest of the body had been consumed.

The indictment charged that the respondent "with force and arms, unlawfully and indecently did take the human body of one

* 9 A. 2d 657 (1939) (Maine Supreme Court).

Harriet P. Bradbury, and then and there indecently and unlawfully put and placed said body in a certain furnace, and then and there did dispose of and destroy the said body of the said Harriet P. Bradbury by burning the same in said furnace, to the great indecency of Christian burial, in evil example to all others in like case offending, against the peace of said State and contrary to the laws of the same."

The offence is not covered by the provisions of Rev. Stat. 1930, Ch. 135, Sec. 47, which makes it an offence to disinter, to conceal, to indecently expose, to throw away or to abandon a human body; and it is important to note that the indictment does not charge the violation of any statute. The question for us to decide is whether this was a crime under the common law.

Judge Holmes, in speaking of the common law as applicable to crimes, has well said: "The first requirement of a sound body of law is, that it should correspond with the actual feelings and demands of the community, whether right or wrong." Holmes, Common Law, p. 41. And in Pierce v. Proprietors of Swan Point Cemetery, 10 R. I. 227, a case involving rights of sepulture, the court discusses the application thereto of the principles of the common law and quotes from a report published in 1836 by Joseph Story, Simon Greenleaf and others on the Codification of the Laws of Massachusetts. With reference to the common law, this says in part: "In truth, the common law is not in its nature and character an absolutely fixed, inflexible system, like the statute law, providing only for cases of a determinate form, which fall within the letter of the language, in which a particular doctrine or legal proposition is expressed. It is rather a system of elementary principles and of general juridical truths, which are continually expanding with the progress of society, and adapting themselves to the gradual changes of trade and commerce, and the mechanic arts, and the exigencies and usages of the country."

It is because the common law gives expression to the changing customs and sentiments of the people that there have been brought within its scope such crimes as blasphemy, open obscenity, and kindred offenses against religion and morality, in short those acts which, being highly indecent, are contra bonos mores. *Rex v. Lynn*.

The proper method for disposal of the dead has been regulated by law from earliest times, on the continent of Europe by the canon law, and in England by the ecclesiastical law. . . . But even in England where the subject has been largely committed to the ecclesiastical courts, the principles of the common law have been held applicable and the courts have not hesitated to apply them to give effect to the well recognized customs of the day and age. *Rex v. Lynn*, supra. In *Reg. v. Stewart*, the rule is broadly laid down in the following language: "We have no doubt, therefore, that the common law casts on some one the duty of carrying to the grave, decently covered, the dead body of any person dying in such a state of indigence as to leave no funds for that purpose. The feelings and the interest of the living require this, and create the duty: . . . ."

In this country the subject is governed quite largely by statute and where no statutory provision is applicable by the principles of the common law; and the general doctrine laid down in *Reg. v. Stewart*, supra, modified only by changing usages, has been almost universally followed.

In our own state some time before the decision in *Reg. v. Stewart*, it was held that the indecent disposal of a human body was an offence at common law. *Kanavan's* Case, 1 Me, 226. The second count of the indictment in this case charged that the respondent "unlawfully and indecently took the body" of a child "and threw it into the river, against common decency." The respondent maintained that the offence was not indictable at common law and filed a motion in arrest of judgment. The indictment was held good. The court said: "From our childhood, we all have been accustomed to pay a reverential respect to the sepulchres of our fathers, and to attach a character of sacredness to the grounds dedicated and enclosed as the cemeteries of the dead. Hence, before the late statute of Massachusetts was enacted, it was an offence at common law to dig up the bodies of those who had been buried, for the purpose of dissection. It is an outrage upon the public feelings, and torturing to the afflicted relatives of the deceased. If it be a crime thus to disturb the ashes of the dead, it must also be a crime to deprive them of a decent burial, by a disgraceful exposure or disposal of the body, contrary to usages so long sanctioned, and which are so grateful to the wounded hearts of friends and mourners."

This case seems to lay down the doctrine that any disposal of a dead body which is contrary to common decency is an offense at common law. But counsel for the respondent in the case before us argues that cremation is now a well recognized method of disposing of a dead body and cites the case of *Reg. v. Price*, as an authority that on the facts of the instant case no crime has been committed. If this case upholds the doctrine for which he contends, it does not represent the law in this country. A careful reading of it, however, satisfies us that the court did not intend to lay down any such principle. The question considered was a very narrow one, "whether," to use the language of the court, "to burn a dead body instead of burying it is in itself an illegal act." The question is answered as follows: "I am of the opinion that a person who burns instead of burying a dead body does not commit a criminal act, unless he does it in such a manner as to amount to a public nuisance at common law." And in the case before us the essence of the offense charged and proved is, not that the body was burned, but that it was indecently burned, in such a manner that, when the facts should in the natural course of events become known, the feelings and natural sentiments of the public would be outraged.

## 5. Yome v. Gorman*

*In this case, does the court proceed by asking whether the widow or the church owns the remains? Would this way of putting the question clarify the case?*

*The court says that the deceased's body should not normally be disturbed if there was "reason to suppose that the conscience of the deceased, were he alive, would be outraged by the change." Is this an interest that Mill's principle allows us to take into account?*

*What is "the interest of the public" that the court refers to, apart from the wishes of the deceased and his survivors?*

*What is the trial court supposed to do when it gets the case back?*

CARDOZO, J., delivered the opinion of the court:

The controversy has its origin in an attempted disinterment of the bodies of the dead.

John D. Yome and the plaintiff, Anna Yome, his wife, bought an eight-grave plot in Holy Cross Cemetery, Brooklyn. They had buried two infant children in the same cemetery many years before. The approach of old age seems to have warned them of the need of providing a resting place for themselves and for others who were close to them. There is a statement by the plaintiff that the plot was taken with the thought of supplying a place of merely temporary burial. Its size, however, the number of its graves, and the use

* 242 N.Y. 395 (New York Court of Appeals, 1926).

thereafter made of it, suggest a purpose more enduring. Holy Cross Cemetery is maintained by the Roman Catholic Diocese of Brooklyn. Burial within the cemetery is a privilege reserved to those who have died in communion with the Roman Catholic Church. The certificate of ownership delivered to the purchasers of plots expressly so provides, and provides also that the right of burial shall be subject to the rules and regulations of the Bishop of the Diocese. In the faith of the Church, plaintiff's mother and brother were buried in the plot so purchased. This was done some years ago while Mr. Yome was yet alive. The end came for him in February, 1925. On his deathbed he received the sacraments of his Church, and he was laid in his grave in accordance with its rites. A rule of the Church forbids the removal of a body from consecrated ground to ground that is unconsecrated, or consecrated to another faith.

There was swiftly a change of heart. Plaintiff, though baptized a Roman Catholic, became the owner of a plot in a non-Catholic cemetery, where it is now her purpose to be buried. She made demand upon the defendants, the Roman Catholic Diocese and the Supervisor of Cemeteries, for permission to remove the bodies. They refused to yield to the demand on the ground that disinterment for the purpose of removal to a cemetery of another faith would be an act of desecration. Plaintiff, seeking to justify her position, insists that her husband was without devotion to the tenets of the Church, and did not care where he was buried if only he was close to her. Defendants remind us on the other hand that he was reared in the faith of the Church, and died in it, sending for a priest upon his deathbed to gain the privilege of burial in consecrated ground. What the plaintiff says of her husband, she says in substance also of her mother and her brother. The infant children, buried long before, were too young to have religious convictions or wishes of their own. The surviving next of kin support the plaintiff in her request that the bodies be removed.

This action is brought to restrain the defendants from preventing the removal. . . .

Upon the record before us, one may draw conflicting inferences of duty and propriety. The wishes of wife and next of kin are not always supreme and final though the body is yet unburied. . . . Still less are they supreme and final when the body has been laid at rest and the aid of equity is invoked to disturb the quiet of the grave. . . . There will then be "due regard to the interest of the public, the wishes of the decedent, and the rights and feelings of those entitled to be heard by reason of relationship or association.". . . A benevolent discretion, giving heed to all those promptings and emotions that men and women hold for sacred in the disposition of their dead, must render judgment as it appraises the worth of the competing forces. . . .

To the making of that appraisal many factors will contribute. One may not fix their values in advance, for in so doing one would overlook the varying force of circumstance. One can do little more than offer the suggestion of example. The wish of the deceased, even though legal compulsion may not attach to it . . . has at least a large significance. . . . Especially is this so when the wish has its origin in intense religious feeling. . . .

Only some rare emergency could move a court of equity to take a body from its grave in consecrated ground and put it in ground unhallowed if there was good reason to suppose that the conscience of the deceased, were he alive, would be outraged by the change. Subordinate in importance, and yet at times not wholly to be disregarded, are the sentiments and usages of the religious body which confers the right of burial. . . . [S]entiments and usages, devoutly held as sacred, may not be flouted for caprice. They must be weighed in the balance with the motives and feelings that sway the acts of the survivors. Removal at the instance of a wife or of kinsmen near in blood to satisfy a longing that those united during life shall not be divided after death may seem praiseworthy and decorous when removal at the instance of distant relatives or strangers would be arbitrary or cruel. The dead are to rest where they have been laid unless reason of substance is brought forward for disturbing their repose. . . .

We have sought not to declare a rule, but to exemplify a process. The considerations we have instanced and others of like order may move a court of equity to keep a grave inviolate against the will of the survivors. They are none of them so absolute, however, that they may not be neutralized by others. The wish expressed during life may have been declared casually or lightly. The bond of religion may have been weak, and the bond of marriage or of kinship may have been strong. Separation after death from the resting place of wife or child may have seemed an evil more poignant than separation after death from the faithful of the church. We are told by Mrs. Yome that so her husband would have felt. Her statement does not control us. To some extent, though not at all conclusively, it is contradicted by his acts. The trier of the facts must probe his state of mind. With this, when it is ascertained and the intensity of his feelings measured, must be compared the sentiments and wishes of wife and kin surviving. A like process must be followed before the other graves may be disturbed. Right must then be done as right would be conceived of by men of character and feeling. [The case was returned to the trial court for its consideration of the factors set out in Judge Cardozo's opinion.]

# B.

# The Transplant Problem: The Gift Act

This section introduces an important legal response to the development of organ transplantation—the Uniform Anatomical Gift Act (UAGA). The excerpt from the Sadler and Sadler article summarizes the traditional law of dead bodies reflected in cases like *Bradbury* and *Yome* and in the Anatomy Acts passed after the nineteenth-century body-snatching scandals. They argue that this set of rules was deficient to meet the need for transplant organs but that the deficiencies have been overcome by the UAGA. The text of the UAGA is then set out, followed by a critique of the Act by Professor Jesse Dukeminier, who argues it does not go far enough in changing the existing law on the subject.

The whole section has two purposes. The first is to pose the issue of whether the values opposed to unrestricted access to the bodies of the newly dead for puposes of organ transplantation are compatible with any version of Mill's principle. Why should the deceased, or their relatives, have any say at all about what is done with their remains? The second purpose is to show the reader the level of detail to which a social and moral problem is reduced when the problem comes to be translated into legal form. In order to give a sense of this, the text of the statute is given in full, and Professor Dukeminier's detailed lawyer's criticisms of the statute are included. The student should read through the statute in order to get a general sense of the legal framework created and then refer back to it in considering each of Dukeminier's criticisms.

## 1. Alfred M. Sadler and Blair L. Sadler, "Transplantation and the Law: The Need for Organized Sensitivity"*

It is difficult to recall any event which so dramatically displayed the many multidisciplinary ramifications of the current scientific revolution than did the first transplantation of a human heart on December 3, 1967. Despite its obvious appeal as a medical landmark, that event and its progeny received a colorful spectrum of epithets ranging from, "a miracle" and "the answer to heart disease," to "exceedingly premature," "immoral," and "criminal." Such emphatic reactions must come as a surprise to some, for many of the ethical, social, and legal questions raised by heart transplantation are not new, but have been raised previously by the transplantation of other organs and the use of human tissue for medical and scientific purposes.[†] . . .

. . . The donation and procurement of human tissue can be effected from both living and dead persons. In the former case, such as in the transplantation of a kidney or the taking of skin for grafting, the primary legal concern is to obtain both adequate and informed consent authorizing the surgical removal. This may become complicated if the prospective donor is a minor or incompetent. The crucial point, however, is that while donation and procurement of tissue from a living donor may produce serious ethical and legal issues, there is no doubt as to the right of a competent adult to make such a donation; thus, there is no need for statutory donation authority.

An altogether different situation arises when an organ or tissue is utilized after the death of the donor and the validity of the individual's donation is unclear. Many additional questions result from the existence of several very important, but frequently competing, interests which the law has endeavored to recognize. In addition to the wishes of the deceased and those of the surviving spouse and other

---

* 57 Geo. L. J. 5 (1968–69). Reprinted with the permission of the Publisher; copyright © 1968 by the Georgetown Law Journal.
[†] Corneas were successfully transplanted in the 1940s; their use as a therapeutic modality today is widely accepted and commonplace. Transplantation of a human kidney in 1954 demonstrated the feasibility of the use of whole organs. Many other tissues are now being successfully transplanted, including skin, cartilage, tendon, nerve, artery, heart valve, and bone. More recently, the pancreas, thymus, liver, and lung have been transplanted in man.

appropriate next of kin, modern medical science's need for organs, tissue, and cadavers and society's requirement that cause of death be determined in certain circumstances must also be taken into account. The attempted reconciliations of these conflicting interests by piecemeal legislation and the many recent technological advances in transplantation and research have produced the legal problems which are the subject of this analysis.

The present law concerning transplantation is an unwieldly morass of archaic common-law principles; related, but not relevant, autopsy, unclaimed body, and medical examiner statutes; and incomplete, highly irregular donation legislation. The Uniform Anatomical Gift Act, prepared by the Commissioners on Uniform State Laws, represents an important step forward in the creation of the needed legal structure to guide the donation and use of organs and tissue for transplantation and other medical purposes. . . . In order to appreciate the present dilemma, it is necessary to understand the void which had existed prior to the appearance of the Uniform Act.

## JUDICIAL INADEQUACIES OF THE COMMON LAW

In medieval England, matters concerning dead bodies were subject to the jurisdiction of the ecclesiastical courts. In keeping with the traditional Western emphasis on the dignity and sanctity of the individual, the body was considered incapable of being owned in the commercial sense, and thus, could not be bought or sold. This resulted in the refusal of early common-law decisions to recognize any property rights in the body of a deceased person. This "no property" doctrine was reiterated in subsequent English cases. In *Williams v. Williams*, the court concluded that since a body is not property, it is not a part of the decedent's estate; thus, a person could not direct the manner of his burial.

Although early decisions in American courts adopted the "no property" rule, the more recent trend is to recognize that an individual has certain interests frequently termed "quasi-property" rights which give some authority to his directing the post-mortem disposition of his body. Generally, these rights have been limited to directing the place and manner of burial or to agreements in insurance policies by which the insured authorizes an autopsy of his body.

As a result of the scarcity of judicial declarations dealing specifically with donations, the existence of any common-law right of an individual to donate his own organs or tissue for use after his death may only be derived by analogy from a closely related situation—where a decedent has directed his manner or place of burial. Unfortunately, an examination of these cases proves similarly inconclusive.

The rights of the next of kin to donate all or part of the deceased's body have also had a curious ancestry. Due to the well recognized right which each individual has to a proper burial and the concomitant societal interest in the adequate disposal of bodies, the next of kin have long been obligated to provide for the decedent's burial. In order that they may adequately discharge this duty, courts have declared that the body must be returned in the same condition it was at the time of death, providing a cause of action if the body should be mutilated. Under this example, an unauthorized removal of organs for transplantation or research would be an actionable wrong.

The right to donate all or part of the decedent's body for medical or scientific purposes is not synonymous with the common-law right to provide the body with a decent burial. However, the practice of obtaining donation consent from next of kin is so widely recognized today that such permission is not likely to be challenged. The wide acceptance of this proposition is evidenced by the fact that several states specifically permit donation by next of kin, while none prohibit this right.

The paucity of cases dealing with donation of tissue, by either the decedent or next of kin, and the conflicting judicial treatment of the questions dealing with the place and manner of burial, provide little assurance that an individual has the authority to control the disposition of his body. The severe time demands requiring the speedy removal of tissue and the reluctance on the part of those involved to resolve disagreements over donations by litigation explain the almost total lack of case law on this subject. Consequently, guidance must be sought from statutory law.

## AUTOPSY STATUTES

A large number of states have enacted autopsy statutes which permit the next of kin to authorize an autopsy on the deceased. These statutes are of substantial help to doctors in that they usually enumerate the appropriate next of kin for obtaining autopsy consent; some even establish an order of priority based upon the degree of familial kinship. Approximately one-half specifically provide an individual the right to authorize an autopsy of his remains.

It is questionable whether present statutory autopsy authority is broad enough to include the procurement of organs and tissue for medical purposes, such as transplantation, since this is clearly beyond the scope of the routine autopsy and none of the statutes have attempted to redefine the term. It has been suggested that permission for an autopsy, in effect, authorizes the removal of tissue for scientific use. Such a view is based upon the belief that permanent removal of certain organs is the customary practice. This presumption is probably not justified; the public is not adequately aware of the non-replacement practices regarding autopsies, and cannot be assumed to have intended such a broad authorization.

## UNCLAIMED BODY STATUTES

In addition to autopsy statutes, a number of jurisdictions have passed legislation providing for the delivery of unclaimed bodies to medical schools and hospitals for educational and scientific purposes. These statutes, known as either "unclaimed body" or "anatomy" statutes, usually contain waiting periods of at least 24 hours, during which time the hospital in possession of the deceased's body must make a reasonable search for the next of kin. Until this has been made, and the waiting period has passed, the body is not "unclaimed" within the meaning of the statute. These requirements, in themselves, preclude the use of unclaimed bodies for transplantation and most medical research purposes.

## MEDICAL EXAMINER AND CORONER STATUTES

It is well established that the rights of the next of kin must yield to the right of the public to investigate the cause of death in certain circumstances. Despite the longstanding tradition of allowing the next of kin to control the disposition of the remains, a complete post-mortem examination of a body is often essential to determine the cause of death, establish the existence of a crime, or provide necessary evidence at trial. Consequently, statutes exist in every jurisdiction which authorize a medical examiner or coroner to perform post-mortem examinations in those situations where he believes death to have occurred as the result of violence or in other suspicious circumstances. Because of the clear public interest involved, he is authorized to perform an autopsy without the next of kin's consent.

The medical examiner would be the ideal person to sanction the procurement of tissue from victims of fatal accidents or other cases over which he has jurisdiction. His stated authority is limited to performing an autopsy, however, and does not include the donation of organs and tissues for transplantation and medical research. Consequently, if such a donation were made by a medical examiner without the consent of the next of kin, it might be successfully challenged. . . .

## THE UNIFORM ANATOMICAL GIFT ACT

In response to these legislative shortcomings and in the face of the increasing number of transplantations and the correlatively increasing need for more human tissue, the Commissioners on Uniform State Laws created a special committee . . . to draft a uniform donation statute, one which would serve as a model for the individual states and provide a uniform, favorable legal setting for the donation and use of organs and tissue in medical research and therapy—specifically, transplantation. Three years later, on July 30, 1968, the Uniform Anatomical Gift Act received final approval from the Commissioners. . . .

The Uniform Act is based on the belief that each individual should be able to control the disposition of his body after death without having his wishes frustrated by anyone, including his next of kin. To encourage donation and to help meet the need for organs and tissue, unnecessary and cumbersome formalities have been eliminated and only those safeguards required to protect the varied interests have been included. An attempt has been made to protect the rights of the appropriate next of kin, doctors working in this area, and the public interest in a dead body. . . .

## 2. *The Uniform Anatomical Gift Act**

*To see if you have a grasp of the basic provisions of the UAGA, the text of which follows, determine for yourself what it provides for in each of the following cases: (a) wife of decedent is willing to donate his kidney, but his parents object; (b) brother of decedent present at time of death is willing to donate organ, but says he knows that parents (who cannot be reached) would object; (c) the deceased has a signed and witnessed organ donation card in his wallet, authorizing use of any of his organs for transplant, but his parents, who*

---

* 57 Geo. L. J. 5 (1968–69). Reprinted with the permission of the Publisher: copyright © 1968 by the Georgetown Law Journal.

*are the only persons present at the time of death, object; (d) deceased has authorized removal of his brain for research purposes by a private non-university-affiliated biological research institution; his spouse objects (see Section 3 of the UAGA).*

SECTION 2. [Persons Who May Execute an Anatomical Gift.]

(a) Any individual of sound mind and 18 years of age or more may give all or any part of his body for any purposes specified in Section 3, the gift to take effect upon death.

(b) Any of the following persons, in order of priority stated, when persons in prior classes are not available at the time of death, and in the absence of actual notice of contrary indications by the decedent, or actual notice of opposition by a member of the same or a prior class, may give all or any part of the decedent's body for any purposes specified in Section 3.

    (1) the spouse.
    (2) an adult son or daughter.
    (3) either parent.
    (4) an adult brother or sister.
    (5) a guardian of the person of the decedent at the time of his death.
    (6) any other person authorized or under obligation to dispose of the body.

(c) If the donee has actual notice of contrary indications by the decedent, or that a gift by a member of a class is opposed by a member of the same or a prior class, the donee shall not accept the gift. The persons authorized by this subsection (b) may make the gift after death or immediately before death.

(d) A gift of all or part of a body authorizes any examination necessary to assure medical acceptability of the gift for purposes intended.

(e) The rights of the donee created by the gift are paramount to the rights of others except as provided by Section 7(d).

SECTION 3. [Persons Who May Become Donees, and Purposes for Which Anatomical Gifts May Be Made.]

The following persons may become donees of gifts of bodies or parts thereof for the purposes stated:

(1) any hospital, surgeon, or physician, for medical or dental education, research, advancement of medical or dental science, therapy or transplantation; or

(2) any accredited medical or dental school, college or university for education, research, advancement of medical or dental science or therapy; or

(3) any bank or storage facility, for medical or dental education, research, advancement of medical or dental science, therapy or transplantation; or

(4) any specified individual for therapy or transplantation needed by him.

SECTION 4. [Manner of Executing Anatomical Gifts.]

(a) A gift of all or part of the body under Section 2(a) may be made by will. The gift becomes effective upon the death of the testator without waiting for probate. If the will is not probated, or if it is declared invalid for testamentary purposes, the gift, to the extent that it has been acted upon in good faith, is nevertheless valid and effective.

(b) A gift of all or part of the body under Section 2(a) may also be made by document other than a will. The gift becomes effective upon the death of the donor. The document, which may be a card designed to be carried on the person, must be signed by the donor, in the presence of 2 witnesses who must sign the document in his presence. Delivery of the document of gift during the donor's lifetime is not necessary to make the gift valid.

(c) The gift may be made to a specified donee or without specifying a donee. If the latter, the gift may be accepted by the attending physician as donee upon or following death. If the gift is made to a specified donee who is not available at the time and place of death, the attending physician upon or following death, in the absence of any expressed indication that the donor desired otherwise, may accept the gift as donee. The physician who becomes a donee under this subsection shall not participate in the procedures for removing or transplanting a part.

(d) Notwithstanding Section 7(b), the donor may designate in his will, card or other document of gift the surgeon or physician to carry out the appropriate procedures. In the absence of a designation, or if the designee is not available, the donee or other person authorized to accept the gift may employ or authorize any surgeon or physician for the purpose.

(e) Any gift by a person designated in Section 2(b) shall be made by a document signed by him, or made by his telegraphic, recorded telephonic, or other recorded message.

SECTION 5. [Delivery of Document of Gift.]

If the gift is made by the donor to a specified donee, the will, card or other document, or an executed copy thereof, may be delivered to the donee to expedite the appropriate procedures immediately after death, but delivery is not necessary to the validity of the gift. The will, card or other document, or an executed copy thereof, may be deposited in any hospital, bank, or storage facility or registry office that accepts them for safekeeping or for facilitation of procedures after death. On request of any interested party upon or after the donor's death, the person in possession shall produce the document for examination.

SECTION 6. [Amendment or Revocation of the Gift.]

(a) If the will, card or other document or executed copy thereof, has been delivered to a specified donee, the donor may amend or revoke the gift by:

(1) the execution and delivery to the donee of a signed statement, or

(2) an oral statement made in the presence of 2 persons and communicated to the donee, or

(3) a statement during a terminal illness or injury addressed to an attending physician and communicated to the donee, or

(4) a signed card or document found on his person or in his effects.

(b) Any document of gift which has not been delivered to the donee may be revoked by the donor in the manner set out in subsection (a) or by destruction, cancellation, or mutilation of the document and all executed copies thereof.

(c) Any gift made by a will may also be amended or revoked in the manner provided for amendment or revocation of wills, or as provided in subsection (a).

SECTION 7. [Rights and Duties at Death.]

(a) The donee may accept or reject the gift. If the donee accepts a gift of the entire body, he may, subject to the terms of the gift, authorize embalming and the use of the body in funeral services. If the gift is of a part of the body, the donee, upon the death of the donor and prior to embalming, shall cause the part to be removed without unnecessary mutilation. After removal of the part, custody of the remainder of the body vests in the surviving spouse, next of kin or other persons under obligation to dispose of the body.

(b) The time of death shall be determined by a physician who attends the donor at his death, or, if none, the physician who certifies the death. This physician shall not participate in the procedures for removing or transplanting a part.

(c) A person who acts in good faith in accord with the terms of this Act, or under the anatomical gift laws of another state [or foreign country] is not liable for damages in any civil action or subject to prosecution in any criminal proceeding for his act.

(d) The provisions of this Act are subject to the laws of this state prescribing powers and duties with respect to autopsies.

## 3. *Jesse Dukeminier, "Critique of the UAGA"**

*In reading Professor Dukeminier's criticism of the UAGA, consider these questions:*

*What does Dukeminier mean when he says that friends and relatives of the deceased have an I-Thou rather than an I-It relationship with the deceased's body?*

*Can you think of any response to Dukeminier's statement that "when liability of the surgeons turns on the intention of a dead man, it would be wise not to foreguess the jury"? Does Section 7(c) of the UAGA deal satisfactorily with this problem?*

*Dukeminier thinks that asking relatives for permission to use an organ of the deceased at the time of death is cruel. Might such an opportunity be consolatory? In any case, is it less cruel to use the deceased as a donor without asking permission and have the family learn later?*

Existing donation statutes, including the Uniform Anatomical Gift Act, contain fundamental defects, both in conception and design, which must be avoided if organ procurement legislation is to be satisfactory.

a. Formulation of the problem. Current donation statutes are based on an overly narrow, anachronistic formulation of the problem. Until the nineteenth century a person had no power to direct disposition of his body at death; the right of disposal was in the next of kin. In time many individuals expressed a desire to be cremated or to be buried in a certain spot; others wished to give their bodies to medical schools for dissection. To give effect to the wishes of the

---

* Jesse Dukeminier, "Supplying Organs for Transplantation" 68 Mich. L. Rev. 811 (1970) copyright © 1970 by The Michigan Law Review Association.

decedent over any objection of the next of kin, statutes permitting a person to direct disposition of his body were passed.

Organ transplantation radically changed the nature of the problem by bringing into the picture for the first time the highest principle of law, medicine, ethics, and religion: saving human life. . . . The basic question today is whether a dead person or his next of kin should have power to withhold life from another. A decision that a dead man or his next of kin should have such power should be reached only after the competing interests are examined and the alternatives evaluated. By beginning with the assumption that the legislative problem is simply to make it possible for a person to transfer "rights" to his cadaver organs, the legislative draftsman begs the fundamental question of what "rights" to cadavers ought to be recognized.

b. Analysis of policies and evaluation of conflicting interests. Because cadaver organs can now be used to save human life, the donation statutes which were drafted without a true awareness of the implications of that fact have the effect of reversing the policy priorities traditionally recognized by western civilization. Saving human life is the first policy priority, but donation statutes give it last priority. This reversal of priorities can best be illustrated by the draftsmen's commentary accompanying the Uniform Anatomical Gift Act. The prefatory note to the Uniform Act contains the following cryptic description of the principles for policy guidance:

> Tissues and organs from the dead can also be used to bring health and years of life to the living. From this source the potential supply is very great. But, if utilization of bodies and parts of bodies is to be effectuated, a number of competing interests in a dead body must be harmonized, and several troublesome legal questions must be answered.
>
> The principal competing interests are: (1) the wishes of the deceased during his lifetime concerning the disposition of his body; (2) the desires of the surviving spouse or next of kin; (3) the interest of the state in determining by autopsy, the cause of death in cases involving crime or violence; (4) the need of autopsy to determine the cause of death when private legal rights are dependent upon such a cause; and (5) the need of society for bodies, tissues, and organs for medical education, research, therapy, and transplantation. These interests compete with one another to a greater or less extent and this creates problems.

This listing of applicable policies does not explicitly rank them in order of importance. Such a ranking, however, is made, either explicitly or implicitly, in the Act itself. First priority is given to autopsying the body for detection of crime and for other purposes prescribed by state statutes. Second priority is given the wishes of the deceased. Third priority is given the wishes of the next of kin. Last priority is given to saving the life of a human being, an interest which is disguised in the quotation above as "the need of society for bodies, tissues, and organs for medical education, research, therapy, and transplantation." This analysis of the interests involved is most curious. The demands for bodies for classroom dissection, for organs for established transplantation operations, such as kidney transplants, and for organs for experimental transplantations are placed together as one interest. Such a grouping implies that the various uses all involve the same moral principle and the same amount of demand, but that implication is inaccurate. Anatomical dissection aids human life only indirectly—through disclosing scientific information. The demand for bodies for complete dissection is limited to, at most, the number of enrolled first year medical students, and medical schools have little difficulty acquiring the necessary number. The transplantation of a kidney or the temporary grafting of skin onto a person suffering from third-degree burns directly saves the life of a person, and the needs are very great. Transplantations of livers and lungs are still in the experimental stages, but they too are undertaken in a direct attempt to save life. It is surprising that the draftsmen of the Uniform Act do not even discuss the distinction between indirect and direct means of saving life, for such a distinction is an ancient one in theology, medicine, and law. But even more remarkable than the failure to separate disparate demands of different ethical ranking is the Aesopian ploy of describing this last interest as "the need of society for . . . organs." Organs are not transplanted into society; organs are transplanted into people! It is human need, and not the need of some amorphous, distant "society," that is at issue. If this last interest is rewritten as "the need of human beings for organs and tissue to save their lives," it becomes clear that the Uniform Act has reversed traditional humanist values and has given last priority to saving human lives. . . .

Removing cadaver organs has a deep emotional and psychological impact on some people. Traditionally we identify the corpse with the living person; it is the focus of all the relationships one had with the person. And just as the body of the living person was inviolate, so too is his corpse. Friends and relatives have an I-Thou relationship with a corpse, not an I-It relationship. Yet the view of the corpse as inviolate does admit some socially conditioned exceptions. Many violations occur, for example, in preparing the body for burial; arteries are cut, blood is removed, and formaldehyde is pumped into the blood vessels. Similarly, eyelids may be sewn closed, and faces may be restored. Practices such as these are accepted largely because people do not think about them; they are routinely performed behind the closed doors of the undertaking establishment and do not interfere with the relatives' I-Thou relationship with the corpse. The acceptance of these practices indicates that other practices which do not disfigure the corpse, such as routine autopsy, might well become acceptable to the public. In any case, remedial legislation should not be based upon some paralyzing supposition as to the popular will. . . .

c. Ritual and evidentiary problems in a gift ceremony. Not only have the proponents of donation statutes failed to analyze thoroughly the policy issues involved in providing organs for transplantation, but they have also introduced counterproductive procedures in the application of this lifesaving treatment. By giving the process of making an organ available the characterization of a "gift," the legislative draftsmen have built into the problem not only the necessity of prescribing by statute the kind of ritual and the kind of evidence required to accomplish the gift, but also the necessity for the transplant team to be able to establish quickly and conclusively that the gift ceremony has been properly performed. In some states the formalities are so cumbersome as to discourage any gift at all. In Delaware, for example, the donor must sign in the presence of two witnesses and must acknowledge his signature before a notary public. . . . The Uniform Anatomical Gift Act attempts to simplify the ritual by providing that the document of gift may be a document or a card signed by the donor in the presence of two witnesses, who must sign the document in his presence.

All lawyers familiar with the law of wills know that when a ceremony is required, extensive litigation over whether the ceremony was properly carried out is possible. Similarly, litigation may arise over the question whether the instrument of gift has been revoked. The standard provision in many wills, "I hereby revoke all prior wills," may unintentionally revoke an earlier instrument authorizing transplantation. A similar problem is caused by the decisions in which it has been held that written gifts of organs at death may be revoked orally. Relying upon a written instrument is therefore perilous, since there is no practical way to find out if the donor ever told anyone that he had changed his mind. The Uniform Anatomical Gift Act seeks to solve this problem by providing that a written document of gift may be revoked orally only if the oral statement is "communicated to the donee"; but the Act does not make clear what acts come within the words, "communicated to the donee." If the donee is a hospital, for example, will nodding to a nurse or telling the patient's physician suffice? The ways of communicating with a hospital range from a registered letter to the president to a whisper to an orderly, but which of these are legal communications will have to be established by litigation. The Uniform Act also permits revocation by "destruction, cancellation, or mutilation" of the document of gift but again it is not at all clear what acts come within that language. Suppose that a donation card has been carried folded in a wallet for several years and at death it is found that the card has been separated at the fold into two pieces. Is the card revoked by mutilation? If the dead donor separated the card with the intention to revoke, it is revoked; if the separation occurred without his knowledge or with his knowledge but without the intention to revoke, it is not revoked. But when liability of the surgeons turns on the intention of a dead man, it would be wise not to foreguess the jury. . . .

d. *Psychological difficulties in giving one's own organs.* Current donation statutes are also based upon an inadequate understanding of the psychological problems involved in giving human organs. . . . As might be expected, younger persons do not think much about death. In one investigation of students, more than ninety percent said they rarely thought about death in a personal way. Older persons, on the other hand, may be apprehensive of death and may try to avoid the matter by thinking, "it won't happen to me this week," or by channeling their thoughts in other directions. In analyzing the attitudes of persons toward death, Freud wrote:

> Our own death is indeed unimaginable, and whenever we make the attempt to imagine it we can perceive that we really survive as spectators. Hence . . . at bottom no one believes in his own death, or to put the same thing in another way, in the unconscious every one of us is convinced of his own immortality.

The psychological barrier to thinking of one's own death affects the testamentary disposition both of property and of organs. In a recent study, Professor Thomas Shaffer explored the attitudes of persons toward death when they talked with their lawyers about their wills. He reports evasion and denial of death by both the lawyers and their clients. If one of the primary reasons that people do not make wills of their property is that they cannot face death, they are even less likely to make wills donating their organs. Organs are so much a part of a person's conception of himself that signing a donation paper usually arouses the deepest and most fearful anxieties. A Gallup poll taken in December 1967 indicated that seven out of ten Americans are willing to donate their organs after death. Yet the waiting lists of sick persons needing organs grow longer. Since people tend to do a poor job of answering realistically hypothetical questions about remote, improbable, and awesome events, the Gallup poll may not be very reliable. But, for whatever the poll is worth, the only useful conclusion from it is that any organ donation statute should infer the consent of decedents to the removal of their organs because seven out of ten Americans favor organ removal, and because it is unrealistic to expect these people to take the steps currently needed for an organ donation when such a procedure causes fearful anxiety. Between expressing a wish to make a will some day and actually doing it lies an inner resistance that serves as a great obstacle to action.

e. The best donors. Consent must come from next of kin at time of shock. Another important fact that must be taken into account in any realistic scheme to salvage cadaver organs is that the best sources for organs are persons who die of cerebral tumors, cerebral injury, or sudden coronary attacks. These persons usually enter the hospital unconscious or with blunted consciousness and, in either case, are unable legally to sign any consent form. Thus any program to present consent forms routinely to all persons admitted to the hospital would have to exclude such individuals even though they make the best donors. Consent for such persons has to come from the next of kin if it is to come at all. In case of accidental death the next of kin may not be available on the spot, so that the request for organs may have to be made over the telephone by a physician not known to the next of kin. It is hard to imagine a physician reaching for a telephone and saying: "Mrs. Smith, I deeply regret having to inform you that your husband Thomas had a car accident on Interstate 5. He was admitted here in a dying condition and he died five minutes ago. We very much need his kidneys for transplantation. Will you give us permission to remove them?" This approach seems callous and uncivilized, but it comes within the language of the Uniform Anatomical Gift Act, which provides that a consent may be by "telegraphic, recorded telephonic, or other recorded message." In many states not even this procedure is possible, for most statutes make no provision for telephonic consent.

f. The destruction of hope. A last consideration in the appraisal of donation statutes is the delicate problem of asking for consent before death. Dr. Irvine Page has written:

> It should also not be forgotten in this age of scientific medicine that the physician himself has become to the patient an important medicine. Therefore, he dare not destroy lightly that most precious of human qualities, *hope*. When consent is asked of the donor, remember what it means to the patient and his family.

Methods other than prior consent may be less destructive of hope for continuing life.

# C.

# Beyond Donation: Routine and Compulsory Salvaging

In the following excerpt from his article, Professor Dukeminier sketches his proposal that organs be routinely available upon death for transplantation unless the deceased has, while alive, expressed objection to serving as an organ donor. In reading it, consider Robert Veatch's objections to routine salvaging:

> The strongest objection to proposals for routine salvaging is really one of human values. Do we want a society which conceives of body parts as essentially property of the state to be taken by eminent domain, or is that a dangerous misordering of moral priorities? If the state can assume that human bodies are its for the taking (unless contested by the individuals or relatives as in the Dukeminier and Sanders proposal), what will be the implications for less ultimate, less sacred possessions? If the body is essential to the individual's identity, in a society which values personal integrity and freedom, it must be the individual's first of all to control, not only over a lifetime, but within reasonable limits after that life is gone

as well. If the body is to be made available to others for personal or societal research, it must be a gift.*

Does the characterization of the salvaging proposal as treating body parts as "property of the state" add clarity to the discussion? In this view, the donation scheme of the Gift Act treats body parts as "property of the family." What about characterizing the salvaging scheme as one that treats body parts as not property at all, but as resources to be distributed according to need?

If we set the property notion to one side, what other objections might there be to routine salvaging, subject to objection by the family or the deceased? The theologian Paul Ramsey argues that it places too great a burden on those opposed to transplantation by requiring them actually to assert their objection, whereas the Gift Act scheme presumes that there will be no transplantation unless permission is affirmatively given:

> . . . The wish to exercise a more ancient wisdom concerning the body ought not to be specially burdened. Jewish people or Jehovah's Witnesses or anyone else holding religious objections, or persons without religious philosophy having deeply felt opinions in this matter, should not have, in hours of grief and suffering, to protrude these objections against the whole edifice of a hospital practice which routinely goes on without their wills.
>
> A society will be a better human community in which giving and receiving is the rule, not taking for the sake of good to come. . . . The positive consent called for by Gift Act, answering the need for gifts by encouraging real givers, meets the measure of authentic community among men. The routine taking of organs would deprive individuals of the exercise of the virtue of generosity.†

In assessing Ramsey's objection, imagine a typical transplant scenario. The central difference is that under the salvaging proposal, organs will be taken without the members of the family being told. If they wish to prevent use for transplantation, they must know that salvage is routine and must object before salvage can be carried out. Does Ramsey's objection, with its preference for "giving" over "taking," beg the question by assuming that the body parts belong to the relatives in the first place?

---

* *Death, Dying, and the Biological Revolution* (1976); pp. 268–269.
† *The Patient as Person* (1970); p. 210.

A large number of "interferences" with the corpse are now carried out routinely, without asking the family's permission. Embalming, for example, is commonly done without affirmative permission. Why is the use of the body as a source of transplant parts different? Professor Dukeminier's proposal follows.

## 1. *Jesse Dukeminier, "Routine Salvaging of Cadaver Organs Unless There Is Objection"*

A significant increase in the supply of organs for transplantation would result if usable organs were removed from cadavers routinely unless, before the time of removal, an objection had been entered, either by the decedent during his life or by his next of kin after the decedent's death. This approach is not as extreme as the proposal to salvage useful organs without regard to objection, since under this approach persons who do not wish to make their organs available may object and opt out. Nor is this approach as radical a departure from traditional humanist values as the Uniform Anatomical Gift Act, for, by making the basic presumption one which favors life, and by thus putting the burden of objecting upon persons who would deny life to another, the policy of saving human life is given first priority and the wishes of persons to preserve a corpse inviolate are also accommodated. This method would produce far more organs for transplantation than are produced by statutes permitting organ donation by the decedent.

Some time ago Dr. David Sanders and the author proposed legislation to make removal of usable cadaver organs routine unless the decedent or his next of kin instructed otherwise. In light of the 1967 Gallup poll results, it appears that a carefully drawn statute embodying such an approach would be acceptable to a majority of people in this country. Indeed, in a recent questionnaire submittted to physicians, Dr. Robert Williams found that the Dukeminier-Sanders proposal was favored by seventy-one percent of those responding. Similar figures from Britain indicate that two-thirds of the British people favor routine removal of cadaver kidneys. A leading kidney transplant surgeon from England, Professor Roy Caine, writes that in his experience most relatives would prefer not to be asked for the kidneys but would rather that the kidneys be removed routinely.

Perhaps the simplest way to provide for routine salvaging of cadaver organs would be to enact a statute permitting prompt autopsies for organ removal on all persons who die in authorized hospitals, unless objection is first entered. In many countries the public already accepts routine autopsies. In France, for example, cadaver organs may be removed without permission of the family if the person dies in a hospital approved by the Minister of Public Health. . . .

If a broad autopsy statute is unacceptable, the best substitute is a statute dealing solely with removal of organs for transplantation. The details of such a statute need to be carefully considered. There are at least four major problems. First, what organs may be routinely removed? The legislative draftsmen might conclude that only those organs with a high degree of transplantation success could be removed—at the present time, corneas and kidneys. . . .

A middle position might be taken between permitting only specified organs to be removed and permitting all usable organs to be removed. For example, a medical board or the state director of public health could be empowered to promulgate administrative regulations specifying the organs that could be removed routinely; the statute could provide a general guideline, such as a provision that the list be limited to organs which can be transplanted with a good chance of success when transplantation is recognized by the medical profession as appropriate therapy. Such an approach, however, would prevent routine removal of organs for experimental purposes, including experiments to save life; and such a limitation on experimentation might be felt to be too restrictive.

The second problem to be solved in drafting an organ removal statute is the determination of which persons are to be authorized to remove organs routinely. . . .

The third problem must be faced in drafting an appropriate statute is whether any bodies should be excluded from routine removal of organs. Section 3 of the British Renal Transportation Bill provided an exclusion for any person who, at the time of his death, was

(a) mentally insane, or
(b) mentally handicapped, or
(c) below the age of 18, or
(d) 65 years old or more than that age, or

(e) deprived of his liberty by the conviction and judgment of a court, or

(f) a permanent resident of a hospital, home or institution for the aged, the disabled, or the handicapped.

The primary purpose of these exclusions was to ensure that only those who are free to object fall within the terms of the bill. A secondary purpose was to set at ease the minds of older persons, who might fear that doctors would hasten their demise in order to transplant their organs into a younger person.

The fourth drafting problem concerns the method of registering objections so that organs cannot be removed after death. There are various possible methods: a card could be carried by the person, a statement could be made to the hospital upon entering, a statement could be made to the physician, or a central computer registry could be established. One of the problems discussed previously in connection with organ donation statutes reappears in another form here. That problem was how to provide a means to aid the surgeon in finding out quickly and conclusively that he has a valid consent. The problem under the approach being examined here is determining how the surgeon can find out quickly and conclusively that there is no objection. Fortunately, the latter is more readily soluble than the former and does not contain within it as many subsidiary problems. The presumption is that there is no objection, and thus the burden of proving that there was an objection which the surgeon knew or ought to have known is on the next of kin. Hence, the problem is narrowed to the determination of what inquiry the surgeon ought to be required to make. The statute could provide that a valid objection must be entered in a specific way, such as through registration with a national computer system. For instance, section 7 of the British Renal Transplantation Bill provided for a central renal registry in the Ministry of Health in which any person might register his objection to the transplantation of his kidneys. With such a provision, the only inquiry the surgeon would have to make would be the computer, and it would be possible for surgeons to ascertain within minutes whether the donor had entered any objection. If a computer error occurs, the next of kin would have a cause of action against the organization responsible for the computer, not against the surgeon. Alternatively, a statute might contain a provision for a compensation fund for the next of kin in cases involving decedent who had filed an objection but whose objection had been ignored by mistake. As a practical matter, few suits would probably be brought as a result of computer malfunction, because if organ removal becomes routine, the practice will become part of the expectations of the next of kin and the public, just as routine autopsies are part of the expectations of persons in some European countries. . . .

A final question which pertains to the filing of objections is whether the next of kin, as well as the decedent, should have the power to object and thereby to prevent removal of organs. The British bill permitted only the decedent to object, but the next of kin could bring the decedent's objection to the attention of the surgeons. In any event, the question is not very important, because if the next of kin objects, either on the ground that the decedent instructed otherwise or for his own personal reasons, it is unlikely that a surgeon will remove the organs. A tug of war for organs with the next of kin would be most unseemly. Nonetheless, a statute in the United States should expressly permit the next of kin to object, since such a provision would help to avoid first amendment difficulties. . . .

### 2. Jesse Dukeminier, *"Removal of Cadaver Organs Regardless of Objection"*

*In this excerpt, Dukeminier considers and rejects a more far-reaching proposal: that cadaver organs should always be available for use, even in the face of explicit objection by the deceased or the next of kin. He examines two constitutional objections that might be made to such a proposal: that it "takes property," and that it might violate the free exercise of religion of those who object to such use on religious grounds.*

*Proponents of compulsory salvaging rely on the analogy of the autopsy in cases of suspicious death. Such autopsies are performed even where there is religiously based objection and have not been held to violate freedom of religion. Is there any basis for different treatment of organ salvaging?*

*Dukeminier rejects the argument that compulsory salvaging might violate constitutional property rights. If the family has no property rights in the body, what is the basis for their religiously based objection? Should the religious objection to transplantation of someone with no legally recognized stake in the body be taken seriously?*

A recent analysis of the problem of supplying organs resulted in the suggestion that legislation be enacted to authorize the removal, with or without consent, of cadaver organs useful for transplantation. The ethical basis for this solution to the problem of organ supply is that saving human life is paramount to all other policies and that no one has the right to deny another the chance to live.

Today, in disposing of the dead, the principle of protecting life requires that a coroner perform an autopsy on a body when homicidal behavior is suspected, even though the next of kin objects. Courts have uniformly held that the rights of the decedent and next of kin are subordinate to the paramount public interest in apprehending killers. In these circumstances the autopsy may be held without the consent of the next of kin or even over his positive objection. Catching a murderer both prevents further homicidal behavior by the man apprehended and deters homicidal behavior by others. The overriding principle is protecting the lives of the survivors.

There are many other instances in which the interest of the next of kin in controlling the body has been held subordinate to another interest, and some of these instances do not involve the primary principle of protecting human life. The competing interest deemed paramount may be public health or convenience, economic benefit to undertakers, or economic liability of employers or insurers. A captain of a ship, for example, may order burial at sea for a person who dies aboard, regardless of objection by the next of kin. Similarly, a surviving spouse may wish to bury the deceased on the back part of the family farm but will not be able to do so if a statute requires that the burial permit specify a particular cemetery. It is also common for statutes to require burial or other disposition within a reasonable time. Furthermore, although embalming might violate the religious beliefs of the deceased and be objectionable to the next of kin, many states require a body to be embalmed if it is shipped across state lines by a common carrier. How the law operates for the economic advantage of the funeral industry, despite the wishes of the next of kin, has been detailed elsewhere. In at least two other situations the interests of the next of kin are not deemed compelling. When a person dies during the course of his employment in circumstances that might lead to the liability of his employer under a workmen's compensation act, the employer or the compensation board has the right to require an autopsy even if the surviving spouse objects. Similarly, accident insurance policies usually contain a provision granting the insurer a right to an autopsy. If the demand by the insurer is seasonably made to a beneficiary who has the right to control the body; and if the beneficiary refuses, the insurer is relieved of liability on the policy. In this situation the next of kin may still prevent an autopsy, but economic pressure to consent is placed upon him.

If one accepts the view that saving human life requires the removal of useful cadaver organs regardless of the wishes of the decedent or next of kin, the question arises whether a statute effectuating that policy would run afoul of any constitutional provisions prohibiting the taking of property without compensation. One recent study concludes that such a statute would constitute a taking of the property of the next of kin, who would have to be paid just compensation for the cadaver organs. . . .

It is, however, extremely troublesome to use property terms [in considering] the taking of cadaver organs, for cadaver organs are not property in any conventional sense. Under modern law the next of kin is given a cause of action for unauthorized dissection, and courts have sometimes characterized this right in the next of kin as a property or a quasi-property right. But as Dean Prosser points out, "It is in reality the personal feelings of the survivors which are being protected under a fiction likely to deceive no one but a lawyer. . . ." In determining the constitutionality of legislation authorizing the removal of cadaver organs regardless of objection it is inappropriate to begin the analysis by accepting a characterization of cadaver organs as property. As Justice Jackson said some years ago with reference to another claim of constitutionally protected "property right": "We cannot start the process of decision by calling such a claim as we have here a 'property right'; whether it is a property right is really the question to be answered."

In striking a balance between the interests of the public and the desires of the decedent and the survivors, legislatures have already subordinated the interests of the decedent and survivors to the public interest in saving human life, to interests of public health and convenience, and to the economic welfare of undertakers, employers, and insurers. In view of that background, it would surely be odd to find that the fourteenth amendment forbids subordinating the interest of the decedent and next of kin to the public interest in saving the life of a human being.

A more serious constitutional objection to removing usable organs over the objection of the decedent or his next of kin is based upon the first amendment: "Congress shall make no law respecting an establishment of religion, or prohibiting the free exercise thereof. . . ." A fundamentalist Christian might consider organ removal inconsistent with the principle of bodily resurrection. A Jehovah's Witness might object to the shedding of blood. Many orthodox rabbis have opposed autopsies, invoking a principle of Judaism that the body must not be violated. . . .

First amendment objections to salvaging cadaver organs can be overcome if the decedent or the next of kin is given the right to object and preclude removal. Although first amendment requirements might be satisfied if the only permissible basis for an objection to organ removal were religious belief, such an approach is not desirable. Determining what is a "religious belief" is clearly a matter that everyone would be wise to avoid. To obviate constitutional problems, then, a statute should permit the decedent or the next of kin to forbid removal of the decedent's organs, and should place no limitation on the reasons therefor. . . .

# D.

# Commerce in Human Organs

### 1. *Jesse Dukeminier, "Sale of Cadaver Parts"*

*This further excerpt from Professor Dukeminier's article introduces the question of the commercial sale of body parts. The question is whether cadaver parts should be subject to sale—either "in advance" by the person whose body it is, or after death by relatives or others to whom the law might assign this property right. To what extent does commercialization of an activity take it outside the sphere of the principle of liberty and subject it to public regulation?*

*Is it clear that the state's refusal to allow body-part sales is an interference with liberty? If I do not own my kidney after I die, I cannot now sell you the right to take that kidney from my body after death; similarly, if my next of kin does not own my body after my death, the question of sale of organs does not arise. Is not the problem of the definition and assignment of property rights necessarily prior to the question of which transfers of rights (or "sales") ought to be allowed?*

*Notice Dukeminier's statement that "apart from the unsavoriness of the idea" of next of kin selling body parts after death, there are rational policy arguments against it. What makes the idea unsavory? Is it the same thing that would make it unsavory for surviving relatives to sell rights to a gossip magazine to cover an otherwise private family service for a deceased celebrity? Is this a reason for prohibition?*

*In his well-known study* The Gift Relationship, *Richard Titmuss concluded that blood for transfusion was more generally available, and less often contaminated by hepatitis, in England, where the system is based entirely on voluntary donation, than in the United States, where sale of blood is allowed and exists alongside the voluntary system. If Titmuss's findings are correct, what might be the explanation for them? Are the same reasons likely to be applicable (as Dukeminier suggests) in the case of sales of the body parts of the deceased by the next of kin? Professor Dukeminier's discussion follows.*

It is the essence of a market economy that goods are transferred from those persons who have them to those who desire them by the medium of a sale. There is, however, nothing traditional about the sale of human organs and, indeed, the initial reaction to such a suggestion is likely to be extreme distaste. Understandably, the subject has not previously been given much analytical attention. But remarkable advances in transplantation, and the consequent increase in the demand for organs, require an examination of the matter.

Today the sale of bodily substances is not unknown. Blood is bought by hospitals and commercial blood banks. The price is usually ten to fifteen dollars a pint. Of the 348,571 units of blood collected in New York City in 1956, forty-two percent was received from paid donors. In 1964 it was estimated that the largest user of blood in New York City, Memorial Hospital, obtained from sixty to seventy percent of its blood from commercial sources. In Chicago it has been estimated that forty-five percent of the blood collected is paid for. Semen for use in artificial insemination is also bought, with prices ranging from five dollars to fifty dollars per ejaculation, and with the average price between fifteen and twenty-five dollars. Pituitary glands from cadavers have also been bought; in Los Angeles, more than 1,000 pituitary glands were removed from cadavers in the coroner's office and were unlawfully sold by an employee to an institute studying abnormal growth. The United States Health Service, largely through the National Institutes of Health, makes research grants in the field of medicine; expenditures by grantees of approved projects may include payment for such personal services as are required to carry out the project. The Public Health Service specifically authorizes payment "to individuals who contribute blood, urine samples, and other body fluids or tissues used for the projects." Payment in money to volunteers for human experimentation is practiced very widely. . . .

In almost all states there are statutes authorizing bequests of bodies, or parts of bodies, to medical science. Few of these statutes prohibit sale. Statutes in Delaware, Hawaii, Nevada, New York, and Oklahoma provide that no remuneration shall be given the deceased; but they do not prohibit the sale of organs by the next of kin. In Georgia it is a misdemeanor to receive remuneration for an eye or to take possession of an eye for which a person has received compensation. Mississippi has a unique statute that permits a person to contract—with or without a money consideration—to donate parts of his body at death to a hospital; it further provides that if the donor revokes the contract, he must repay any monetary consideration with six percent interest. Only Massachusetts prohibits the payment of compensation to any person for any cadaver organ. The Uniform Anatomical Gift Act contains no provision forbidding the sale of organs.

Regardless of the general policy decisions, there are practical problems in buying organs from living persons with delivery to take place after death, and these problems may prove insurmountable. Few persons would pay for an organ unless they were certain of its delivery in usable condition. Accordingly, bargains could be reached only with persons fatally ill in hospitals. In most circumstances, however, psychological considerations would be such that doctors would be extremely reluctant to approach such patients. Hence, it appears that few organs would be obtained by buying them from a person prior to his death. However, the psychological considerations which would inhibit conversations with a patient about the sale of his organs may not affect the willingness of doctors to talk with a patient's next of kin. . . .

Sale of cadaver organs by the next of kin appears to be more objectionable than is sale by the decedent himself, but such sales are prohibited by statute only in Massachusetts and Georgia. Apart from the unsavoriness of the idea, permitting sales by the next of kin may well result in great anxiety and fear on the part of a patient that his doctors and next of kin would not do everything possible to save him. It does not seem likely that such sales would lead to murder, as happened when cadavers were bought in the early nineteenth century in Edinburgh; organs will be useful only if they are removed immediately after death, and thus, as a practical matter, organs for transplantation can be removed only from persons who die in hospitals. Nonetheless, permitting sales by the next of kin would increase the possibility that the dead man's wishes would not be carried out. The financial benefit from a sale might be irresistible to the next of kin, and even a statutory provision that the rights of the donee created by the gift of the dead donor are paramount to the rights of the next of kin will probably not be enforceable if the next of kin demands payment. Because of the risk that the donation ceremony was not properly performed or that the donation has been revoked, surgeons will not remove an organ over the positive objection of the next of kin. Moreover, if sales were permitted, donations by the next of kin would probably decline. If payment is made to the next of kin in one case, the next of kin may well demand it in the next, and that demand will usually have to be met so that consent can be obtained. If donation of organs declines as a result, economic resources that could have been used elsewhere in medicine would have to be allocated to payment for organs so that transplantation can continue.

It may be contended that it is ethically permissible to offer the next of kin, as the consideration for removing the organs, payment for services that benefited the dead man during his life. For example, if the decedent dies of a brain tumor and has incurred large hospital bills during his life, the next of kin might consent to removing the decedent's kidneys in exchange for the cancellation of the hospital bill. This kind of remuneration would result in different valuations for each person's kidney in accordance with his hospital bill, but that is not the most disturbing element of such an approach. Rather, the primary difficulty in approving such a means of payment lies in the consequences. The decedent may not wish his body cut open and may prefer that his estate pay the hospital bill; an economic incentive would be given his next of kin not to carry out his wishes. Indeed, this consequence characterizes all proposals to permit the sale of cadaver organs by the next of kin. . . .

## 2. Jesse Dukeminier, "Sales by Living Persons with Delivery During Life"

*The following excerpt from Professor Dukeminier's article departs from the theme of treatment of dead bodies to raise the related question whether people should be allowed to sell their "spare" body parts for removal while they are still alive. The issue raises the question, standard in debate over Mill's principle, of the legitimacy of paternalistic regulation, in both a commercial and noncommercial context.*

*What is the difference between selling your labor as a racing driver or a coal miner and selling your kidney, which leaves you in good health but with the risk that the remaining kidney may malfunction? Notice the distinction between "direct" and "indirect" consequences mentioned by Dukeminier. Does it make any sense in this context? Is there an important difference between allowing someone to sell an eye or a kidney and allowing him to sell blood or bone marrow?*

In some foreign countries live persons are not permitted either to give or to sell their spare organs when delivery is to take place during life. In Italy, such a statutory provision exists as a result of an incident which occurred in the 1930s when a rich man bought a testis from a young Neapolitan and had it transplanted by a surgeon. The public outrage resulted in the passage of a law prohibiting the sale or gift by a live person of an organ if removal of the organ could produce a permanent deficiency. The Italian law was modified in 1967 to permit the removal of kidneys from live persons for transplantation. . . .

[In America, general] criminal law sets limits on the ability of a patient to give his informed consent to a surgical operation that is not for his benefit, but . . . exactly what those limits are is unclear. It is clear that one cannot consent to the infliction of death, and consequently an unpaired vital organ such as the liver may not be consensually removed. Under some circumstances, a person cannot consent to serious bodily injury; the removal of an organ, even with the donor's consent, may constitute the crime of assault and battery or the crime of mayhem. . . .

Mayhem is the crime of intentionally and maliciously maiming or disfiguring a person. At common law, mayhem was limited only to deprivation of such a man's organs "as may render him the less able, in fighting, either to defend himself or to annoy his adversary." Included were a man's hand, his finger, his foot, his testicle, or his eye. The significance of the organs in fighting is irrelevant today, and modern statutes have extended the crime of mayhem to disfigurings in general and to the disfiguring of women as well as of men. Under modern law, it is possible to contend that surgically removing an internal organ from a person constitutes mayhem.

Again the question arises whether, if removing a kidney for transplantation is mayhem, consent by the donor is a defense to the charge. Only two cases are even remotely relevant, and in both of those the victim's consent had no effect. In Wright's Case, recorded by Lord Coke in 1603, "a strong and lustie rogue" directed his companion to cut off the rogue's left hand so that he might get out of work and beg more effectively. Both the rogue and his companion were convicted of mayhem; consent was held to be no defense to the crime. In *State v. Bass*, a man wanted his fingers cut off so that he could collect insurance money. With full knowledge of the purpose, a physician deadened four fingers of the man's left hand, which were then cut off by another man using an electric saw. The physician was convicted of being an accessory to mayhem. The court held that consent of the person was no defense to the charge. Although the opinion of the court in *State v. Bass* was extremely vague, the court apparently thought that cutting off the fingers was no "benefit" to the man and that the conduct was "antisocial." . . .

Inasmuch as the decided cases are not very helpful in the transplant situation, it is particularly useful to see how the problem is solved by the American Law Institute's Model Penal Code, which represents a decade of work by distinguished scholars to define the appropriate criteria for criminal punishment. The Code abolishes the crime of mayhem, submitting it under aggravated assault. A person commits aggravated assault when he knowingly causes serious bodily injury to another. Since a surgeon who removes a kidney for transplantation does so knowingly, the act is aggravated assault if it causes serious bodily injury. "Serious bodily injury" is, in turn, defined by the Code to include "protracted loss or impairment of the function of any bodily member or organ." Removing a kidney for transplantation therefore comes within the definition of aggravated assault under the Model Penal Code.

Under the Code consent is not a defense to aggravated assault; consent is a defense only if the bodily harm consented to is not serious. . . . [But] Section 3.02 of the Model Penal Code provides that an action which a person believes to be necessary to avoid a harm or evil is justifiable if "the harm or evil sought to be avoided by such conduct is greater than that sought to be prevented by the law defining the offense charged." If the doctor who removes a spare kidney for transplantation relies on the general defense of justification, a judge or jury must balance the evils. . . .

[This] general defense of justification under section 3.02 . . . would be applicable to a purchase of an organ and in the application of that defense some most difficult and hitherto answered questions arise. When the surgeon balances the plight of the prospective recipient against the loss to the donor, is he justified in offsetting against that loss any monetary gain by the donor? Furthermore, in weighing the donor's net gain or loss, must the surgeon look into the adequacy of the remuneration and into the uses which the donor intends to make of any monetary payment? Suppose patient A offers to sell a kidney for 5,000 dollars in order to invest in the stock market, patient B offers a kidney for 1 million dollars in order to invest in Government bonds, patient C offers a kidney for 200,000 dollars in order to set up a trust fund to care for his mentally retarded child, and patient D offers a kidney for 25,000 dollars in order to pay for plastic surgery of his horribly scarred face. If all four patients are ordinary workers with an income of 7,000 dollars a year each, is acceptance of any one of these offers justified? . . .

[Generally, in determining whether organ sale should be allowed, two principles compete.] The first is . . . the general ethical principle of preservation of life. That principle, simply stated, is that an individual should not endanger his life except for the love of another or in a case such that the danger is an indirect consequence of the activity. This position has deep roots in Judaeo-Christian, and even earlier, teachings that man should not seek his own destruction. Unlike the Eskimos, who encourage suicide by the elderly when they can no longer contribute to the family larder, most western societies have long condemned taking one's own life. In ancient Athens a man who unsuccessfully attempted suicide was punished by the cutting off of his hand. In medieval England a stake was driven through the heart of a man who committed suicide and all his property was forfeited to the crown; Christians who committed suicide could not be buried in consecrated ground. Remnants of this attitude can still be found in laws against abetting and, in some places, attempting suicide.

However, the principle of preserving life does permit some exceptions. Society condones, and even praises, some acts of heroism and self-sacrifice, such as that of the man who gives up his seat in the lifeboat, the passerby who enters a burning building to save the occupants, or the mother who jumps into the rapids to save her child. These are heroic acts motivated by the desire to help others. Under this view, the sole motivation for risking one's life by giving up an organ must be the love of one's fellow man, and a gift of a spare organ to a specific donee is permissible so long as such a motivation exists. Otherwise, allowing the removal of an organ for transplantation is condemned.

Yet, if a charitable motive is so important in judging conduct in situations involving a risking of one's life, how can we permit men to risk their lives in driving racing cars, in entering boxing contests, and in pursuing all kinds of paid risky occupations and still object to the paid kidney donor? When confronted with this question many moral theologians draw a line between direct and indirect effects. For race car drivers and others in risky occupations, dying or being functionally impaired is an indirect consequence, which is foreseen as only possible. In the transplantation case, they argue, removal of the organ from the donor is a life-risking procedure which is the necessary means to an end. If, however, the direct-indirect distinction is accepted, the conclusion that it is unethical to pay a man for a kidney to save life, even though the risks to him are small, but ethical to pay a race car driver at the Indianapolis 500 for entertainment, even though the risks to him are great, can hardly be avoided. Such a principle is troubling indeed.

The second position from which the problem of organ sale can be approached may be characterized as one of "free will." This position is based upon the principle that a person should be able to do whatever he chooses, so long as he does not harm another. Particularly among the young, this position is now much in vogue. It underlies much of the current trend to liberate "sins," such as private deviate sexual conduct and fornication by the unmarried, from criminal sanction. Undoubtedly this principle has also influenced the judicial decisions which have relaxed old proscriptions against obscenity, and it is the base of the recent decisions holding that statutes requiring motorcyclists to wear helmets are unconstitutional since the state may not require a citizen to protect his health alone. As applied to organ sales, the argument would be that an individual has the right to decide for himself whether to sell an organ.

A [principal] difficulty with this view is that in harming himself a person may harm society; a person who gives or sells a kidney might, if his other kidney fails, have to be maintained by the government on an artificial kidney machine. If he gives or sells other spare organs, the risk that he will disable himself is greater and the resulting harm to society may be substantial. To represent society's interest, a person other than the donor, such as a judge or a physician, must appraise the possible harm to society at large.

A variation of the free-will view is that free will, or informed consent as it is known in medico-legal terminology, should be the ethical criterion, but that a monetary payment for an organ would constitute economic coercion so that the consent would not really represent an act of free will. This is merely a conclusion, however, and is not a reason. What is really at issue is the determination of criteria by which to measure "unfair inducement" or "economic coercion" in situations involving the risking of life. Why is it unfair to induce a man to sell a kidney and not unfair to induce him into the boxing ring or into a coal mine?

## F.

## The Implications of "Brain Death"

These materials have so far assumed that the line between life and death was clear. On that assumption, there is one set of problems in regulating the use living persons make, or allow to be made, of their bodies; there is another set of problems involving the use of dead bodies.

But modern technology has rendered the concept of death an uncertain one. The respirator makes it possible to sustain respiration and circulation of the blood where the brain is so damaged that without artificial aid these functions, and with them all signs of life, would cease.

This development did not by itself lead to a redefinition of death. The patient with the destroyed brain on the respirator was considered alive; the difficult question raised was the standard to be used by doctors in deciding when to "pull the plug" and thus "let the patient die." There came to be widespread agreement that the use of extraordinary measures to prolong "life" could be discontinued when there was irreversible coma.

The first successful heart transplant was performed in 1967. Heart-transplant technology requires that respiration and circulation be maintained in the donor body right up to the time that the heart is removed. In 1968, the famous "Harvard definition" of death was proposed for general acceptance in the transplant age by a committee of Harvard Medical School professors. Their proposal was that "brain death" or "irreversible coma" should be accepted as the legal definition of death, and they listed a number of criteria that should be jointly present before brain death could be found to exist. With modifications, the Harvard criteria have come to be widely accepted in the years since. In some jurisdictions, the concept of brain death has been enacted into law.

## 1. The California Brain Death Statute*

*The California Brain Death statute, enacted in 1974, follows. What is the fear at which Section 7181 is directed? If it is a real fear, is the measure that Section provides for sufficient?*

Section 7180. A person shall be pronounced dead if it is determined by a physician that a person has suffered a total and irreversible cessation of brain function. There shall be independent confirmation of the death by another physician.

Nothing in this chapter shall prohibit a physician from using other usual and customary procedures for determining death as the exclusive basis for pronouncing a person dead.

Section 7181. When a part of the donor is used for direct transplantation pursuant to the Uniform Anatomical Gift Act . . . and the death of the donor is determined by determining that the person has suffered a total and irreversible cessation of brain function, there shall be an independent confirmation of the death by another physician. Neither the physician making the determination of death under Section 7155.5 nor the physician making the independent confirmation shall participate in the procedures for removing or transplanting a part.

## 2. The "Neomort" Proposal

The brain death concept means that the person can be declared dead while respiration and circulation are being artificially maintained. Normally, once death is declared, these artificial means of maintaining function will be discontinued; or if the brain-dead body is to be used as a transplant source, this will be done after the organ to be transplanted has been removed.

* Calif. Ann. Health and Safety Code 7180-7181.

But there is no obvious reason why artificial respiration and circulation must be terminated, and many practical reasons why they might be maintained. In an article written in 1975, Dr. Willard Gaylin listed a number of uses that might be made of the physiologically functioning dead body, reasons that might justify sustaining the body as a functioning entity for years. Dr. Gaylin coined the term "neomort" to refer to these legally dead but "warm, respiring, pulsating, evacuating and excreting bodies requiring nursing, dietary, and general grooming attention." The neomorts could be used as objects for training nervous medical students in various procedures; as objects for the testing of the toxicity of new drugs; for basic experimentation, as through the injection of cancer viruses; as banked sources of organs for transplants; and as manufacturing systems for useful products like blood, skin, cartilage, hormones, and antibodies. Given the number of people who die each year with healthily functioning bodies but destroyed brains—particularly head injury and stroke victims—this could be a vast new source of useful medical knowledge, training, and material.

Would prohibition of the use of neomorts in the ways suggested be consistent with Mill's principle? Is there any ground for objection other than the revulsion that in the Devlinite view properly supports morals legislation? Gaylin himself sympathized with those "who will defend that revulsion as a quintessentially human factor whose removal would diminish us all, and extract a price we cannot anticipate in ways yet unknown and times not yet determined." Can you articulate what the price might be?

## 3. Hans Jonas, "Philosophical Reflections on Experimenting with Human Subjects"*

*In this excerpt, the philosopher-theologian Hans Jonas registers his strenuous objection to the use of the brain death concept as a justification for treating "dead" but functioning bodies as sources of organs or objects of research. He urges that full, traditional death must ensue before such uses are made of the body of the deceased. Suppose that once brain death has occurred, the respirator is turned off, as Jonas wishes, and respiration and circulation cease. Now suppose that technology makes possible the restarting of the mechanisms of circulation and respiration, perhaps by electrical stimulation of*

* *Daedalus*, Spring 1969, pp. 243–245. Reprinted by permission of *Daedalus*, Journal of the American Academy of Arts and Sciences, Boston, Mass.

*the nerves. Would Jonas's objections be met? Or is his real point the same one Congressman Moss stated in the first excerpt in this chapter—that this use of human remains is in itself inappropriate? Is that objection more forceful here than in that first excerpt? Are the Jonas objections based on different grounds to those that were lodged against dissection in anatomy classes, or later against autopsies in cases of suspicious death?*

My other emphatic verdict concerns the question of the redefinition of death—acknowledging "irreversible coma as a new definition for death." I wish not to be misunderstood. As long as it is merely a question of when it is permitted to cease the artificial prolongation of certain functions (like heartbeat) traditionally regarded as signs of life, I do not see anything ominous in the notion of "brain death." Indeed, a new definition of death is not even necessary to legitimize the same result if one adopts the position of the Roman Catholic Church, which here for once is eminently reasonable—namely that "when deep unconsciousness is judged to be permanent, extraordinary means to maintain life are not obligatory. They can be terminated and the patient allowed to die." Given a clearly defined negative condition of the brain, the physician is allowed to allow the patient to die his own death by any definition, which of itself will lead through the gamut of all possible definitions. But a disquietingly contradictory purpose is combined with this purpose in the quest for a new definition of death, in the will to advance the moment of declaring him dead: Permission not to turn off the respirator, but, on the contrary, to keep it on and thereby maintain the body in a state of what would have been "life" by the older definition (but is only a "simulacrum" of life by the new)—so as to get at his organs and tissues under the ideal conditions of what would previously have been "vivisection."

Now this, whether done for research or transplant purposes, seems to me to overstep what the definition can warrant. Surely it is one thing when to cease delaying death, but another when to start doing violence to the body; one thing when to desist from protracting the process of dying, but another when to regard that process as complete and thereby the body as a cadaver free for inflicting on it what would be torture and death to any living body. For the first purpose, we need not know the exact borderline with absolute certainty between life and death—we leave it to nature to cross it whenever it is, or to traverse the whole spectrum if there is not just one line. All we need to know is that coma is irreversible. For the second purpose we must know the borderline; and to use any definition short of the maximal for perpetrating on a possibly penultimate state what only the ultimate state can permit is to arrogate a knowledge which, I think, we cannot possibly have. Since we do not know the exact borderline between life and death, nothing less than the maximum definition of death will do—brain death plus heart death plus any other indication that may be pertinent—before final violence is allowed to be done.

It would follow then, for this layman at least, that the use of the definition should itself be defined, and this in a restrictive sense. When only permanent coma can be gained with the artificial sustaining of functions, by all means turn off the respirator, the stimulator, any sustaining artifice, and let the patient die; but let him die all the way. Do not, instead, arrest the process and start using him as a mine while, with your own help and cunning, he is still kept this side of what may in truth be the final line. Who is to say that a shock, a final trauma, is not administered to a sensitivity diffusely situated elsewhere than in the brain and still vulnerable to suffering? A sensitivity that we ourselves have been keeping alive? No fiat of definition can settle this question. But I wish to emphasize that the question of possible suffering (easily brushed aside by a sufficient show of reassuring expert consensus) is merely a subsidiary and not the real point of my argument; this, to reiterate, turns on the indeterminacy of the boundaries between life and death, not between sensitivity and insensitivity, and bids us to lean toward a maximal rather than a minimal determination of death in an area of basic uncertainty.

There is also this to consider: The patient must be absolutely sure that his doctor does not become his executioner, and that no definition authorizes him ever to become one. His right to this certainty is absolute, and so is his right to his own body with all its organs. Absolute respect for these rights violates no one else's rights, for no one has a right to another's body. Speaking in still another, religious vein: The expiring moments should be watched over with piety and be safe from exploitation.

I strongly feel, therefore, that it should be made quite clear that the proposed new definition of death is to authorize only the one and not the other of the two opposing things: only to break off a sustaining intervention and let things take their course, not to keep up the sustaining intervention for a final intervention of the most destructive kind.

# THE DUTY TO RESCUE

In the parable of the good Samaritan, the priest and the Levite passed by an injured man lying beside the road before the Samaritan stopped and helped him. In an episode in New York in 1964 that has taken on the status of a contemporary parable, there was no Samaritan. Thirty-eight neighbors listened to the screams for help of Kitty Genovese and watched as she was pursued and repeatedly stabbed by an assailant outside their windows. Only after thirty-five minutes did one of them finally call the police, who found Miss Genovese dead when they responded to the call. Both of the stories are meant to teach unequivocal *moral* lessons; we are meant to conclude that the priest and the Levite, and Kitty Genovese's neighbors, failed to live up to the elementary standards of proper conduct.

The implications of the stories for *law* have been regarded, by contrast, as problematic. It is no coincidence that the parable of the good Samaritan is reported to us as Jesus' answer to a lawyer's question. The lawyer, seeking an interpretation of the new commandment "Love thy neighbor as thyself," asked "Who is my neighbor?" Jesus gave the parable as his answer and extracted the lawyer's agreement that the commandment must have universal scope.

But the Christian commandment has never been the law; nowhere have persons been legally required to act on behalf of strangers as though motivated by an instinct of self-preservation. Indeed in New York in 1964 the failure of Kitty Genovese's neighbors to take even the small step of calling the police violated no law. Even where some legal duty to act on behalf of others has been imposed, it has applied only in extreme circumstances. and it has remained controversial whether such duties should be imposed at all. The source of the controversy has not been primarily over the moral requirements of rescue, but over the extent to which the law should intrude upon individual autonomy to enforce conceded moral standards. It is this feature that links the rescue issue to those we have dealt with in Chapters 2 and 3.

# A.

## The Traditional Anglo-American Doctrine

The following case contains a striking statement of the traditional rule that there is no duty to rescue a stranger. In its opinion the court

157

says that there is "a broad gulf" in law between causing and failing to prevent an injury. Is there, as the court also says, a similar broad gulf "in reason"? Consider these alternative scenarios: Y has a heart attack and reaches for the bottle of medicine that will save him. What difference does it make "in reason" if (a) X pushes the bottle out of his reach or (b) it is just out of his reach, and X could easily give it to him, but does not? Are not the morally relevant features of the situation X's state of mind and the consequences? Yet in both versions these are the same: X wants Y dead, and he dies. The only difference is that in version (a) a slight movement is required of X to cause Y's death while in (b) X can achieve his desires without moving a muscle. Is this a morally significant difference? Can you think of any reason to make it a legally significant difference?

## 1. *Buch v. Amory Manufacturing Co.** ═══════════

[An eight-year-old child visited his 13-year-old brother while the latter was working in a mill. The older brother tried to show the younger one how to operate the machinery. An overseer told the younger brother to leave, but the boy understood no English. The overseer took no further action to remove or protect the boy, though the danger to a child his age from attempting to operate machinery was obvious. The young boy's hand was crushed in the machine and the company was sued for the resulting damages. The court ruled for the company, as follows:]

CARPENTER, C. J.:

Actionable negligence is the neglect of a legal duty. The defendants are not liable unless they owed to the plaintiff a legal duty which they neglected to perform. With purely moral obligations the law does not deal. For example, the priest and Levite who passed by on the other side were not, it is supposed, liable at law for the continued suffering of the man who fell among thieves, which they might and morally ought to have prevented or relieved. Suppose A, standing close by a railroad, sees a two-year-old babe on the track and a car approaching. He can easily rescue the child with entire safety to himself, and the instincts of humanity require him to do so. If he does not, he may, perhaps, justly be styled a ruthless savage and a moral

* 44 Atl. 809 (1897) (Supreme Court of New Hampshire).

monster; but he is not liable in damages for the child's injury, or indictable under the statute for its death. . . .

There is a wide difference—a broad gulf—both in reason and in law, between causing and preventing an injury; between doing by negligence or otherwise a wrong to one's neighbor, and preventing him from injury himself; between protecting him against injury by another and guarding him from injury that may accrue to him from the condition of the premises which he has unlawfully invaded. The duty to do no wrong is a legal duty. The duty to protect against wrong is, generally speaking and excepting certain intimate relations in the nature of a trust, a moral obligation only, not recognized or enforced by law. . . . I scc my neighbor's two-year-old babe in dangerous proximity to the machinery of his windmill in his yard, and easily might, but do not, rescue him. I am not liable in damages to the child for his injuries, nor, if the child is killed, punishable for manslaughter by the common law or under the statute because the child and I are strangers, and I am under no legal duty to protect him. Now suppose I see the same child trespassing in my own yard and meddling in like manner with the dangerous machinery of my own windmill. What additional obligation is cast upon me by reason of the child's trespass? The mere fact that the child is unable to take care of himself does not impose on me the legal duty of protecting him in the one case more than in the other. Upon what principle of law can an infant by coming unlawfully upon my premises impose upon me the legal duty of a guardian? None has been suggested, and we know of none. . . .

## 2. Thomas B. Macaulay, "Notes on the Indian Penal Code"*

*In this classic argument for limiting legal duties to rescue, Macaulay says it would be "preposterous" to "attempt to punish men by law for not rendering to others all the service which it is their duty to render to others." What would be preposterous about it? Is it only that it would involve the courts in making judgments of degree—of how much inconvenience, expense, or risk the rescuer could reasonably be expected to incur in rescuing?*

*If that is the main argument, consider that the law of homicide provides a defense where one kills another in self-defense. In order to invoke self-defense, the killer must have acted "reasonably" in the circumstances. In particular, he*

* *Works of Lord Macaulay*, Trevelyan, ed. Vol. 7 (1866), pp. 493–497.

*must retreat if he can reasonably do so and avoid the threat to himself; he may use deadly force only if it is "reasonable" in the circumstances to conclude that lesser force would not suffice. Are not these judgments of reasonableness just as much matters of degree as the judgment, alluded to by Macaulay, of how far one should have to walk in the midday heat to save the life of another?*

Early in the progress of the Code it became necessary for us to consider the following question: When acts are made punishable on the ground that those acts produce, or are intended to produce, or are known to be likely to produce, certain evil effects, to what extent ought omissions which produce, which are intended to produce, or which are known to be likely to produce, the same evil effects to be made punishable?

Two things we take to be evident; first, that some of these omissions ought to be punished in exactly the same manner in which acts are punished; secondly, that not all these omissions ought to be punished. It will hardly be disputed that a jailer who voluntarily causes the death of a prisoner by omitting to supply that prisoner with food, or a nurse who voluntarily causes the death of an infant entrusted to her care by omitting to take it out of a tub of water into which it has fallen, ought to be treated as guilty of murder. On the other hand, it will hardly be maintained that a man should be punished as a murderer because he omitted to relieve a beggar, even though there might be the clearest proof that the death of the beggar was the effect of this omission, and that the man who omitted to give the alms knew that the death of the beggar was likely to be the effect of the omission. It will hardly be maintained that a surgeon ought to be treated as a murderer for refusing to go from Calcutta to Meerut to perform an operation, although it should be absolutely certain that this surgeon was the only person in India who could perform it, and that if it were not performed, the person who required it would die. It is difficult to say whether a penal code which should put no omissions on the same footing with acts, or a penal code which should put all omissions on the same footing with acts, would produce consequences more absurd and revolting. There is no country in which either of these principles is adopted. Indeed, it is hard to conceive how, if either were adopted, society could be held together.

It is plain, therefore, that a middle course must be taken; but it is not easy to determine what that middle course ought to be. The absurdity of the two extremes is obvious. But there are innumerable intermediate points; and wherever the line of demarcation may be drawn it will, we fear, include some cases which we might wish to exempt, and will exempt some which we might wish to include. . . .

What we propose is this, that where acts are made punishable on the ground that they have caused, or have been intended to cause, or have been known to be likely to cause, a certain evil effect, omissions which have caused, which have been intended to cause, or which have been known to be likely to cause the same effect, shall be punishable in the same manner, provided that such omissions were, on other grounds, illegal. An omission is illegal . . . if it be an offense, if it be a breach of some direction of law, or if it be such a wrong as would be a good ground for a civil action.

We cannot defend this rule better than by giving a few illustrations of the way in which it will operate. A. omits to give Z. food, and by that omission voluntarily causes Z.'s death. Is this murder? Under our rule it is murder if A. was Z.'s gaoler, directed by the law to furnish Z. with food. It is murder if Z. was the infant child of A., and had, therefore, a legal right to sustenance, which right a Civil Court would enforce against A. It is murder if Z. was a bedridden invalid, and A. a nurse hired to feed Z. It is murder if A. was detaining Z. in unlawful confinement, and had thus contracted . . . a legal obligation to furnish Z., during the continuance of the confinement, with necessaries. It is not murder if Z. is a beggar, who has no other claim on A. than that of humanity.

A. omits to tell Z. that a river is swollen so high that Z. cannot safely attempt to ford it, and by this omission voluntarily causes Z.'s death. This is murder, if A. is a peon stationed by authority to warn travellers from attempting to ford the river. It is a murder if A. is a guide who had contracted to conduct Z. It is not murder if A. is a person on whom Z. has no other claim than that of humanity.

A savage dog fastens on Z. A. omits to call off the dog, knowing that if the dog not be called off, it is likely that Z. will be killed. Z is killed. This is murder in A., if the dog belonged to A., inasmuch as his omission to take proper order with the dog is illegal. But if A. be a mere passer-by, it is not murder.

We are sensible that in some of the cases which we have put, our rule may appear too lenient; but we do not think that it can be made more severe without disturbing the whole order of society. It is true that the man who, having abundance of wealth, suffers a fellow creature to die of hunger at his feet, is a bad man, a worse man, probably, than many of those for whom we have provided very severe punishment. But we are unable to see where, if we make such a man legally punishable, we can draw the line. If the rich man who refuses to save a beggar's life at the cost of a little copper is a murderer, is the poor man just one degree above beggary also to be a murderer if he omits to invite the beggar to partake his hard-earned rice? Again, if the rich man is a murderer for refusing to save the beggar's life at the cost of a little copper, is he also to be a murderer if he refuses to save the beggar's life at the cost of a thousand rupees? Suppose A. to be fully convinced that nothing can save Z.'s life unless Z. leave Bengal and reside a year at the Cape; is A., however wealthy he may be, to be punished as a murderer because he will not, at his own expense, send Z. to the Cape? Surely not. Yet it will be difficult to say on what principle we can punish A. for not spending an anna to save Z.'s life, and leave him unpunished for not spending a thousand rupees to save Z.'s life. The distinction between a legal and an illegal omission is perfectly plain and intelligible; but the distinction between a large and a small sum of money is very far from being so, not to say that a sum which is small to one man is large to another.

The same argument holds good in the case of the ford. It is true that none but a very depraved man would suffer another to be drowned when he might prevent it by a word. But if we punish such a man, where are we to stop? How much exertion are we to require? Is a person to be a murderer if he does not go fifty yards through the sun of Bengal at noon in May in order to caution a traveller against a swollen river? Is he to be a murderer if he does not go a hundred yards?—if he does not go a mile?—if he does not go ten? What is the precise amount of trouble and inconvenience which he is to endure? The distinction between the guide who is bound to conduct the traveller as safely as he can, and a mere stranger who will not give a halloo to save a man's life, and a stranger who will not run a mile to save a man's life, is very far from being equally clear.

It is, indeed, most highly desirable that men should not merely abstain from doing harm to their neighbours, but should render active services to their neighbours. In general, however, the penal law must content itself with keeping men from doing positive harm, and must leave to public opinion, and to the teachers of morality and religion, the office of furnishing men with motives for doing positive good. It is evident that to attempt to punish men by law for not rendering to others all the service which it is their duty to render to others would be preposterous. We must grant impunity to the vast majority of those omissions which a benevolent morality would pronounce reprehensible, and must content ourselves with punishing such omissions only when they are distinguished from the rest by some circumstance which marks them out as peculiarly fit objects of penal legislation. Now, no circumstance appears to us so well fitted to be the mark as the circumstance which we have selected. It will generally be found in the most atrocious cases of omission; it will scarcely ever be found in a venial case of omission; and it is more clear and certain than any other mark that has occurred to us. That there are objections to the line which we propose to draw, we have admitted. But there are objections to every line which can be drawn, and some lines must be drawn . . .

### 3. *Richard Epstein, "A Theory of Strict Liability"* *

*Macaulay's argument draws on the traditional liberal view that rules defining criminal liability should be relatively clear and precise, so that the prosecuting authorities' discretionary use of the weapon of criminal prosecution can be closely confined. There is no comparable tradition of requiring clear rules defining civil liability. Indeed, in tort law the prevailing standard of liability governing most injuries is that the person causing the injury will be liable for it if he has not exercised "reasonable care," with the question of what is reasonable largely left to determination by a jury on a case-by-case basis. Given this basic test of reasonableness, governed by the standards of popular common sense, might not it make sense to impose tort liability on one who failed to take "reasonable" steps to rescue another? In the following excerpt, Richard Epstein argues against the legal duty to rescue in the tort situation. What does he add to Macaulay's argument that a duty to rescue requires judgments of degree in its administration? What is the connection between Epstein's account of the "two lines of belief" that have characterized Western ethics and his opposition to a duty to rescue?*

*Is there a meaningful sense in which duties to rescue are more intrusive into personal liberty than other requirements? Might it be argued that being forced under threat of legal sanction to help others in need is somehow akin to slavery—the state is forcing you to work for someone else? Is it more of a deprivation of liberty to be told you have to call the police if you see a person in danger than to be told you cannot turn right against a red traffic light?*

* 2 J. of Legal Studies 151 (1973). Published by the University of Chicago Press.

*Both Epstein and Macaulay worry that a general duty to rescue means that a solvent person can be punished or be held civilly liable for refusing to supply the means of subsistence to someone who otherwise might starve—a result they apparently regard as impossible to administer. Is not a modern income-maintenance system, paid for out of taxes collected from those able to pay, precisely the administration of just such a general duty? And would not the existence of a welfare system justify precluding individual actions by the poor against the rich for subsistence, if such duty to rescue were established?*

The common law position on the good Samaritan question does not appeal to our highest sense of benevolence and charity, and it is not at all surprising that there have been many proposals for its alteration or abolition. Let us here examine but one of these proposals. After concluding that the then (1908) current position of the law led to intolerable results, James Barr Ames argued that the appropriate rule should be that:

> One who fails to interfere to save another from impending death or great bodily harm, when he might do so with little or no inconvenience to himself, and the death or great bodily harm follows as a consequence of his inaction, shall be punished criminally and shall make compensation to the party injured or to his widow and children in case of death.

. . . Even those who argue, as Ames does, that the law is utilitarian must in the end find some special place for the claims of egoism which are an inseparable byproduct of the belief that individual autonomy—individual liberty—is a good in itself not explainable in terms of its purported social worth. It is one thing to allow people to act as they please in the belief that the "invisible hand" will provide the happy congruence of the individual and the social good. Such a theory, however, at bottom must regard individual autonomy as but a means to some social end. It takes a great deal more to assert that men are entitled to act as they choose (within the limits of strict liability) even though it is certain that there will be cases where individual welfare will be in conflict with the social good. Only then is it clear that even freedom has its costs: costs revealed in the acceptance of the good Samaritan doctrine.

But are the alternatives more attractive? Once one decides that as a matter of statutory or common law duty, an individual is required under some circumstances to act at his own cost for the exclusive benefit of another, then it is very hard to set out in a principled manner the limits of social interference with individual liberty. Suppose one claims, as Ames does, that his proposed rule applies only in the "obvious" cases where everyone (or almost everyone) would admit that the duty was appropriate: to the case of the man upon the bridge who refuses to throw a rope to a stranger drowning in the waters below. Even if the rule starts out with such modest ambitions, it is difficult to confine it to those limits. Take a simple case first. X as a representative of a private charity asks you for $10 in order to save the life of some starving child in a country ravaged by war. There are other donors available but the number of needy children exceeds that number. The money means "nothing" to you. Are you under a legal obligation to give the $10? Or to lend it interest-free? Does $10 amount to a substantial cost or inconvenience within the meaning of Ames' rule? It is true that the relationship between the gift to charity and the survival of an unidentified child is not so apparent as is the relationship between the man upon the bridge and the swimmer caught in the swirling seas. But lest the physical imagery govern, it is clear in both cases that someone will die as a consequence of your inaction in both cases. Is there a duty to give, or is the contribution a matter of charity?

Consider yet another example where services, not cash, are in issue. Ames insists that his rule would not require the only surgeon in India capable of saving the life of a person with a given affliction to travel across the subcontinent to perform an operation, presumably because the inconvenience and cost would be substantial. But how would he treat the case if some third person were willing to pay him for all of his efforts? If the payment is sufficient to induce the surgeon to act, then there is no need for the good Samaritan doctrine at all. But if it is not, then it is again necessary to compare the costs of the physician with the benefits to his prospective patient. It is hard to know whether Ames would require the forced exchange under these circumstances. But it is at least arguable that under his theory forced exchanges should be required, since the payment might reduce the surgeon's net inconvenience to the point where it was trivial.

Once forced exchanges, regardless of the levels of payment, are accepted, it will no longer be possible to delineate the sphere of activities in which contracts (or charity) will be required in order to

procure desired benefits and the sphere of activity in which those benefits can be procured as of right. Where tests of "reasonableness"—
stated with such confidence, and applied with such difficulty—
dominate the law of tort, it becomes impossible to tell where liberty
ends and obligation begins; where contract ends, and tort begins. In
each case, it will be possible for some judge or jury to decide that
there was something else which the defendant should have done, and
he will decide that on the strength of some cost-benefit formula that is
difficult indeed to apply. These remarks are conclusive, I think,
against the adoption of Ames' rule by judicial innovation, and they
bear heavily on the desirability of the abandonment of the good
Samaritan rule by legislation as well. It is not surprising that the law
has, in the midst of all the clamor for reform, remained unmoved in
the end, given the inability to form alternatives to the current
position.

But the defense of the common law rule on the good Samaritan
does not rest solely upon a criticism of its alternatives. Strong
arguments can be advanced to show that the common law position on
the good Samaritan problem is in the end consistent with both moral
and economic principles.

The history of Western ethics has been marked by the development of two lines of belief. One line of moral thought emphasizes the
importance of the freedom of the will. It is the intention (or motive)
that determines the worth of the act; and no act can be moral unless it
is performed free from external compulsion. Hence the expansion of
the scope of positive law could only reduce the moral worth of human
action. Even if positive law could insure conformity to the appropriate external standards of conduct, it, like other forms of external
constraints, destroys the moral worth of the act. Hence the elimina-
tion of the positive law becomes a minimum condition for moral
conduct, even if it means that persons entitled to benefits (in
accordance with some theory of entitlements respected but not
enforced) will not receive them if their fellow men are immoral.

On the other hand, there are those theories that concern themselves not with the freedom of the will, but with the external effects of
individual behavior. There is no room for error, because each act
which does not further the stated goals (usually, of the maximization
of welfare) is in terms of these theories a bad act. Thus a system of
laws must either require the individual to act, regardless of motive, in
the socially desired manner, or create incentives for him to so

behave. Acceptance of this kind of theory has as its corollary the acceptance, if necessary, of an elaborate system of legal rules to insure compliance with the stated goals of maximization even if individual liberty (which now only counts as a kind of satisfaction) is sacrificed in the effort.

At a common sense level, neither of these views is accepted in its pure form. The strength of each theory lays bare the weaknesses of the other. Preoccupation with the moral freedom of a given actor ignores the effects of his conduct upon other persons. Undue emphasis upon the conformity to external standards of behavior entails a loss of liberty. Hence, most systems of conventional morality try to distinguish between those circumstances in which a person would be compelled to act for the benefit of his fellow man, and those cases where he should be allowed to do so only if prompted by the appropriate motives. To put the point in other terms, the distinction is taken between that conduct which is required and that which, so to speak, is beyond the call of duty. If that distinction is accepted as part of a common morality, then the argument in favor of the good Samaritan rule is that it, better than any possible alternatives, serves to mark off the first class of activities from the second. Compensation for harm caused can be demanded in accordance with the principles of strict liability. Failure to aid those in need can invoke at most moral censure on the ground that the person so accused did not voluntarily conform his conduct to some "universal" principle of justice. The rules of causation, which create liability in the first case, deny it in the second. It may well be that the conduct of individuals who do not aid fellow men is under some circumstances outrageous, but it does not follow that a legal system that does not enforce a duty to aid is outrageous as well. . . .

# B.
## The European Civil-Law Tradition

The laws of most European countries are set out in comprehensive codes derived more or less distantly from Roman law. Despite this difference of form and background, they are not on most issues all that different in content from Anglo-American law. One often-noted substantive difference is that European legal systems characteristically reject the common-law doctrine of no legal duty to rescue a stranger. The following excerpts sketch the treatment of this issue in several European legal systems.

## 1. *John P. Dawson, "Negotiorum Gestio: The Altruistic Intermeddler"** *

*In this passage, Professor John Dawson describes the treatment of refusal to rescue in French and German law. Defenders of the traditional Anglo-American rejection of duties to rescue have found support for their position in the fact that the German and French legal systems first adopted their general requirements of rescue under the Nazi and the pro-Nazi Vichy governments respectively. On the other hand, almost all European countries now have general duties to rescue, some dating from the nineteenth century; and postwar France and West Germany have deliberately decided to continue imposing rescue requirements. It is sometimes said that the absence of duties to rescue in Anglo-American law reflects a peculiarly callous and selfish individualism in English-speaking cultures. Does a duty to rescue conflict with the spirit of Mill's principle?*

The German Criminal Code of 1870 made it a criminal offense for a private citizen to disobey the police when they requested the citizen's aid "in cases of accident, common danger, or necessity" and he could give such aid without serious danger to himself. By legislation of the Nazi regime in 1935 this provision was greatly expanded. Refusal of aid requested by the police was made merely a particular instance of a much broader crime, punishable by money fine without limit or imprisonment up to two years and defined as refusal of "aid in cases of accident, common danger or necessity where there is a duty to aid according to the sound sense of the people (*gesundes Volksempfinden*)." The official statement of motives for this legislation explained that "the sound sense of the people" was

> a sufficient standard; it will not make excessive demands or exact heroism to the extent of self-sacrifice, though it may in some cases require economic injury through loss of time and under some circumstances also a danger of bodily injury that is small in relation to the harm threatened. The feeling of togetherness (*Zusammengehorigkeit*) obviously requires,

* 74 Harv. L. Rev. 817 1073 (1961). Copyright © 1961 by The Harvard Law Review Association.

for example, that a passerby who sees a boat sinking should throw to the person who is struggling for life a lifebelt that is nearby or otherwise bestir himself to secure prompt help.

During the Nazi period—and later—prosecutions for failure to aid have been brought chiefly against physicians and those failing to aid victims in traffic accidents, if one can judge from reported cases. As to physicians, the alarm generally felt by the medical profession was assuaged by decisions that construed "accident" to mean a situation that was "suddenly" produced, thus excluding continuing illness, and also by decisions that permitted a considerable measure of professional discretion in deciding the nature and the timing of the medical care required. Nevertheless physicians are occasionally sent to jail, and the affirmative duty to intervene when their aid is requested goes well beyond the requirements usually imposed on the medical profession by our own criminal law. In the traffic-accident cases, on the other hand, the crime of refusing aid is in many respects the same as the crime, well-known to us, of leaving the scene of an accident. Yet the duty is more extensive, and it extends to persons who were themselves in no way responsible for causing the accident. The cases reported so far do not throw much light on the question how much sacrifice or risk the potential but delinquent rescuer is expected to undergo. In most of them the aid that was needed could have been given without any risk of injury to the rescuer, at most with slight inconvenience.

After the collapse of the Nazi regime the question arose whether the regulations of the allied military governments invalidated the duty-to-aid legislation as imposing criminal liability without adequate standards. On this question two intermediate courts of appeal disagreed, one of them holding that "the sound sense of the people" was the only operative provision in cases where the police had not asked for aid and that as a standard it was too vague. When the Supreme Court of West Germany faced the question in 1951, it declared that the standard provided was not too indefinite and that the legislation was still in force. When the question was then fully reexamined in 1954 by the Great Criminal Senate, this view was confirmed. The duty to give aid in emergencies was declared to be "a moral obligation that has existed from time immemorial. Aid to neighbors in need was, in particular, always an imperative command of Christian doctrine." The court declared that the idea of criminal sanctions to enforce the duty was not invented by the Nazis, as was shown by legislative proposals seriously made before 1933, though never actually adopted. The legislation of 1935 had therefore remained in force during the period after the second war and applied to a refusal of aid, occurring in 1951, by a husband whose wife had attempted suicide.

The task of the Great Criminal Senate in this case had been made much easier by an amendment of article 330c of the German Criminal Code in 1953. This amendment struck out "the sound sense of the people" as a standard and rearranged the wording to read as follows:

> Whoever does not render help in case of accident, common danger or necessity although help is required and under the circumstances is exactable, and in particular is possible without danger of serious injury to himself and without violation of other important [*wichtige*] duties, will be punished by imprisonment up to one year or by fine.

It should be observed that similar legislation has been adopted in most of western Europe. In Holland, as early as 1886, the Criminal Code provided for imprisonment up to three months and a money fine up to 300 florins for one who refused aid to a person "in danger of death" if aid could be given "without reasonable fear of danger to himself or another" and if the death of the person in distress followed. Similar provisions for criminal liability for refusing aid to persons "in peril" or "in danger of death" were adopted in Turkey, Italy, Poland, Denmark, Rumania, Norway, and Portugal. The draft proposals of 1934 for revision of the French Criminal Code included a clause authorizing criminal punishment of a person who could "without prejudice or risk to himself or his near relatives" give aid to a person in peril if this person for lack of aid subsequently died or suffered serious bodily injury. This clause was not adopted in France until 1941, and it was then included as one of a group of measures introduced by the Vichy government under pressure of the German occupying forces in France. But again, as in Germany, when the matter was reconsidered by the French government in 1945, these basic provisions were retained, with penalties reduced but coverage extended. The French courts in applying them have been mainly concerned, like the German courts, with physicians and with fleeing drivers, and the solutions reached in the two countries have been on the whole quite similar.

One question inevitably raised by legislation of this kind is whether the standard of conduct defined by the criminal law is carried over to the law of tort to permit recovery of damages against the person who commits a crime in refusing aid. I have found no German decisions that permit this translation of criminal into civil liability. In one trial-court decision in France, however, the accused in a criminal case had walked away from the scene when his son-in-law fell through ice into a deep canal. The accused also refused, despite the son-in-law's "peril of death," to join with a third person in handing out to him a nearby iron bar to which the son-in-law might cling. For this unkindness, excessive even in a father-in-law, the accused was sent to jail for three years. But the son-in-law had apparently managed to scramble out of the icy water, for he appeared in the action as *partie civile* and recovered 25,000 francs from his impervious father-in-law. The general conclusion that the standards of the criminal law define fault for the purposes of damage liability has the strong support of the leading modern French authors on tort liability. It may be, therefore, that through the indirect route of the criminal law French courts will reach a solution of the problem, much discussed in our own law, of tort liability for refusal of aid in emergencies. . . .

## 2. Note, "Stalking the Good Samaritan: Communists, Capitalists and the Duty to Rescue"*

*This excerpt describes the treatment of the duty-to-rescue issue in the legal systems of two European communist states, the Soviet Union and Czechoslovakia. Note the respective influences of socialist ideology and of bourgeois European code traditions in the two countries. Are communist legal systems more likely to adopt a rule allowing a victim to sue a refuser to rescue for money damage suffered as a result of the refusal? Would you expect the communist system to provide more serious criminal treatment of rescue refusal than do systems in capitalist countries?*

In the Soviet Union, the question of whether the civil law of tort should be used to enforce the acknowledged moral duty to rescue a person in peril has been the subject of a controversy similar to that in the United States. The controversy arose soon after the U.S.S.R.

---

* 1976 Utah Law Rev. 529. Reprinted by permission of the Utah Law Review.

Constitution of 1936 went into effect. Article 130 of the Constitution provides that all citizens shall have the affirmative duty to "respect the rules of socialist intercourse." . . .

The duty to be a good Samaritan was quickly defined as one of the rules of socialist intercourse, and in 1938 Professor Agarkov became the first to assert that article 130 created a legally enforceable duty to rescue. He suggested that the constitution would be violated if a "healthy person who knew how to swim failed to render aid in the summer time to another person who was drowning in a river not far from its bank." Subsequent authors of official textbooks retreated from this position. In 1948, however, a short article was published urging that the constitution required a duty to rescue, and suggesting a statute to that effect. The proposed statute imposed on citizens a duty to notify competent authorities or to personally intervene if necessary to protect life, health, or property if the danger to the rescuer was not severe. The statute made the potential rescuer liable to the victim in tort for damages caused by his failure to rescue. The victim was also required to compensate his rescuer for injury he sustained during the rescue. The proposed statute was never enacted.

During the 1950s several authors spoke out against a duty to rescue. Vil'nianskii, for example, objected on principle to the legal enforcement of altruism. Fleishits seemed to interpret the words "to *respect* the rules of socialist intercourse" by contrasting them with the words "to *obey* the law" and found they contained no mandate but merely expressed fundamental moral principles.

In spite of the scholarly controversy on the subject, there has yet been no judicial enforcement of a duty to rescue under article 130. Moreover, the article's general duty has never been enacted in the Civil Code as a duty to rescue, with specifications of the legal consequences of breach. . . .

It would seem that the Soviet Union, because of its political and philosophical stance, would be more receptive to a legally enforced duty to rescue than the United States. Infringement of personal freedoms is tolerated in the Soviet Union to a great degree, in deference to the collective good. The common law theoretical reluctance to punish omissions is practically nonexistent in the Soviet Union, where the law imposes numerous affirmative duties. The Soviet Constitution lists not only the rights of each citizen, but his obligations as well, following Engels' view that "[e]qual obligations are for us a particularly important addendum to bourgeois-democratic equal rights, an addendum removing the specifically bourgeois meaning from the latter." In spite of this philosophy, the duty to rescue, although generally recognized as included within article 130's admonition to "respect the rules of socialist intercourse," has failed to inspire legal sanctions.

The basic objection of Soviet legal thought to an enforced duty to rescue seems to parallel the common law view: that it is somehow wrong, or, perhaps, unnecessary to add legal sanctions to a recognized moral law. Orlovskii's 1961 civil law textbook states that "[t]he selflessness, with which citizens come to aid with the goal of saving another's life or socialist property, is characteristic of Soviet reality." Whether true or not at present, the theory is that the obligations of communist morality will eventually be recognized and voluntarily performed by everyone without the coercion of the state. . . .

The 1964 Czechoslovak Civil Code created a comprehensive duty to prevent "injury to health and damage to property or undue enrichment to the detriment of society or individuals." Although some European countries have found civil liability for failure to rescue following from a duty imposed by the criminal law, the Czechoslovak provisions represent the first broad statutory use of tort law to mandate Good Samaritan behavior. Thus, the civil provisions are intended to supplement the limited criminal liability Czechoslovakia imposes for failure to render aid where there is danger of death.

The Code provisions create two specific duties for citizens when there is a threat of "serious damage to life, health, or property . . . or when undue enrichment" appears imminent. First, the citizen must immediately notify the appropriate authorities of the danger. Second, if immediate action is urgently required to avert the danger, he must personally intervene unless "he is prevented from doing so by a serious circumstance or if he would thereby expose himself or persons close to him to a serious danger." No such qualifications, of course, excuse the citizen from notifying the authorities.

The citizen who fails to act to prevent damage to life, health, or property will be required to compensate the victim for damage to "an extent appropriate to the circumstances of the case," if fulfillment of his duty would have prevented the damage. . . .

To further encourage fulfillment of the duty to rescue and to prevent damage, the Code provides that a rescuer who causes damage during the course of a rescue shall not be liable therefore in most cases. He will, however, be liable if the threat clearly could have been averted in a way which would entail less damage, or if the damage he caused was "obviously" as serious or more serious than that which threatened. In addition, if the rescuer suffers injury, the one rescued must compensate him for "effectively expended costs and . . . damages suffered by him."

In Czechoslovakia, as in the U.S.S.R., the duty to rescue is recognized as one of the "principles of socialist intercourse." Reflected in the Preamble to the 1964 Civil Code, these principles demand of the socialist citizen that he not be indifferent to potential harm to his neighbor. Unlike the U.S.S.R., however, Czechoslovakia has decided that, in this instance, the dictates of communist morality must be reinforced through legal sanctions.

The reason for the differing views on enforcement between two nations, both of which agree that socialism imposes a specific moral duty to rescue, seems to lie in the extensive influence of German civil law in Czechoslovakia's history. The duty to rescue provisions of the 1964 Civil Code, when viewed as hortatory rather than mandatory, closely resemble the elements of the Roman law doctrine of *negotiorum gestio*, which has received its most extensive modern development in German law.

The doctrine of *negotiorum gestio* effectively encourages altruism without requiring it. Simply stated, when a man voluntarily undertakes to "manage another's affair," for the other's benefit and without request or authorization, he is entitled to compensation for his trouble. Although the concept originated in an implied agency to look after an absent person's property or business affairs, it has been extended to the voluntary rescue of human life or health. An early German case allowed the rescuer to recover only money expended for the rescue, but later decisions extended recovery to damages for personal injuries to or for the wrongful death of the rescuer.

The language and approach of the 1964 Czechoslovak Civil Code provisions regarding prevention of injury to life, health, or property reflect the German tradition of *negotiorum gestio*. The statute is not narrowly directed to the typical rescue situation, which requires rescue only when there is immediate danger to life—an issue addressed in the Czechoslovak and most other European criminal codes. Instead, the statute covers both immediate and remote threats of damage, and applies broadly to life, health, and property, all of which have traditionally been susceptible of "management" by a *gestor.* The inclusion of property, whether socialist or personal, is particularly revealing, since *negotiorum gestio* is extensively applied to management of another's property. Also, the provision relieving the rescuer from liability for reasonable damage done during the course of the rescue incorporates a right traditionally belonging to the *gestor.* In sum, if a citizen *voluntarily* undertook the duties specified in the new Code, in the absence of a legal duty to do so, the consequences in terms of compensation to the *gestor* prescribed in these provisions would automatically flow from application of the doctrine of *negotiorum gestio.*

The tradition of *negotiorum gestio,* therefore, prepared the way in Czechoslovakia for the imposition of a duty to rescue. The influence of a socialist system with its articulation of strict rules of communist morality probably helped to persuade Czechoslovakia to add the gloss of obligation to what had traditionally been a method of encouraging voluntary altruism. In any event, without the historical influence of the German development of *negotiorum gestio,* the Soviet Union is still struggling with the question of whether or not to add legal sanctions to a recognized obligation of communist morality. In Czechoslovakia, the combined influence of two systems of legal thought has provided a possible answer.

## C.

# The Common-Law Rescue Doctrine in Application

It is a fair first generalization that individuals in European civil code jurisdictions are generally subject to a legal duty to come to the aid of a stranger in distress, whereas individuals in Anglo-American common-law jurisdictions have no such duty. But that first generalization needs much qualification. On the European side, we have seen that civil-law systems do not generally grant damage recovery to individuals injured by others' failure to rescue. The criminal penalties imposed by European codes for nonrescue are minor, and in practice it seems that prosecutions are rare.

On the Anglo-American side, the "no duty to rescue" doctrine has been much qualified in application, and increasingly so in recent years, as the following seven cases suggest. The first case, *Hurley,* decided at the turn of the century, represents the classic common-law doctrine in its full individualist rigor, applied in the context of a doctor's refusal to treat an emergency patient. The next two cases, *O'Neill* and *Manlove*, show how that rigor has recently been relaxed to place substantial duties in emergency cases upon hospitals and doctors. There then follows the famous *Tarasoff* case, in which a doctor-patient relation is held to impose a duty on the doctor to rescue a stranger from the patient. The fifth case, *Farwell*, shows how far another contemporary court is willing to go, in this instance in a nonmedical context, to find a special relationship that overrides the "no duty" doctrine. The final two cases point to another context— danger at sea—in which Anglo-American courts have departed from their traditional individualism.

Apart from the substantive questions it raises, this section is meant to provide a sustained illustration of the method of the common law in action. In one sense, each of these cases is—like the hypothetical cases created by philosophers and lawyers for use in teaching and argument—an "example," an "illustration," of the application of a general rule or principle that is our central focus of attention. But in another sense, each case involves the representation in story form of a concrete human dispute, which it is the primary task of the court to settle in a peaceful, practical, and fair way. Seen from the latter perspective, the story, the facts of the case, become the primary focus; and the principles and rules of law (or of morals) are important only as auxiliaries to the main job of dispute settlement. The common law, and perhaps the business of case decision or practical reasoning generally, is better understood when this "bottom-up" perspective has been recognized as different from and equal in importance to the more familiar "top-down" perspective.

At the same time, you should keep the broader question behind all these materials in mind. Is liberty threatened by the extensions of duty to rescue imposed by these decisions? If not, do their further implications threaten any of the values implicit in Mill's principle of liberty—as contemporary libertarians argue?

## 1. *Hurley v. Eddingfield*＊ ═══════════════

*In the following case, the court holds that a physician has an absolute right to refuse treatment to a patient in an emergency, however urgent the need, however trivial the physician's reasons for refusal. Do you see the argument for this position implicit in the court's statement that "the alleged wrongful act*

＊ 59 N.E. 1058 (1901) (Supreme Court of Indiana).

*was [the doctor's] refusal to enter into an employment contract"? If the law forces you to go to work for other people on their say-so, doesn't it make you in some sense their servant against your will—more dramatically, their slave? Recall Epstein's argument for the common-law doctrine.*

*The court's rejection of plaintiff's analogy to the obligations of "innkeepers, common carriers, and the like" has the following background. Traditionally at common law, persons following certain occupations, such as innkeepers and "common carriers" (for example, those operating regular coach service), were not allowed to refuse paying customers without reasonable cause. These duties arose before the high laissez-faire period of the law in the late nineteenth century. But physicians were never included within these traditional categories, and the court here is expressing an unwillingness to extend by analogy any of the ancient occupation-based restrictions on freedom of contract. Are there reasonable grounds on which an innkeeper might be required to accept guests, but physicians not required to treat emergency patients?*

*The first paragraph of the opinion describes the procedures that brought the case to the Indiana Supreme Court. The plaintiff was the personal representative of the estate of the deceased, who had died "intestate"—that is, without a will. The plaintiff sued the defendant doctor by filing with the court a complaint, a document alleging that certain facts were true and that they entitled plaintiff to $10,000. Defendant "demurred" to the complaint—which means that he argued, in effect, "even if what you allege as facts really are facts, you aren't entitled to any recovery." Such a "demurrer" raises a pure question of law—given the hypothetical facts as alleged by plaintiff, can he recover? The trial court "sustained the demurrer," ruling that plaintiff could not recover even if the facts were as he alleged. This ended the case in defendant's favor, and plaintiff appealed the ruling, which the appellate court now affirms in this decision. If the Supreme Court of Indiana had held that the demurrer was not valid, so that the plaintiff's allegations would support recovery, the defendant would still have had the opportunity to contest the facts as plaintiff alleged them at a trial.*

BAKER, J.

The appellant sued appellee for $10,000 damages for wrongfully causing the death of his intestate. The court sustained appellee's demurrer to the complaint, and this ruling is assigned as error.

The material facts alleged may be summarized thus: At and for years before decedent's death appellee was a practicing physician at Mace, in Montgomery county, duly licensed under the laws of the state. He held himself out to the public as a general practitioner of medicine. He had been decedent's family physician. Decedent became dangerously ill, and sent for appellee. The messenger informed appellee of decedent's violent sickness, tendered him his fee for his services, and stated to him that no other physician was procurable in time, and that decedent relied on him for attention. No other physician was procurable in time to be of any use, and decedent did rely on appellee for medical assistance. Without any reason whatever, appellee refused to render aid to decedent. No other patients were requiring appellee's immediate service, and he could have gone to the relief of decedent if he had been willing to do so. Death ensued, without decedent's fault, and wholly from appellee's wrongful act. The alleged wrongful act was appellee's refusal to enter into a contract of employment. . . . In obtaining the state's license (permission) to practice medicine, the state does not require, and the licensee does not engage, that he will practice at all or on other terms than he may choose to accept. Counsel's analogies, drawn from the obligations to the public on the part of innkeepers, common carriers, and the like, are beside the mark. Judgment affirmed.

## 2. *O'Neill v. Montefiore Hospital**

*The procedural circumstances in the following case are different from those in* Hurley. *Here the plaintiff, Mrs. O'Neill, actually introduced her evidence at trial. At the close of her case, the trial court ruled that even if all the testimony in her favor was believed, she had no legal case against the hospital; hence there was nothing for the jury to decide and judgment was granted to the hospital. The doctor, however, was required to give his evidence in defense. After that evidence was heard, the court made a similar decision for the doctor: even if the jury believed the plaintiff's evidence on all factual issues in which there was conflict, there still was not an adequate case for her under the law.*

*In discussing the case against the doctor, the court invokes the general rule that once there is any action by a potential rescuer on which the victim or other potential rescuers might rely, the potential rescuer can no longer argue that he is merely leaving the situation unaltered; by his intervention he has "acted," so that any subsequent abandonment of the rescue is no longer a mere failure to rescue. It is often argued that drawing the line in this way creates perverse incentives for potential rescuers; do you see what they are? Do you see any way around those perverse incentives, within the bounds of the "no duty to rescue" doctrine?*

*The possible liability of the hospital is premised on the same basis, that it began a rescue and hence undertook a duty of reasonable care. Here there is an additional factual question—whether the nurse's conduct in telephoning the doctor was only "a personal favor" or was undertaken in her role as a hospital employee. Why does this matter? How would one go about deciding this question—what kind of evidence might you look for that would be relevant? If*

* 202 N.Y.S. 2d 436 (1960) (Appellate Division, New York).

*the hospital had an absolute right to refuse treatment, how could the nurse's refusal of Mrs. O'Neill's request for a doctor's examination of Mr. O'Neill be a basis for recovery, as the last quoted sentence of the majority opinion suggests?*

PER CURIAM. In this action for the wrongful death of John J. O'Neill, who died of a heart attack on the morning of June 29, 1952, the widow sought recovery against a hospital for failure to render necessary emergency treatment, and against a physician for his failure and refusal to treat the deceased. Since the complaint against the hospital was dismissed at the trial at the close of plaintiff's case and the complaint against the doctor was dismissed at the conclusion of all of the evidence, the question posed on this appeal is whether plaintiff made out a prima facie case sufficient for submission to the jury. In other words, the issue presented is whether, under the circumstances hereinafter described, there was a duty owing respectively by the hospital and the doctor to examine and treat plaintiff's deceased husband.

Briefly, the facts, as they appear in the record, are that the plaintiff awoke shortly before 5:00 A.M., and saw her husband standing at the window, rubbing his arms and chest. His mouth was open "and he was trying to get as much air as he possibly could." He was perspiring, his face was white as contrasted with his normally ruddy complexion, and he complained of severe pains in his chest and arms. With the assistance of the plaintiff, O'Neill dressed and walked to the hospital, which was three blocks away. He stopped frequently on the way in order to rest and to find a taxicab, but none was available.

It appears that the hospital maintained an emergency room or clinic. When Mr. and Mrs. O'Neill arrived at the hospital, the doorman conducted them to the nurse in charge of the emergency room. The plaintiff told the nurse that the deceased was very ill, was suffering chest and arm pains, and she thought he was having a heart attack, and she requested the services of a doctor. At that point, Mr. O'Neill mentioned that they were members of the Hospital Insurance Plan (hereinafter referred to as HIP). Thereupon the nurse stated that the hospital had no connection with HIP and did not take care of HIP patients. After reflecting for a minute or two, the nurse stated, "I'll try and get you a HIP doctor," and then telephoned the defendant Graig, telling him that the deceased was in the emergency room of the hospital, complaining of the pains hereinbefore described. She then handed the telephone to Mr. O'Neill who described his pains to Dr. Graig, and then, after a pause, stated, "Dr. Kirstein." After another pause Mr. O'Neill said, "Well I could be dead by 8 o'clock." When the deceased concluded the telephone conversation, he informed the nurse that Dr. Graig had told him to go home and come back when HIP was open. Mrs. O'Neill, however, asked the nurse to have a doctor examine her husband since it was an emergency. Disregarding the request, the nurse told her that their family doctor would see Mr. O'Neill at 8 o'clock, to which he again replied, "I could be dead by 8 o'clock."

When the examination or treatment at the hospital was refused, the plaintiff and the deceased left and returned home on foot, pausing occasionally to permit him to catch his breath. After they arrived at their apartment, and as the plaintiff was helping her husband to disrobe, he fell to the floor and died before any medical attention could be obtained.

Insofar as the cause of action against Dr. Graig is concerned, the proof indicates and the court found that the plaintiff and her husband were members of the Montefiore Group of HIP. Two of the doctors composing that group, and under contract with HIP to treat its members, were Doctors Kirstein and Graig, the former being the physician ordinarily consulted by the O'Neills, while the latter was the doctor on call on the morning in question.

Dr. Graig confirmed Mrs. O'Neill's testimony that he received a phone call from the Montefiore Hospital emergency room and spoke to the deceased. Dr. Graig testified in some detail concerning that conversation, and related the inquiries he made concerning symptoms, prior episodes, electrocardiograms, and other items of the patient's medical history. He then went on to state that he offered to come to the emergency room and make an examination, but Mr. O'Neill declined, stating that he felt better and would prefer to wait to see Dr. Kirstein who would be available at 8 o'clock.

We are not called upon to decide whether, by his contract with HIP, Dr. Graig assumed to examine and treat the deceased and failed to do so as distinguished from whether he, defendant Graig, independently undertook or assumed to examine and treat and failed to exercise due care in so doing. Perhaps a more complete development of the facts in that regard might have been desirable. Thus whether, as the plaintiff claimed, there was an abandonment of the patient by the doctor, or as the defendant claimed there was a refusal to accept a proffered examination presents a question of fact which should have been submitted to the jury.

However, from the proof in the record, we must hold that the jury could have concluded that Dr. Graig undertook to diagnose the ailments of the deceased and could have decided whether he abandoned the patient, inadequately or improperly advised him, or, conversely, made a proper diagnosis fully appropriate under the circumstances, or offered an examination which was rejected.

The law is settled that a physician who undertakes to examine or treat a patient and then abandons him, may be held liable for malpractice.

With respect to the action against the hospital, there is also a question of fact presented which should have been submitted to the jury. That question is whether the conduct of the nurse in relation to the deceased was in the nature of a personal favor to him or whether her conduct was that of an attaché of the hospital trying to discharge her duty, and if so, whether what she did was inadequate. So, too, whether the alleged request of the nurse for an examination of Mr. O'Neill, following the telephone conversation with Dr. Graig, and the nurse's refusal to have Mr. O'Neill examined at the hospital constituted negligent conduct, would also be a question for the jury. . . .

[MCNALLY, Justice]

I concur in the order for reversal and for a new trial as against defendant Frank Graig. I dissent and vote to affirm the dismissal of the complaint against defendant Montefiore Hospital. Through the efforts of the hospital's nurse, the decedent had been enabled to communicate by telephone with Dr. Graig who had knowledge of the decedent's presence at the hospital. Dr. Graig did not indicate in any manner that emergency treatment was required nor did he direct or request the admittance of the decedent as a patient to the hospital. Any action by the nurse contrariwise would not have been in keeping with her position. It is my view that the conduct of the nurse was by way of favor and I fail to see any legal basis for liability on the part of the hospital.

3.  *Wilmington General Hospital v. Manlove**

*In the following case, we have still another procedural situation. Plaintiffs have sued defendant hospital for refusing emergency treatment to their now*

---

* 174 A. 2d 135 (1961) (Supreme Court of Delaware).

*deceased child. The case has not yet come to trial, but certain evidence has been developed in pretrial proceedings; specifically witnesses have made "depositions" (sworn statements given out of court) of what they know about the facts in the case. On the basis of these depositions, the defendant hospital has moved for "summary judgment": in effect, a ruling that even if the facts are all found in the way most favorable to the plaintiff, still the plaintiff will not have a legally sufficient case. The trial court has denied the motion, which has the effect of allowing the case to proceed to trial. But the defendant has appealed the denial of summary judgment to the state Supreme Court, arguing that the trial can serve no purpose. (In most states, such appeals are not allowed; can you see the practical grounds for and against allowing the progress of trial court proceedings to be interrupted by an appeal before they run their course?)*

*Does the court here go beyond the court in* O'Neill *in imposing a duty on a hospital to accept emergency patients? What is the basis for the court's departure from the general rule, which it states, that private hospitals have no duty to accept patients they don't want?*

*What are the implications of this decision for the duty of the private physician? Suppose the facts of* Hurley *arose in Delaware today; would the physician be liable? Does the rationale offered by the court for imposing a duty on the hospital in this case extend to a private physician? Recall that the defendant in* Hurley *was alleged to be the deceased's regular family doctor and the only physician available in the circumstances. What would be the relevance of each of these facts, given the rationale in this case?*

This case concerns the liability of a private hospital for the death of an infant who was refused treatment at the emergency ward of the hospital. The facts are these:

On January 4, 1959, Darien E. Manlove, the deceased infant, then four months old, developed diarrhea. The next morning his parents consulted Dr. Hershon. They asked whether the medicine they had for him was all right and the doctor said that it was. In the evening of the same day Mrs. Manlove took the baby's temperature. It was higher than normal. They called Dr. Hershon, and he prescribed additional medication (streptomycin), which he ordered delivered by a pharmacy.

Mrs. Manlove stayed up with the child that night. He did not sleep. On the morning of January 6th the parents took the infant to Dr. Hershon's office. Dr. Thomas examined the child and treated him for sore throat and diarrhea. He prescribed a liquid diet and some medicine.

When Mr. Manlove returned home that night, the baby's condition appeared to be the same. His temperature was still above normal, and again he did not sleep during the night.

On the morning of January 7th (a Wednesday) his temperature was still above normal—102. Mr. and Mrs. Manlove determined to seek additional medical assistance. They knew that Dr. Hershon and Dr. Thomas were not in their offices on Wednesdays, and they took their infant to the emergency ward of the Wilmington General Hospital.

There is no real conflict of fact as to what occurred at the hospital. The parents took the infant into the reception room of the emergency ward. A nurse was on duty. They explained to the nurse what was wrong with the child, that is, that he had not slept for two nights, had a continuously high temperature, and that he had diarrhea. Mr. Manlove told the nurse that the child was under the care of Dr. Hershon and Dr. Thomas, and showed the nurse the medicines prescribed. The nurse explained to the parents that the hospital could not give treatment because the child was under the care of a physician and there would be danger that the medication of the hospital might conflict with that of the attending physician. The nurse did not examine the child, take his temperature, feel his forehead, or look down his throat. The child was not in convulsions, and was not coughing or crying. There was no particular area of body tenderness.

The nurse tried to get in touch with Dr. Hershon or Dr. Thomas in the hospital and at their offices, but was unable to do so. She suggested that the parent bring the baby Thursday morning to the pediatric clinic.

Mr. and Mrs. Manlove returned home. Mrs. Manlove made an appointment by telephone to see Dr. Hershon or Dr. Thomas that night at eight o'clock.

At eight minutes past three o'clock in the afternoon the baby died of bronchial pneumonia.

The foregoing facts are taken mainly from the deposition of the plaintiff.

Plaintiff, as administrator, brought suit against the hospital to recover damages for wrongful death. The complaint charged negligence in failing to render emergency assistance, in failing to examine the baby, in refusing to advise the intern about the child or permit the parents to consult him, and in failing to follow reasonable and humane hospital procedure for the treatment of emergency cases. Defendant answered denying negligence and averring that, pursuant to its established rule, and community practice, plaintiff was advised by its employee that it was unable to accept the infant for care.

Discovery proceedings were taken by both parties, eliciting the facts set forth above. Defendant then moved for summary judgment, and attached an affidavit from the nurse on duty when the infant was brought to the hospital. Her statement concerning the refusal of treatment is:

> I then told Mr. and Mrs. Manlove that the rules of the hospital provided that in such cases, where a person is under attendance and medication by a private doctor, and there is no frank indication of emergency, no treatment or medication may be given by doctors employed by the hospital until the attending doctor has been consulted. . . .

We are of opinion that the defendant is a private and not a public hospital, in so far as concerns the right of a member of the public to demand admission or treatment.

What, then, is the liability of a private hospital in this respect?

Since such an institution as the defendant is privately owned and operated, it would follow logically that its trustees or governing board alone have the right to determine who shall be admitted to it as patients. No other rule would be sensible or workable. Such authority as we have found supports this rule.

> A private hospital owes the public no duty to accept any patient not desired by it, and it is not necessary to assign any reason for its refusal to accept a patient for hospital service. 41 C.J.S. Hospitals § 8, p. 345. . . .

In *Levin v. Sinai Hospital*, above cited, the court said:

> A private hospital is not under a common law duty to serve every one who applies for treatment or permission to serve. 46 A. 2d 301.

The above authorities announce a general rule governing the question of admissions to a private hospital. Does that rule apply to the fullest extent to patients applying for treatment at an emergency ward? . . .

It may be conceded that a private hospital is under no legal obligation to the public to maintain an emergency ward, or, for that matter, a public clinic. Cf. *Taylor v. Baldwin*, Mo., 247 S.W. 2d 741, 751.

But the maintenance of such a ward to render first-aid to injured persons has become a well-established adjunct to the main business of a hospital. If a person, seriously hurt, applies for such aid at an emergency ward, relying on the established custom to render it, is it still the right of the hospital to turn him away without any reason? In such a case, it seems to us, such a refusal might well result in worsening the condition of the injured person, because of the time lost in a useless attempt to obtain medical aid. . . .

We are of opinion that liability on the part of a hospital may be predicated on the refusal of service to a patient in case of an unmistakable emergency, if the patient has relied upon a well-established custom of the hospital to render aid in such a case. The hospital rule with respect to applicants already under the care of a physician may be said to be an implied recognition of this duty.

Applying this rule here, we inquire, was there an unmistakable emergency?

We do not think that the record made below satisfactorily developed the pertinent facts. What is standard hospital practice when an applicant for aid seeks medical aid for sickness at the emergency ward? Is it the practice for the nurse to determine whether or not an emergency exists, or is it her duty to call the intern in every case? Assuming (as seems probable) that it is her duty to make such a determination, was her determination in this case within the reasonable limits of judgment of a graduate nurse, even though mistaken, or was she derelict in her duty, as a graduate nurse, in not recognizing an emergency from the symptoms related to her? To resolve these questions additional evidence, probably expert opinion, would seem to be required.

In the circumstances we think the case should go back for further proceedings. . . .

## 4. *Tarasoff v. University of California**

*This celebrated case involves a somewhat different question from the last three: can a doctor's (here a psychiatrist's) acceptance of a patient for treatment create a legal duty on the doctor to rescue a third party, a stranger to the doctor, who the doctor learns is in danger from the patient? The California*

* 17 Cal. 3d 425 (1976).

*Supreme Court's answer is yes, in some circumstances. You should note that the case, like* Hurley, *reached the state Supreme Court after a demurrer had been granted in favor of defendant—that is, the lower court had ruled that even if the facts as alleged by plaintiff were true, plaintiff had no case. Hence the "facts" discussed in the case are not really proven facts, but only the allegations in the plaintiff's complaint.*

*First, note the court's reaffirmance of the basic common-law doctrine that there is no duty to rescue a stranger. But, second, note the court's skeptical attitude toward the doctrine, reflected explicitly in a footnote and implicitly in its entire opinion.*

*What are the further implications of this decision? Suppose a bartender had heard Poddar make a credible-sounding threat to kill Tarasoff while he was drinking at the bar. Might he be held liable for failure to warn Tarasoff? (We may suppose he knew who she was; we may also suppose that Poddar was a customer of long standing, known to be an unstable character.) If the bartender would* not *be liable, is it not anomalous to impose liability in these circumstances upon a psychotherapist, who unlike a bartender has an important professional duty of confidentiality toward his patient?*

*How should a California court rule, after this decision, in a case where the patient threatened suicide, the therapist did not warn the parents, and the patient did take her own life? In fact, a lower court refused to extend the* Tarasoff *doctrine to instances where the threat was only of self-harm; the case is* Bellah v. Greenson, *81 Cal. App. 3d 614 , 146 Cal. Rptr. 535 (1978). Is that a justifiable distinction?*

[Prosenjit Poddar told his psychotherapist, Dr. Moore, that he intended to kill Tatiana Tarasoff. Moore took the threat seriously, but was prevented from warning Miss Tarasoff by the chief of the psychiatric service. Poddar then did kill Miss Tarasoff, and her parents sued the University of California—which was responsible for the psychiatric service—for negligently causing her death. The lower court dismissed the suit on the ground that there is no duty to rescue a stranger. The Supreme Court of California ruled as follows:]

TOBRINER, J.:

Although . . . under the common law, as a general rule, one person owed no duty to control the conduct of another[†] nor to warn

---

[†] [Footnote by the court:] This rule derives from the common law's distinction between misfeasance and nonfeasance, and its reluctance to impose liability for the latter. . . . Morally questionable, the rule owes its survival to "the difficulties of setting any standards of unselfish service to fellow men, and of making any workable rule to cover possible situations where fifty people might fail to rescue. . . . " Because of these practical difficulties, the courts have increased the number of instances in which affirmative duties are imposed not by direct rejection of the common law rule, but by expanding the list of special relationships which will justify departure from that rule.

those endangered by such conduct, the courts have carved out an exception to this rule in cases in which the defendant stands in some special relationship to either the person whose conduct needs to be controlled or in a relationship to the foreseeable victim of that conduct.

Although plaintiff's pleadings assert no special relation between Tatiana and defendant therapists, they establish as between Poddar and defendant therapists the special relation that arises between a patient and his doctor or psychotherapist. Such a relationship may support affirmative duties for the benefit of third persons. Thus, for example, a hospital must exercise reasonable care to control the behavior of a patient which may endanger other persons. A doctor must also warn a patient if the patient's condition or medication renders certain conduct, such as driving a car, dangerous to others. . . .

Defendants contend, however, that imposition of a duty to exercise reasonable care to protect third persons is unworkable because therapists cannot accurately predict whether or not a patient will resort to violence. . . .

We recognize the difficulty that a therapist encounters in attempting to forecast whether a patient presents a serious danger of violence. . . . Within the broad range of reasonable practice and treatment in which professional opinion and judgment may differ, the therapist is free to exercise his or her own best judgment without liability; proof, aided by hindsight, that he or she judged wrongly is insufficient to establish negligence. . . .

In our view, however, once a therapist does, in fact, determine, or under applicable professional standards reasonably should have determined, that a patient poses a serious danger of violence to others, he bears a duty to exercise reasonable care to protect the foreseeable victim of that danger. While the discharge of this duty of due care will necessarily vary with the facts of each case, in each instance the adequacy of the therapist's conduct must be measured against the traditional negligence standard of the rendition of reasonable care under the circumstances. . . .

Weighing the uncertain and conjectural character of the alleged damage done the patient by such a warning against the peril to the victim's life, we conclude that professional inaccuracy in predicting violence cannot negate the therapist's duty to protect the threatened victim.

The risk that unnecessary warnings may be given is a reasonable price to pay for the lives of possible victims that may be saved. We would hesitate to hold that the therapist who is aware that his patient expects to attempt to assassinate the President of the United States would not be obligated to warn the authorities because the therapist cannot predict with accuracy that his patient will commit the crime.

Defendants further argue that free and open communication is essential to psychotherapy. . . . The giving of a warning, defendants contend, constitutes a breach of trust which entails the revelation of confidential communications.

We recognize the public interest in supporting effective treatment of mental illness and in protecting the rights of patients to privacy . . . and the consequent public importance of safeguarding the confidential character of psychotherapeutic communication. Against this interest, however, we must weigh the public interest in safety from violent assault. The Legislature has undertaken the difficult task of balancing the countervailing concerns. In Evidence Code Section 1014, it established a broad rule of privilege to protect confidential communications between patient and psychotherapist. In Evidence Code Section 1024, the Legislature created a specific and limited exception to the psychotherapist-patient privilege: "There is no privilege . . . if the psychotherapist has reasonable cause to believe that the patient is in such mental or emotional condition as to be dangerous to himself or to the person or property of another and that disclosure of the communication is necessary to prevent the threatened danger."

We realize that the open and confidential character of psychotherapeutic dialogue encourages patients to express threats of violence, few of which are ever executed. Certainly a therapist should not be encouraged routinely to reveal such threats; such disclosures could seriously disrupt the patient's relationship with his therapist and with the persons threatened. To the contrary, the therapist's obligations to his patient require that he not disclose a confidence unless such disclosure is necessary to avert danger to others, and even then that he do so discreetly, and in a fashion that would preserve the privacy of his patient to the fullest extent compatable with the prevention of the threatened danger.

The revelation of a communication under the above circumstances is not a breach of trust or a violation of professional ethics; as stated in the Principles of Medical Ethics of the American Medical Association (1957), Section 9: "A physician may not reveal the confidence entrusted to him in the course of medical attendance . . . unless he is required to do so by law or unless it becomes necessary in order to protect the welfare of the individual or of the community." We conclude that the public policy favoring protection of the confidential character of patient-psychotherapist communications must yield to the extent to which disclosure is essential to avert danger to others. The protective privilege ends where the public peril begins.

Our current crowded and computerized society compels the interdependence of its members. In this risk-infested society we can hardly tolerate the further exposure to danger that would result from a concealed knowledge of the therapist that his patient was lethal. If the exercise of reasonable care to protect the threatened victim required the therapist to warn the endangered party or those who can reasonably be expected to notify him, we see no sufficient societal interest that would protect and justify concealment. The containment of such risks lies in the public interest. . . .

## 5. Farwell v. Keaton*

*In the following case, there are two grounds of decision. You will see from the statement of facts that two friends, Siegrist and Farwell, went out for the evening together, and Farwell was attacked and beaten up. Siegrist picked him up, drove him around, and finally left him "asleep" in the car. Farwell later died from his injuries. In the subsequent suit against Siegrist, the jury found for the plaintiff. As one ground for its affirming the judgment, the court invoked the doctrine that once you commence a rescue you must then act reasonably. The jury might have found that Siegrist commenced a rescue by picking Farwell up, and that his subsequent abandonment of him without seeking further help was negligent. This part of the court's opinion is omitted.*

*The court goes on, in the part of the opinion excerpted below, to rule that in any event Siegrist had a duty to rescue Farwell in the first place, based on their social association for the evening. Note that here as elsewhere, the duty is only to take reasonable steps to aid the victim; if the jury had believed that Siegrist had no reason to suspect that Farwell was seriously injured, it would have ruled in Siegrist's favor.*

*After this decision, what is left of the "no duty to rescue" doctrine? Should this exception to the no-duty doctrine apply whenever the potential rescuer knows the victim? Would Siegrist have had an obligation to rescue Farwell when he found him on the ground even if they had not been social companions*

* 240 N.W. 2d 217 (1976) (Supreme Court of Michigan).

*on that evening? In a small town where "everyone knows everyone else" does this decision impose a universal duty to rescue? Would a community living under such a legal doctrine not be a free community?*

*You may have a question why Farwell's parents are suing his friend Siegrist rather than the thugs who beat him up. The answer is that the assailants were sued, also; one of them, Keaton, is the named defendant in the case. But it is often the case that the more serious wrongdoers have no money to pay damages and no insurance covering their liability; probably that was true here.*

LEVIN, Justice.

On the evening of August 26, 1966, Siegrist and Farwell drove to a trailer rental lot to return an automobile which Siegrist had borrowed from a friend who worked there. While waiting for the friend to finish work, Siegrist and Farwell consumed some beer.

Two girls walked by the entrance to the lot. Siegrist and Farwell attempted to engage them in conversation; they left Farwell's car and followed the girls to a drive-in restaurant down the street.

The girls complained to their friends in the restaurant that they were being followed. Six boys chased Siegrist and Farwell back to the lot. Siegrist escaped unharmed, but Farwell was severely beaten. Siegrist found Farwell underneath his automobile in the lot. Ice was applied to Farwell's head. Siegrist then drove Farwell around for approximately two hours, stopping at a number of drive-in restaurants. Farwell went to sleep in the back seat of his car. Around midnight Siegrist drove the car to the home of Farwell's grandparents, parked it in the driveway, unsuccessfully attempted to rouse Farwell, and left. Farwell's grandparents discovered him in the car the next morning and took him to the hospital. He died three days later of an epidural hematoma.

At trial, plaintiff contended that had Siegrist taken Farwell to the hospital, or had he notified someone of Farwell's condition and whereabouts, Farwell would not have died. A neurosurgeon testified that if a person in Farwell's condition is taken to a doctor before, or within half an hour after, consciousness is lost, there is an 85 to 88 per cent chance of survival. Plaintiff testified that Siegrist told him that he knew Farwell was badly injured and that he should have done something.

The jury returned a verdict for plaintiff and awarded $15,000 in damages. The Court of Appeals reversed, finding that Siegrist had not assumed the duty of obtaining aid for Farwell and that he neither knew nor should have known of the need for medical treatment. . . .

Siegrist contends that he is not liable for failure to obtain medical assistance for Farwell because he had no duty to do so.

Courts have been slow to recognize a duty to render aid to a person in peril. Where such a duty has been found, it has been predicated upon the existence of a special relationship between the parties; in such a case, if defendant knew or should have known of the other person's peril, he is required to render reasonable care under all the circumstances. . . .

Farwell and Siegrist were companions on a social venture. Implicit in such a common undertaking is the understanding that one will render assistance to the other when he is in peril if he can do so without endangering himself. Siegrist knew or should have known when he left Farwell, who was badly beaten and unconscious, in the back seat of his car that no one would find him before morning. Under these circumstances, to say that Siegrist had no duty to obtain medical assistance or at least to notify someone of Farwell's condition and whereabouts would be "shocking to humanitarian considerations" and fly in the face of "the commonly accepted code of social conduct." "[C]ourts will find a duty where, in general, reasonable men would recognize it and agree that it exists."

Farwell and Siegrist were companions engaged in a common undertaking; there was a special relationship between the parties. Because Siegrist knew or should have known of the peril Farwell was in and could render assistance without endangering himself he had an affirmative duty to come to Farwell's aid.

FITZGERALD, Justice (dissenting).

The unfortunate death of Richard Farwell prompted this wrongful death action brought by his father against the defendant, David Siegrist, a friend who had accompanied Farwell during the evening in which the decedent received injuries which ultimately caused his death three days later. The question before us is whether the defendant, considering his relationship with the decedent and the activity they jointly experienced on the evening of August 26-27, 1966, by his conduct voluntarily or otherwise assumed, or should have assumed, the duty of rendering medical or other assistance to the deceased. We find that defendant had no obligation to assume, nor did he assume, such a duty. . . .

Defendant did not voluntarily assume the duty of caring for the decedent's safety. Nor did the circumstances which existed on the evening of August 26, 1966, impose such a duty. Testimony revealed that only a qualified physician would have reason to suspect that Farwell had suffered an injury which required immediate medical attention. The decedent never complained of pain and, in fact, had expressed a desire to retaliate against his attackers. Defendant's inability to arouse the decedent upon arriving at his grandparents' home does not permit us to infer, as does plaintiff, that defendant knew or should have known that the deceased was seriously injured. While it might have been more prudent for the defendant to insure that the decedent was safely in the house prior to leaving, we cannot say that defendant acted unreasonably in permitting Farwell to spend the night asleep in the back seat of his car.

The close relationship between defendant and the decedent is said to establish a legal duty upon defendant to obtain assistance for the decedent. No authority is cited for this proposition other than the public policy observation that the interest of society would be benefited if its members were required to assist one another. This is not the appropriate case to establish a standard of conduct requiring one to legally assume the duty of insuring the safety of another. Recognizing that legal commentaries have expressed moral outrage at those decisions which permit one to refuse aid to another whose life may be in peril, we cannot say that, considering the relationship between these two parties and the existing circumstances, defendant acted in an unreasonable manner.

Plaintiff believes that a legal duty to aid others should exist where such assistance greatly benefits society and only a reasonable burden is imposed upon those in a position to help. He contends further that the determination of the existence of a duty must rest with the jury where questions of foreseeability and the relationship of the parties are primary considerations.

It is clear that defendant's nonfeasance, or the "passive inaction or a failure to take steps to protect [the decedent] from harm" is urged as being the proximate cause of Farwell's death. We must reject plaintiff's proposition which elevates a moral obligation to the level of a legal duty where, as here, the facts within defendant's knowledge in no way indicated that immediate medical attention was necessary and the relationship between the parties imposes no affirmative duty to render assistance. . . . The posture of this case does not permit us to create a legal duty upon one to render assistance to another injured or imperiled party where the initial injury was not caused by the person upon whom the duty is sought to be imposed.

## 6. *Ploof v. Putnam**

*The following well-known case is not normally thought to raise a duty to rescue issue. The defendant did not simply fail to rescue the plaintiff when the latter was in trouble from a storm; he rather cast the plaintiff's boat off from his dock, thereby actively causing injury. But suppose the facts had been as follows: plaintiff, driven toward shore by the approaching storm, had asked for safe mooring through the storm and been refused ("If you try to moor to my dock, I'll evict you as a trespasser!"); and plaintiff's boat had then been wrecked by the storm and himself and his wife and children injured. Is there any basis in the court's reasoning for treating this hypothetical case differently from the actual facts here?*

*The "doctrine of necessity" stated by the court means that a potential victim may turn a stranger into an involuntary rescuer by making use of his property in an emergency. Does it make sense to draw a line between the mere property and the personal aid of a potential rescuer? Is there an element of "slavery" in making someone act to rescue someone that is not present in merely requiring him to share his property temporarily? Would, for instance, the case be entirely different if plaintiff had needed defendant to throw him a line from the dock before he could safely secure his boat against the storm, and defendant had refused?*

MUNSON, J.

It is alleged as the ground of recovery that on the 13th day of November, 1904, the defendant was the owner of a certain island in Lake Champlain, and of a certain dock attached thereto, which island and dock were then in charge of the defendant's servant; that the plaintiff was then possessed of and sailing upon said lake a certain loaded sloop, on which were the plaintiff and his wife and two minor children; that there then arose a sudden and violent tempest, whereby the sloop and the property and persons therein were placed in great danger of destruction; that, to save these from destruction or injury, the plaintiff was compelled to, and did, moor the sloop to defendant's dock; that the defendant, by his servant, unmoored the sloop, whereupon it was driven upon the shore by the tempest, without the plaintiff's fault; and that the sloop and its contents were thereby destroyed, and the plaintiff and his wife and children cast into the lake and upon the shore, receiving injuries. . . .

There are many cases in the books which hold that necessity, and an inability to control movements inaugurated in the proper exercise of a strict right, will justify entries upon land and interferences with

* 71 A. 188 (1908) (Supreme Court of Vermont).

personal property that would otherwise have been trespasses. . . . A traveler on a highway who finds it obstructed from a sudden and temporary cause may pass upon the adjoining land without becoming a trespasser because of the necessity. . . . In *Procter v. Adams*, 113 Mass. 376, 18 Am. Rep. 500 the defendant went upon the plaintiff's beach for the purpose of saving and restoring to the lawful owner a boat which had been driven ashore, and was in danger of being carried off by the sea; and it was held no trespass. . . .

This doctrine of necessity applies with special force to the preservation of human life. One assaulted and in peril of his life may run through the close of another to escape from his assailant. . . . One may sacrifice the personal property of another to save his life or the lives of his fellows. In *Mouse's Case*, 12 Co. 63, the defendant was sued for taking and carrying away the plaintiff's casket and its contents. It appeared that the ferryman of Gravesend took 47 passengers into his barge to pass to London, among whom were the plaintiff and defendant; and the barge being upon the water a great tempest happened, and a strong wind, so that the barge and all the passengers were in danger of being lost if certain ponderous things were not cast out, and the defendant thereupon cast out the plaintiff's casket. It was resolved that in case of necessity, to save the lives of the passengers, it was lawful for the defendant, being a passenger, to cast the plaintiff's casket out of the barge; . . .

It is clear that an entry upon the land of another may be justified by necessity, and that the declaration before us discloses a necessity for mooring the sloop. The case was sent back for trial in order to determine if the facts as alleged by plaintiff were indeed true.

## 7. *Warschauer v. Lloyd Sabaudo S.A.* *

*In the following case we deal with the law of the sea, a body of doctrine in many respects separate from the common law. A long tradition treats the law of the sea as part of international law, made up of general principles recognized by all seagoing peoples. However, maritime law is here brought to bear in a common-law suit: an action for damages against a shipowner, based on the allegation that the ship's officers failed to give plaintiff assistance though they saw him adrift in a disabled small boat on the high seas. Why does*

* 71 F. 2d 146 (1934) (U.S. Court of Appeals 2d Circuit).

*the court say the plaintiff may not recover? What if the suit had been brought against the captain of the* Conte Biancamano?

*The principle of "respondeat superior" referred to by the court in the third paragraph of the opinion is a generally accepted common-law doctrine to the effect that an employer is liable for damage caused by the negligence of his employees. The principle referred to in the last paragraph of the opinion is also a general one: where a criminal statute imposes some duty in the name of safety, one who violates that statutory duty and thereby injures someone will normally be held liable for civil damages to his victim. It is often said that violation of a safety statute or regulation is "negligence* per se." *Given the principles of "respondeat superior" and "negligence* per se," *can you state why the court does not hold the owner of the ship liable to the plaintiff?*

*Are there special reasons, not applicable on land, why a rule of no duty to rescue is inappropriate at sea?*

SWAN, Circuit Judge.

This is an action at law by the plaintiff Warschauer, a citizen of the United States and a resident of New York City, against an Italian corporation which owned and operated the steamship Conte Biancamano. In substance the complaint alleges that on the afternoon of October 31, 1931, the plaintiff and a companion were adrift on the high seas in a disabled motorboat, without gasoline and without food, when the defendant's steamer passed within hailing distance; that he exhibited a recognized signal of distress and requested the steamer to come to his assistance, and the defendant's servants on said steamer, particularly its operating personnel, clearly observed his signals of distress, but refused to heed them or to stop and take the plaintiff aboard, although they could have done so without peril to themselves or their vessel; that two days later the plaintiff was rescued by a Coastguard cutter. In the meantime and in consequence of the exposure and deprivations to which he was subjected by the failure of the defendant's steamship to render the requested aid, the plaintiff suffered permanent physical injuries for which, together with the attendant pain and subsequently incurred medical expenses, he demands damages. On motion to dismiss, equivalent to a demurrer, the District Court held the complaint insufficient, and the correctness of this ruling is the issue presented by this appeal.

Argument of counsel has taken a wider range than the precise issue presented by the pleadings requires. The question chiefly debated was whether the common law or the law of the sea recognizes the existence of a legal duty coextensive with the universally admitted moral duty to rescue a stranger from peril, when this can be done without risk to the one called upon for help. This interesting problem we pass by as unnecessary to the decision, as did the District Court.

The precise issue is whether a shipowner is liable for damages to a stranger in peril on the high seas to whom the ship's master has failed to give aid. This situation, it may be noted, involves no personal dereliction of a moral duty by the person sought to be held to respond in damages. Such dereliction was that of the master, and only by applying the doctrine of respondeat superior can it be imputed to the ship's owner; moral obliquity is not imputed to one personally innocent. It is conceded that no authority can be found which has imposed legal liability on the owner in such circumstances. . . . The absence of specific precedent, however, is no insuperable barrier, for the law of the sea can grow by judicial decision no less than the common law. . . . But a court should be slow to establish a new legal principle not in harmony with the generally accepted views of the great maritime nations.

Their views on this subject are disclosed in the International Salvage Treaty, which was drafted by representatives of more than twenty nations, meeting at Brussels in 1910, and to which both Italy and the United States are parties. . . . Articles 11 and 12 of the treaty relate to the matter under consideration and read as follows. . . .

## ARTICLE 11.

Every master is bound, so far as he can do so without serious danger to his vessel, her crew and passengers, to render assistance to everybody, even though an enemy, found at sea in danger of being lost.

The owner of the vessel incurs no liability by reason of contravention of the foregoing provision.

. . . The treaty was ratified by the United States in 1912, to become effective on March 1, 1913. In the meantime Congress passed legislation in fulfillment of the obligation imposed by Article 12 of the treaty. Section 2 of the Act of August 1, provides as follows:

Sec. 2. That the master or person in charge of a vessel shall, so far as he can do so without serious danger to his own vessel, crew, or passengers, render assistance to every person who is found at sea in danger of being lost; and if he fails to do so, he shall, upon conviction, be liable to a penalty of not exceeding $1,000 or imprisonment for a term not exceeding two years, or both.

The appellant contends that the declaration in Article 11 that the shipowner "incurs no liability by reason of contravention" of the master's obligation to render assistance refers only to criminal liability of the owner. Such an interpretation would seem a most unlikely meaning. Unless it was intended to cover civil liability, no reason is apparent for mentioning the shipowner's exemption from liability. It is almost inconceivable that criminal responsibility should be imputed to an owner who had not directed the dereliction of his agent. In the United States, at least, imputed crime is substantially unknown. A penal statute is construed to apply only to the class of persons to whom it specifically refers. . . . The same principle should be equally applicable to the construction of a treaty. Hence if the first sentence of Article 11 refers only to the master's public duty, breach of which is to be enforced by the criminal law, there was no need to express the owner's exemption from responsibility. If, however, the master's liability may be civil as well as criminal, then the provision referring to the owner serves a purpose and clearly relieves him from civil liability.

It is further urged that the treaty is not self-executing, that Article 11 is no more than an expression of policy and by the very terms of Article 12 requires legislation to carry it into effect . . . and that Congress in enacting such legislation dealt only with the criminal liability of the master, leaving untouched the civil liability of both master and owner, so that no implication can be drawn, either from the treaty or the statute, that civil liability does not exist. On the contrary, the argument proceeds, the enactment of a criminal statute for the protection of a class creates a right of civil action in a member of the class who is caused harm by an infraction of the statute. . . . Granting all this, the appellant advances no further than to establish a cause of action against the violator of the criminal statute; that is, the master. He must still prove that the master's breach of duty is imputable to his employer. It is at this point that the absence of precedent and the declaration of the treaty against liability on the part of the owner stands in his way. . . .

Judgment affirmed.

# D.

## Conclusion: Vermont Joins Europe?

As the facts of some of the cases in the last section suggest, the common-law doctrine creates a perverse incentive. A potential rescuer who does nothing cannot be legally liable; but one who tries to help may be liable for mere carelessness in carrying out the rescue or for changing his mind and withdrawing. Hence the nurse's willingness to phone the doctor in the O'Neill case exposed the hospital to liability; it appears from the court's reasoning that if she had done nothing for Mr. O'Neill the hospital would have been legally free and clear.

Doctors have often pointed to this anomaly and argued that it served to deter them from volunteering their services in emergencies. In response a number of states have enacted so-called good Samaritan statutes, under which volunteer rescuers cannot be liable for injuries caused to victims by their mere negligence.

In one American state, Vermont, doctors' efforts to have a statute of this sort passed boomeranged. Legislators argued that the anomalous treatment of volunteers vis-à-vis refusers to rescue should be resolved not by easing the duties of the former, but by departing from common-law tradition and imposing a duty to rescue on the latter. The state then enacted a statute that provides:

> A person who knows that another is exposed to grave physical harm shall, to the extent that the same can be rendered without danger or peril to himself or without interference with important duties owed to others, give reasonable assistance to the exposed person unless that assistance or care is being provided by others.

The statute provides a maximum fine of one hundred dollars for violations.

Recall the doctrine you encountered in the *Warschauer* case, that one who violates a criminal statute designed to further safety will be considered negligent for purposes of civil damages in a tort suit brought by one who is injured by the violation. (A typical example of the application of this doctrine is that someone who injures another because he is driving above the speed limit is considered automatically negligent.) There are as yet no reported cases in which the plaintiff invokes this new rescue statute in a civil damage suit. Should the statute be applicable in civil suits for damages?

Examine the following hypothetical case, drawn from a law school examination. In a suit by Victim against Rescuer for the very large money damages that can flow from brain damage, does the statute make Rescuer's safety from a damage award turn on his ability to convince a jury, looking at the matter in hindsight, that his failure to give assistance earlier was "reasonable"? (Consider in particular the phrase "unless that assistance or care is being provided by others"—what is the referent of "that"?) Is human liberty in jeopardy in Vermont if Rescuer could be found liable in these circumstances?

A timid young man (Rescuer) is eating alone in a restaurant when a stranger (Victim) in a large party of businessmen at a nearby table chokes on a piece of food. When Victim is unable to dislodge the particle after a few seconds, his companions begin to show concern, gathering around him, slapping him on the back, and so on. Patrons from other tables gather around as well, forming a considerable crowd. Advice is shouted, and further attempts are made to dislodge the food, but without success. Victim's companions ask if a doctor is present, but no one comes forward. Those nearest Victim keep shouting for quiet and for space. Rescuer gets up during the commotion and comes to the outer limit of the crowd that has formed. He makes a few ineffectual attempts to be heard and to push forward. Only after many minutes have passed and Victim's lips have been blue for some time does one of his companions obtain relative quiet and ask if anyone knows of any way that has not been tried to dislodge the food. At this point Rescuer comes forward. He grasps Victim around the chest from behind, and with a sharp squeeze manages to eject the food particle. This maneuver has been attempted several times already by others who had read about it, but they had not directed the force of the squeeze at the right spot. Rescuer also knew about the technique only from reading, but recalled the details of its proper execution with unusual accuracy.

Victim lives, but suffers brain damage as a result of his several minutes of oxygen starvation. There is expert testimony both that Victim would have died had his breath not been restored before the ambulance arrived, and that the brain damage could have been averted if the food had been dislodged earlier.

# Bibliographic Essay

## Chapter 1

The classic statement of the argument around which this entire book is organized is John Stuart Mill, *On Liberty* (1859), available in many editions. Not nearly so generally available is the classic nineteenth-century critique of Mill, James FitzJames Stephen, *Liberty, Equality, Fraternity* (1873). The contemporary revival of the Mill-Stephen exchange is represented on the liberal side by H.L.A. Hart, *Law, Liberty and Morality* (1963), and on the conservative side by the essays collected in Patrick Devlin, *The Enforcement of Morals* (1965).

Joel Feinberg has written extensively in elaboration and defense of Mill's principle. See especially Chapters 2 and 3 of his *Social Philosophy* (1973) and Chapters 3, 4, and 5 of his *Rights, Justice, and the Bounds of Liberty* (1980). Ronald Dworkin has departed further from Mill, though still arguing recognizably in his spirit, in Chapters 10 and 12 of his *Taking Rights Seriously* (1977). Rolf Sartorius has been unusual among contemporary defenders of Mill in basing his defense on utilitarian grounds; see Chapter 8 of his *Individual Conduct and Social Norms* (1975).

John Rawls states a doctrine of liberty close to Mill's as the "first principle of liberty" in his greatly influential elaboration of liberal theory, *A Theory of Justice* (1971). Rawls's views on liberty are sympathetically restated by H.L.A. Hart in "Rawls on Liberty and Its Priority," 40 *University of Chicago Law Review* 534 (1973). Rawls is often paired in discussion of contemporary political theory with Robert Nozick, who embeds Millian liberty in a more general libertarian system of natural rights in his *Anarchy, State and Utopia* (1974).

Many of Mill's contemporary defenders are at the same time critics of his doctrine, proposing modifications of his theory where they believe it cannot be defended. There is also a smaller literature joining Lord Devlin in straightforward disavowal of Mill's doctrine. This position is represented, from the point of view of American legal realism, by Eugene Rostow in Chapter 2 of his *The Sovereign Prerogative* (1962), and from a radical communitarian perspective by Robert Paul Wolff in *The Poverty of Liberalism* (1968).

## Chapter 2

The connections between liberal moral and political theory, sexual freedom, and the right to privacy in American constitutional law have been extensively explored by David Richards. In addition to the full text of his article excerpted in Chapter 2 of this book, see his "Unnatural Acts and the Constitutional Right to Privacy: A Moral Theory," 45 *Fordham Law Review* 1281 (1977). A book-length treatment of the legal issues is Walter Barnett, *Sexual Freedom and the Constitution* (1973). A valuable earlier treatment is Louis Henkin, "Morals and the Constitution: The Sin of Obscenity," 63 *Columbia Law Review* 391 (1963). For a thoughtful account of the place of the right of privacy in American constitutional law see Chapters 11 and 15 of Laurence Tribe, *American Constitutional Law* (1978). A useful collection of philosophical writings on sexual morality is Robert Baker and Frederick Elliston (eds.), *Philosophy and Sex* (1975).

## Chapter 3

The issues of the legal treatment of dead bodies and human tissues are given a lively and comprehensive survey in Russell Scott, *The Body as Property* (1981). A more philosophical treatment of these issues is contained in Robert Veatch, *Death, Dying and the Biological Revolution* (1976). A valuable study of death and burial customs from the perspective of anthropology is Richard Huntington and Peter Metcalf, *Celebrations of Death* (1979). An article by a philosopher addressing the issue of organ availability at death is James Muyskens, "An Alternative Policy for Obtaining Cadaver Organs for Transplantation," 8 *Philosophy and Public Affairs* 88 (1978).

## Chapter 4

The comprehensive treatment of issues surrounding the duty to rescue is the collection edited by James Ratcliffe, *The Good Samaritan and the Law* (1966). A later and valuable philosophical discussion is John Kleinig, "Good Samaritanism," 5 *Philosophy and Public Affairs* 382 (1976). A legal-philosophical treatment based on the Vermont statute in the text is D'Amato, "The 'Bad Samaritan' Paradigm," 70 *Northwestern U. Law Review* 798 (1975). An interesting analysis of the rescue problem from an economic point of view is William Landes and Richard Posner, "Salvors, Finders, Good Samaritans, and Other Rescuers: An Economic Study of Law and Altruism," 7 *Journal of Legal Studies* 83 (1978).

# Index

Abortion, 58–59
American Law Institute's Model Penal Code.
  *See* Model Penal Code
Ames, James Barr, 164
Anatomy Bill (1832), 111
*Antigone* (Sophocles), 105
Antimiscegenation laws, 55–56, 81, 83
Augustine, 74, 75

Baker, J., 176–178
Baker, Richard John, 79
*Baker* v. *Nelson,* 79–81
*Bellah* v. *Greenson* (1978), 186
Bentham, Jeremy, 34, 110
Bickel, Alexander, 63
Bill of Rights, 9, 42–43, 45, 55, 69, 73
Black, Hugo L., 51–54
Blackmum, Harry A., 58, 73
Blackstone, William, 18
"Bodysnatchers and Benthamites" (Durey), 108–111
Bradbury, Frank E., 112
Bradbury, Harriet P., 112, 113
Brain death
  California statute concerning, (1974), 150
  "neomort" proposal and, 150–151
Brennan, W. J., Jr., 57, 66–67
British Renal Transportation Bill, 136–137
*Buch* v. *Amory Manufacturing Co.* (1897), 158–159
Burger, Warren, E., 62

**203**

Cadavers, 105–118
  brain death and, 149–153
  commerical sale of, 141–149
  organ donation by, 133–141
  organ transplantation and, 118–133
  property rights over, 16–19
  research uses of, 105–108
  wishes of deceased vs. public interest, 115–118
Caine, Roy, 135
California Brain Death statute (1954), 150
Calton, William B., 86*n*, 87
Cardozo, J., 115–118
*Carey* v. *Population Services International* (1977), 57
Carpenter, C. J., 158–159
Causation, 25–29
  "but-for," concept of, 27
  necessary condition test for, 27
Child custody, and sexual freedom, 92–97
Claybrook, Joan, 106
Coma, irreversible, 149, 152
*Commentaries on the Constitution of The United States* (Story), 44
Consensual behavior, 9, 48, 66, 68, 71, 72, 77, 91
Constitution, U.S., Amendments to
  First, 7, 42, 56, 62, 64–65, 67, 141
  Fourteenth, 7, 40–42, 45–47, 50, 51, 56, 58, 59, 61, 65, 71, 73, 80, 81
  Fourth, 42, 52
  Fifth, 7, 42–43, 45
  Ninth, 40, 43–44, 53, 55, 58, 80
  Tenth, 55
  Third, 42
Contraception, 42, 43, 45, 47–48, 50–51, 56–57
Cremation, 112–115
"Critique of the UAGA" (Dukeminier), 127–133

*Dandridge* v. *Williams*, 82
David, Richard, 74–78
Dawson, John P., 168–171
Dead, treatment of
  commerce in human organs and, 141
  implications of brain death for, 149
  law of cadavers concerning, 105–118
  salvaging, cadaver parts and, 133–141
  Uniform Anatomical Gift Act and, 118–133
*Death, Dying, and the Biological Revolution* (Veatch), 133–134
Death, Harvard definition of, 149–150
Decency and offense, in moral conduct, 13–16
Devlin, Patrick, 4, 11, 23

"Disintegration thesis," 30
*Doe* v. *Commonwealth's Attorney for City of Richmond* (1975), 68-74
Douglas, William O., 40, 55, 80
   *Griswold Case* and, 41-43
Due process clause, 7, 40, 42, 45-47, 51, 53-56, 59, 61, 71-73,
   81
Dukeminier, Jesse, 118, 127-133
   "Removal of Cadaver Organs Regardless of Objection," 138-141
   "Routine Salvaging of Cadaver Organs Unless There Is Objection,"
      135-138
   "Sale of Cadaver Parts," 141-144
   "Sales by Living Persons with Delivery During Life," 144-149
Durey, M. J., 108-111
Dworkin, Ronald, 6, 8

*Eisenstadt* v. *Baird* (1972), 57, 65, 71, 72
Employment, and sexual freedom, 85-92
*Enforcement of Morals, The* (Devlin), 5
Epstein, Richard, 163-167
Equal Protection Clause, 7, 81
"Eros, Civilization and the Burger Court" (Grey), 98-102

Family life
   nuclear vs. extended forms of, 59-60
   privacy of, 59-60
*Farwell* v. *Keaton* (1976), 189-192
*Ferguson* v. *Skrupa*, 54
Fitzgerald, Justice, 191-192
Free will, 64-65
Freud, Sigmund, 22, 23, 99-101

Gaylin, Willard, 151
Genovese, Kitty, 157
German Criminal Code (1870), 168
*Gift Relationship, The* (Titmuss), 142
Gill, William, 109
Goldberg, Arthur, 40, 69, 81
   *Griswold Case* and, 43-45
Goldenhersh, Chief Justice, 96-97
Good Samaritan doctrine. *See* Rescue, duty to
Grave, desecration of, 107-108
Grey, Thomas, 98-102
*Griswold* v. *Connecticut* (1965), 7, 65, 69, 71, 76, 80, 84
   historical background to, 40-41
   Justice Black's opinion in, 51-54
   Justice Douglas' opinion in, 41-43
   Justice Goldberg's opinion in, 43-45

Justice Harlan's opinion in, 45–50
Justice Stewart's opinion in, 54–55
Justice White's opinion in, 50–51

Habitual Criminal Sterlization Act (Oklahoma), 80
Harlan, John Marshall, 40, 69, 71, 72
  *Griswold Case* and, 45–50
Harm, concept of, 13–14
Hart, H. L. A, 4–5, 14, 15, 21, 23
Hart-Devlin debate, 6–8
Hill-Link Minority Report of the Commission on Obscenity and Por-
  nography, 63
*Hollenbaugh* v. *Carnegie Free Library* (1978), 60
Holmes, Oliver W., 8, 40–41, 59, 113
Home, privacy of, 56
Homosexuality
  naturalness v. unnaturalness of, 77–78
  privacy and, 67–78
Homosexual marriage, 178–185
Hunt, Henry, 111
*Hurley* v. *Eddingfield* (1901), 176–178

International Salvage Treaty (1910), 196–197
"It All Comes Out in the End" (film), 62

Jarett, Jacqueline, 93
*Jarrett* v. *Jarrett* (1979), 93–97
Jarett, Walter, 93
Jonas, Hans, 151–153

*Kanavan's Case,* 114
Kant, Immanuel, 34
*Kelley* v. *Johnston* (1976), 61
King, Albert I., 106

Laissez faire, 20
Lasch, Christopher, 101
*Law, Liberty and Morality* (Hart), 5
"Legality of Homosexual Marriage," 82–85
Levin, Justice, 190–191
*Levin* v. *Sinai Hospital,* 184
Liberty
  action and, 3
  concept of, 43, 45
  conscience and, 3
  protection of, 3
  vs. right to privacy, 40–41, 61

*Liberty, Equality, Fraternity* (Stephen), 5
Lifestyles and the right to privacy, 60–61
*Lochner* v. *New York* (1905), 40, 42, 54, 59
*Loving* v. *Virginia* (1967), 55, 65, 81

Macaulay, Thomas B., 159–163
McConnell, James Michael, 79
McNally, Justice, 181
Madison, James, 44, 45
"Magic Mirror" (film), 62
*Marbury* v. *Madison (1803)*, 53
Marcuse, Herbert, 101
Marijuana, 61
Marriage, 55–56
   laws regarding, 48
   privacy of, 43, 48
Marriage and Dissolution of Marriage Act (Illinois), 95
Marshall, Thurgood 56, 60, 61
Mayhem, 145–147
Merhige, District Judge, 71–72
*Meyer* v. *Nebraska* (1923), 59
Mill, John Stuart, 3, 8, 20, 99
   causing vs. allowing harm and, 25
   on decency and offense, 13–16
   economic freedom and, 20–25
   exploitation and, 24–25
   influence of, on legislative development, 6
   medical and biological issues and, 9–10
   paternalism and, 23–24
   policy vs. principle and, 10–13
   property rights to cadavers and, 16–19
   protection of collective institutions and, 29–35
   sexual issues and, 6–9
Model Penal Code, 4, 146
*Moore* v. *East Cleveland* (1977), 59
Morality
   criminal law and, 4–5. *See also* Hart-Devlin debate
   sexual, 39
   as a state concern, 47–48, 66
*Morrison* v. *State Board of Education* (1969), 87–89
Moss, John E., 106, 107
*Mouse's Case*, 194
Munson, J., 193
Murder Act (1752), 109

Necessary condition test, 27
Necessity, doctrine of, 193–194

Negligence per se, 195
*Negotiorum gestio,* doctrine of, 174–175
"Negotiorum Gestio: The Altruistic Intermeddler ' (Dawson), 168–171
Nelson, Gerald, 79
"Neomort" proposal, 150–151
New Deal and Supreme Court, 7
"Notes on the Indian Penal Code" (Macauley), 159–16ɔ
Nozick, Robert, 6, 20
*Nye* v. *Nye* (1952), 96

Obscenity, 56
   and privacy, 61–67
*O'Neill* v. *Montefiore Hospital* (1960), 178–181
*On Liberty* (Mill), 3, 8
Ordinary language analysis, 5
Organs, cadaver, sale of, 141–149
   from brain-dead patients, 151–153
Ownership, 18–19

Page, Irvine, 133
*Paris Adult Theater* v. *Slaton*, 61–67
   Justice Brennan's opinion in, 66–67
   Justice Burger's opinion in, 62–66
Paternalism, 23–25
*Patient as Person, The* (Ramsey), 134
Peckham, Rufus W., 59
*Pettit* v. *State Board of Education* (1973), 86–92
"Philosophical Reflections on Experimenting with Human Subjects"
   (Jonas), 151–153
*Pierce* v. *Proprietors of Swan Point Cemetery,* 113
*Pierce* v. *Society of Sisters* (1925), 59
*Plott* v. *Putnam* (1908), 193–194
Poddar, Prosenjit, 186, 187
*Poe* v. *Ullman* (1961), 45–50, 69, 71, 72
Police, uniformity of appearance of, 61
Poor Law Amendment Act, 111
Pornography, 61–67
Powell, Lewis F., 60
Pregnancy, term of, 58
Privacy, right to
   abortion and, 58–59
   constitutional debate over, 39
   contraception and, 56–58
   court's development of, 6–9
   defined, 52
   family life and, 59–60
   *Griswold* v. *Connecticut* (1965) and, 41–55

in the home, 56
vs. liberty, 40–41, 61
"lifestyles" and, 60–61
limits of, 54
marriage and, 55–56
Privileges and Immunities Clause, 46
Procreation, free choice in, 56–58
*Proctor* v. *Adams,* 194
Progressive era, and Supreme Court, 7
Property, defined, 18
Prosser, Dean, 140
Psychotherapist-patient privilege, 188–189

"Quick, the Dead and the Cadaver Population, The," (Wade), 105–107

Ramsey, Paul, 134
*Ravin* v. *State* (1975), 60
Rawls, John, 5, 8
*Reg.* v. *Price,* 114
*Reg.* v. *Stewart,* 114
Rehnquist, William H., 58, 61
Reich, Wilhelm, 101
"Removal of Cadaver Organs Regardless of Objection" (Dukeminier), 138–141
Rescue, duty to
  Ames' rule concerning, 164
  Anglo-American doctrine concerning, 157–167
  beliefs concerning, 166–167
  common-law applications concerning, 175–198
  in Czechoslovakia, 173–175
  by doctor of third party, 185–189
  doctrine of necessity and, 193–194
  European civil-law tradition concerning, 167–175
  in Germany, 168–170
  hospital obligation to accept emergency patients and, 181–185
  interrupted rescue, liability resulting from, 178–181
  limiting legal, 159–163
  physician's right to refuse treatment and, 176–178
  protecting third persons and, 187–188
  social association and, 189–192
  in Soviet Union, 171–173
  in Vermont, 198–199
*Respondeat superior,* 195, 196
*Rex* v. *Lynn* (1788), 107–108, 114
*Roe* v. *Wade* (1973), 8, 58, 71–73
*Roth* v. *United States* (1957), 56

"Routine Salvaging of Cadaver Organs Unless There Is Objection" (Dukeminier), 135–138
Sadler, Alfred M., 119–123
Sadler, Blair L., 119–123
"Sale of Cadaver Parts" (Dukeminier), 141–144
"Sale by Living Persons with Delivery During Life" (Dukeminier), 144–149
Sanders, David, 135
Select Committee of Inquiry into Anatomy, 110
Self-Incrimination Clause, 42–43
"Sexual Autonomy and the Constitutional Right to Privacy: A Case Study in Human Rights and the Constitution" (Richards), 74–78
*Sexual Behavior in the Human Female* (Kinsey), 90
Sexual freedom
  child custody and, 92–97
  employment and, 85–92
  Grey's views on, 97–102
  homosexuality and privacy and, 67–78
  homosexual marriage and, 78–85
  obscenity and privacy and, 61–67
  right to privacy and, 40–61
Sexual love, procreational model of, 74–76
*Skinner* v. *Oklahoma ex rel. Williamson*, 80, 81, 84
Social disintegration, 31
Social philosophy, contemporary, 5–6
*Social Statics* (Spencer), 8
Sodomy, 68
Spencer, Herbert, 8
"Stalking the Good Samaritan: Communists, Capitalists and the Duty to Rescue" (1976), 171
*Stanley* v. *Georgia* (1969), 56, 62, 65, 73
*Stanley* v. *Illinois* (1972), 59, 60,
*State* v. *Bass*, 146
*State* v. *Bradbury* (1939), 112–115
Stephen, James Fitzjames, 5, 11
Stewart, Potter, 54–55
Story, J., 44, 45
Swan, Judge, 195–197

Tarasoff, Tatiana, 186, 187
*Tarasoff* v. *University of California* (1976), 185–189
*Taylor* v. *Baldwin, Mo.,* 184
Thaxter, Justice, 112–115
*Theory of Justice, A* (Rawles), 8
"Theory of Strict Liability, A" (Epstein), 163–167
Titmuss, Richard, 142
Tobriner, J., 89–62, 186–189

"Transplant and the Law: The Need for Organized Sensitivity" (Sadler and Sadler), 119–120
Transplantation, organ
common law and, 120–121
freedom of religion and, 140–141
as mayhem, 146
medical examiner and coroner statutes concerning, 122–123
property rights and, 138–140
rights to donate, of deceased persons and, 120–121
salvaging of cadaver for, 135–141
state autopsy statutes concerning, 121–122
unclaimed body statutes and, 123
Uniform Anatomical Gift Act and, 123–127

Uniform Anatomical Gift Act (UAGA), 118, 120, 123–127
critique of, 127–133
sale of organs and, 143
Utilitarianism, in ethics and law, 33–34

Veatch, Robert, 133
Victimless crimes, 29, 31
Vil'nianskii, 172
Vyvyan, Richard, 111

Wade, N., 105–107
Wage, minimum, 20–21
Warburton, Henry, 110
Warren, Earl, 63, 81
*Warschauer* v. *Lloyd Sabaudo* (1934), 194–197
Weber, Max, 100–101
Williams, Robert, 135
*Williams* v. *Williams*, 120
*Wilmington General Hospital* v. *Manlove* (1961), 181–185
White, Byron R., 40, 58, 59
*Griswold Case* and, 150–51
Wolfenden Committee, 4–5
Wright, J. Skelly, 83
*Wrights Case* (1603), 146

Yome, Anna, 115, 117
*Yome* v. *Gorman* (1926), 115–118
Yome, John D., 115

*Zablocki* v. *Redhail* (1978), 55

### About the Author

THOMAS GREY is professor of law at Stanford Law School, where he teaches torts, and teaches and writes about constitutional law and jurisprudence. He was an undergraduate at Stanford and Oxford and studied law at Yale. This is his first book.


### A Note on the Type

The text of this book was set in a computer version of Times Roman, designed by Stanley Morison for *The Times* (London) and first introduced by that newspaper in 1923.

Among typographers and designers of the twentieth century, Stanley Morison has been a strong forming influence as typographical adviser to the English Monotype Corporation, as a director of two distinguished English publishing houses, and as a writer of sensibility, erudition, and keen practical sense.

Typography by Barbara Sturman. Cover design by Maria Epes. Composition by The Saybrook Press, Inc., Old Saybrook, Connecticut. Printed and bound by Banta Company, Menasha, Wisconsin.

# BORZOI BOOKS
# IN LAW AND AMERICAN SOCIETY

## Law and American History

### EARLY AMERICAN LAW AND SOCIETY
Stephen Botein, *Michigan State University*

This volume consists of an essay dealing with the nature of law and early American socioeconomic development from the first settlements to 1776. The author shows how many legal traditions sprang both from English experience and from the influence of the New World. He explores the development of transatlantic legal structures in order to show how they helped rationalize intercolonial affairs. Mr. Botein also emphasizes the relationship between law and religion. The volume includes a pertinent group of documents for classroom discussion, and a bibliographic essay.

### LAW IN THE NEW REPUBLIC: *Private Law and the Public Estate*
George Dargo, *Brookline, Massachusetts*

Though the American Revolution had an immediate and abiding impact on American public law (e.g., the formation of the federal and state constitutions), its effect on private law (e.g., the law of contracts, tort law) was less direct but of equal importance. Through essay and documents, Mr. Dargo examines post-Revolutionary public and private reform impulses and finds a shifting emphasis from public to private law which he terms "privatization." To further illustrate the tension between public and private law, the author develops a case study (the Batture land controversy in New Orleans) in early nineteenth century legal, economic, and political history. The volume includes a wide selection of documents and a bibliographic essay.

### LAW IN ANTEBELLUM SOCIETY: *Legal Change and Economic Expansion*
Jamil Zainaldin, *Washington, D.C.*

This book examines legal change and economic expansion in the first half of the nineteenth century, integrating major themes in the development of law with key historical themes. Through a series of topical essays and the use of primary source materials, it describes how political, social, and economic interests and values influence law making. The book's focus is on legislation and the common law.

### LAW AND THE NATION, 1865–1912
Jonathan Lurie, *Rutgers University*

Using the Fourteenth Amendment as the starting point for his essay, Mr. Lurie examines the ramifications of this landmark constitutional provision on the economic and social development of America in the years following the Civil War. He also explores important late nineteenth-century developments in legal education, and concludes his narrative with some insights on law and social change in the first decade of the twentieth century. The volume is highlighted by a documents section containing statutes, judicial opinions, and legal briefs, with appropriate questions for classroom discussion. Mr. Lurie's bibliographic essay provides information to stimulate further investigation of this period.

# ORDERED LIBERTY: *Legal Reform in the Twentieth Century*
## Gerald L. Fetner, *University of Chicago*

In an interpretive essay, the author examines the relationship between several major twentieth-century reform movements (e.g., Progressivism, New Deal, and the Great Society) and the law. He shows how policy makers turned increasingly to the legal community for assistance in accommodating economic and social conflict, and how the legal profession responded by formulating statutes, administrative agencies, and private arrangements. Mr. Fetner also discusses how the organization and character of the legal profession were affected by these social changes. Excerpts from relevant documents illustrate issues discussed in the essay. A bibliographic essay is included.

# Law and Philosophy

## DISCRIMINATION AND REVERSE DISCRIMINATION
### Kent Greenawalt, *Columbia Law School*

Using discrimination and reverse discrimination as a model, Mr. Greenawalt examines the relationship between law and ethics. He finds that the proper role of law cannot be limited to grand theory concerning individual liberty and social restraint, but must address what law can effectively discover and accomplish. Such concepts as distributive and compensatory justice and utility are examined in the context of preferential treatment for blacks and other minorities. The analysis draws heavily on the Supreme Court's Bakke decision. The essay is followed by related documents, primarily judicial opinions, with notes and questions, and a bibliography.

## THE LEGAL ENFORCEMENT OF MORALITY
### Thomas Grey, *Stanford Law School*

This book deals with the traditional issue of whether morality can be legislated and enforced. It consists of an introductory essay and legal texts on three issues: the enforcement of sexual morality, the treatment of human remains, and the duties of potential rescuers. The author shows how philosophical problems differ from classroom hypotheticals when they are confronted in a legal setting. He illustrates this point using material from statutes, regulations, judicial opinions, and law review commentaries. Mr. Grey reviews the celebrated Hart-Devlin debate over the legitimacy of prohibiting homosexual acts. He places the challenging problem of how to treat dead bodies, arising out of developments in the technology of organ transplantation, in the context of the debate over morals enforcement, and discusses the Good Samaritan as an issue concerning the propriety of the legal enforcement of moral duties.

## LEGAL REASONING
### Martin Golding, *Duke University*

This volume is a blend of text and readings. The author explores the many sides to legal reasoning—as a study in judicial psychology and, in a more narrow sense, as an inquiry into the "logic" of judicial decision making. He shows how judges justify their rulings, and gives examples of the kinds of arguments they use. He challenges the notion that judicial reasoning is rationalization; instead, he argues that judges are guided by a deep concern for consistency and by a strong need to have their decisions stand as a measure for the future conduct of individuals. *(Forthcoming in 1984)*

# Law and American Literature

## LAW AND AMERICAN LITERATURE
### A one-volume collection of the following three essays:

### Law as Form and Theme in American Letters
#### Carl S. Smith, *Northwestern University*

The author explores the interrelationships between law aned literature generally and between American law and American literature in particular. He explores first the literary qualities of legal writing and then the attitudes of major American writers toward the law. Throughout, he studies the links between the legal and literary imaginations. He finds that legal writing has many literary qualities that are essential to its function, and he points out that American writers have long been wary of the power of the law and its special language, speaking out as a compensating voice for the ideal of justice.

### Innocent Criminal or Criminal Innocence: The Trial in American Fiction
#### John McWilliams, *Middlebury College*

Mr. McWilliams explores how law functions as a standard for conduct in a number of major works of American literature, including Cooper's *The Pioneers,* Melville's *Billy Budd,* Dreiser's *An American Tragedy,* and Wright's *Native Son.* Each of these books ends in a criminal trial, in which the reader is asked to choose between his emotional sympathy for the victim and his rational understanding of society's need for criminal sanctions. The author compares these books with James Gould Cozzens' *The Just and the Unjust,* a study of a small town legal system, in which the people's sense of justice contravenes traditional authority.

### Law and Lawyers in American Popular Culture
#### Maxwell Bloomfield, *Catholic University of America*

Melding law, literature, and the American historical experience into a single essay, Mr. Bloomfield discusses popular images of the lawyer. The author shows how contemporary values and attitudes toward the law are reflected in fiction. He concentrates on two historical periods: antebellum America and the Progressive era. He examines fictional works which were not always literary classics, but which exposed particular legal mores. An example of such a book is Winston Churchill's *A Far Country* (1915), a story of a successful corporation lawyer who abandons his practice to dedicate his life to what he believes are more socially desirable objectives.